PRAISE FOR *COMPLETE KITTEN CARE*

"Another great book from Amy Shojai . . . *Complete Kitten Care* should be as important to the owner as kitten food is to the kitten."
—Bob Vella, host of nationally syndicated *Pet Talk America* radio and author of *300 Incredible Things for Pet Lovers on the Internet*

"A wealth of information for first-time kitten owners. Amy Shojai shows you how to enjoy kittenhood."
—Pam Johnson-Bennett, feline behaviorist and author of *Think Like a Cat* and *Psycho Kitty?*

"*Complete Kitten Care* will give you all the information you need to successfully grow your young feline. Informative and fun to read."
—John C. Wright, Ph.D., certified applied animal behaviorist and author of *Is Your Cat Crazy?*

"A must-have for anyone considering kittenhood. . . . This book covers it all, from selecting a compatible kitten to handling emergencies, in a comprehensive and understandable manner."
—H. Ellen Whitley, D.V.M., author of *Understanding and Training Your Cat or Kitten*

"Thorough, entertaining, and authoritative . . . a primer on the feline mystique, one that owners are sure to turn to again and again as their kitten grows into cathood."
—Kim Thornton, president, Cat Writers' Association

continued . . .

MORE PRAISE FOR *COMPLETE KITTEN CARE*

"Amy Shojai has once again given the cat-loving public a concise, easy-to-understand book. I wish it could accompany every kitten going to a new home."

—Kitty Angell, secretary, Cat Fanciers' Association Inc.

"Amy Shojai, the doyenne of pet care books, has come up with another winner. There's something here for everyone, whether you're a newbie at kitten care or an old pro. This book is an extremely comprehensive resource that will ensure selection of your perfect kitten and guide you in helping him become a happy, healthy, lifelong companion."

—Sally Bahner, freelance writer and feline expert

"Contains a wealth of information about kittens and cats . . . a must-read for anyone contemplating a first kitty as well as those who already know the joys of living with cats."

—Lenny Southam, D.V.M., practicing veterinarian, moderator of Compuserve's PetsForum Group, Inc., and coauthor of *The Pill Book: Guide to Medication for Your Dog and Cat*

"A book that will be regarded as a must in the library of any cat lover. . . . There are, quite simply, no questions left to ask about the acquiring of and caring for a kitten after one has read this book."

—Karen Lawrence, CFA Allbreed judge

COMPLETE
KITTEN
CARE

AMY D. SHOJAI

NEW AMERICAN LIBRARY

NEW AMERICAN LIBRARY
Published by New American Library, a division of
Penguin Putnam Inc., 375 Hudson Street,
New York, New York 10014, U.S.A.
Penguin Books Ltd, 80 Strand,
London WC2R 0RL, England
Penguin Books Australia Ltd, Ringwood,
Victoria, Australia
Penguin Books Canada Ltd, 10 Alcorn Avenue,
Toronto, Ontario, Canada M4V 3B2
Penguin Books (N.Z.) Ltd, 182–190 Wairau Road
Auckland 10, New Zealand

Penguin Books Ltd, Registered Offices:
Harmondsworth, Middlesex, England

First published by New American Library, a division of Penguin Putnam Inc.

First Printing, June 2002
1 3 5 7 9 10 8 6 4 2

REGISTERED TRADEMARK—MARCA REGISTRADA

LIBRARY OF CONGRESS CATALOGING-IN-PUBLICATION DATA:

Shojai, Amy, 1956–
Complete kitten care / Amy D. Shojai.
p. cm.
ISBN 0-451-20634-7 (alk. paper)
1. Kittens. 2. Cats. I. Title.

SF447 .S476 2002
636.8'07—dc21   2001058707

Set in Berkeley Book
Designed by Eve L. Kirch

Printed in the United States of America

For the people who make a difference—

Dedicated shelter staffs,
Caring veterinarians and volunteers,
Loving fanciers, responsible breeders,
Devoted cat-parents everywhere.

And for the kittens who share our lives—

Those from planned births and "accidents,"
Throwaways and foundling strays,
Chosen fur-kids and rescued waifs,
All those serendipity sends our way.

But most especially,
For the kittens that never find a home.

In loving memory.

ACKNOWLEDGMENTS

Many people helped make this book a reality. Darlene Arden and Cheryl S. Smith, great friends and respected colleagues, provided lots of support when I needed it most. The Colorado Gang—Judy Gharis, Bobby Grant, Sherrie McLeroy, Jackye Meineke, Margie Morris, Carol Shenold, Jessie Stephens, and Cherie Wallis—your warm, healing laughter, steadfast friendship, and sound advice keep me sane when the world goes nuts. Love you guys. Most especially my husband, Mahmoud, reminds me what's important; my cat Seren teaches me to live in the moment; and my furry muse, Fafnir, never leaves my heart.

Heartfelt appreciation goes to all the shelter staff and volunteers, cat fanciers, veterinarians, and feline lovers I've met over the past several years. The incredible family of volunteers at CatsForum provides a valuable service to cat lovers around the globe. Thanks for allowing me to be a part of your special community. I'm proud to be part of the Purina Cat Chow Way of Life team—thank you Ken Wilhelm, Julie Kahn, Libby Ottiger and all the traveling mentors, and the sixty-plus shelters with whom we've partnered in the past three years. Y'all are doing the work of the angels.

I'd especially like to thank Cat Writers' Association member Wendy Christensen, whose kitten illustrations bring the text to life, and Jane Popham for smoothing the way for photo releases. My brother, Laird Monteith, prepared professional scans of my images that make my kitten photos look *purr*-fect—many thanks!

I will be forever grateful to Ellen Edwards for adopting my orphaned baby and turning it into *Complete Kitten Care*. And as always, my deepest gratitude goes to my agent, Meredith Bernstein, who makes sure I always land on my feet. Finally, thanks be to the kittens—may this book help them find *and keep* a loving home for all their nine lives.

CONTENTS

PART 3: KITTEN CARE 101

11. Ten Common Emergencies and What to Do   198

PART 4: KITTEN SOCIABILITY AND TRAINING

12. Making Sense of Kitten Talk   213

PART 5: FELINE FASCINATIONS— TOP TEN LISTS

INTRODUCTION

Welcome to *Complete Kitten Care*, the most easy-to-use, up-to-date reference available on one of the most mysterious, endearing, and extraordinary pets you could choose.

First and foremost, this book celebrates kittens. Beyond cute stories and cuter pictures—both of which you'll find here—this book's solid information will arm you with the tools you'll need to build a lasting, loving relationship with the special cat babies in your life.

Kittenhood is a unique period that demands special attention. Kittens are works in progress that must receive proper care if they are to achieve their full potential. The physical and emotional needs of kittens are very specific and impact not only the present, but also the future. What happens to your kitten today—for good or ill—defines everything she can expect to be as an adult.

And so, cherish these days, weeks, and months—for kittenhood is a fleeting treasure. It comes only once in each cat's life, and is even more precious because of its transient nature.

Kittenhood is the period during which affection takes root. With the proper care, affection blooms into a lifetime of shared love.

Nothing Beats Kitten Love

I have testified to kitten love in countless articles and quite a few books over my fifteen-plus years as a pet writer. Kittens are different from their adult counterparts. Not better—just different.

Obviously, a kitten's appearance and behavior set her apart from her parents. More than that, adult cats have already developed many habits, whether good or bad, and their personality traits become more fixed as they mature. Kitten personality and habits, on the other paw, remain malleable and can be shaped by the world around them. The most important difference between cats and kittens is that the tiny kitten brain is a sponge with an insatiable thirst for knowledge. As responsible caretakers, we must make the most of this wonderful opportunity.

Kittens aren't born knowing how the world works or what's expected of them. A kitten is dependent upon the humans in her life to offer guidance and structure as she matures, and help her develop positive personality traits and habits. It's up to you to mold that nonstop dynamo into a respectable and affectionate member of your family. You will be repaid a hundredfold in loving purrs, head bumps and whisker kisses, and unquestioned trust and respect. Kitten compliments don't come any higher than that!

Love 'Em and *Don't* Leave 'Em!

Loving kittens is easy—especially when their purr rumbles, they chase the feather toy with full-tilt energy, or they curl into a sleepy ball of fluff on your lap. You don't need a book to tell your heart how to feel.

But kittens have no off switch. Their high jinks can turn tolerant human smiles into nervous tics, especially when they want to play get-the-toes at 3:00 A.M., their claws target your furniture, or they leave bathroom "deposits" outside the litter box.

Kittens can't explain why they do the things they do. And humans don't automatically know how to teach kittens acceptable behavior. We don't speak the same language, and our cultures are foreign to each other. That's why thousands upon thousands of kittens lose their homes—and their lives—every year. People love 'em and then leave 'em because of unrealistic expectations, misunderstandings, and miscommunication.

That's where this book comes in. Consider *Complete Kitten Care* the Miss Manners for teaching proper feline etiquette to your kitten, and a handy guide for you to understand what makes kitty tick. Believe me, the more you know about the extraordinary creature you've chosen to love, the stronger will become the attachment, and the greater your commitment to fix any transient "problems." That's the best way to ensure that your relationship endures.

The Cute Factor and Disposable Pets

The "cute factor" protects even the most mischievous feline prankster from a scolding. Human scowls and anger dissolve into helpless amusement with one look from an innocent, big-eyed kitten face. She didn't *mean* to trip you on the stairs, ruin your pantyhose, or fall in the toilet. It doesn't take these babies long to learn to clown for our enjoyment, or just how far to push the limits of human patience.

But as kittens mature, their "cute quotient" changes. While allowances may be made for the fuzzy eight-week-old baby who dabbles a paw in your coffee or swings from the drapes, the four- or five-month-old adolescent kitten receives less tolerance when she spills the cup or pulls curtains off the wall. Sometimes people even characterize normal kitten antics at this age as "vindictive" behavior.

Once this desirable "cute factor" fades away, the kitten finds that everything that worked before to gain loving attention from her special human now lands her in the doghouse. And there's nothing worse for a cat, especially when the baby hasn't a clue what she did wrong. A large majority of the young cats relinquished to shelters are these in-between "teenage" kittens—not yet adults, but disposable because their cute factor has betrayed them.

I believe that's what happened with my cat, Seren (short for Serendipity). She was dumped at that "tweener" age, probably when her original backyard or "accidental" breeder lost hope she'd fetch a good price—or find another home—as her cute factor faded. This attitude promotes disposable pets, and the idea that kittens are replaceable. Sadly, this attitude has become all too common. I know readers will be horrified, as I am, by those who routinely "trade in" these wonderful creatures to shelters and then seek out another baby that better fits their notion of the perfect kitten.

Kittenhood lasts about a year—longer for some breeds. But all cats retain that kitten-on-the-inside attitude even when they are mature on the outside, especially when the furry baby receives the proper attitude-shaping attention at the right time. While I abhor that Seren's original caretakers cast her off, I feel blessed that she came into my life. After our three years together, I still see the kitten inside every time I look into her blue-jeans-colored eyes. And I treasure the kitten attitude she owns in abundance.

Kitten attitude—outrageous curiosity, boundless energy, unlimited affection, unending trust—is fragile, often fleeting, and so easily destroyed. That makes understanding and providing for the physical and emotional needs of your kitten even more important. It's up to us to preserve the best parts of kittenhood for all of a pet's life. Seren constantly reminds me of that fact.

Kitten Preparedness—Why You Need This Book

To love a kitten seems simple, but it gets complicated if you want to do things right. A whole lot more goes into kitten preparedness than plopping food in a bowl or setting up a litter box.

There are some terrific guides out there for *cat* care—but *kittens* are different from adults, and they have quite specific requirements. Care information constantly evolves and improves, and expert recommendations of the past often give way to more current knowledge. And quite frankly, there's no one "right" way of doing things (no matter what some books may tell you) because every kitten, owner, or home situation is unique.

Complete Kitten Care has been written with flexibility in mind. The book incorporates the expertise and latest recommendations from more than three hundred veterinary experts in behavior, conventional care, holistic treatments, and emergency protocols whom

(Photo credit: Amy D. Shojai)

Cats remain eternal kittens. Serendipity (here at four months) has never grown up.

I've been fortunate to interview over the past few years. It's important to offer a consensus of opinion and the available options to consider, rather than forcing a one-size-fits-all-kittens philosophy.

Of course, kittens can't read—and even if they could, they would probably prefer to sleep on the open pages of this book than to learn from it. You, on the other hand, are able to learn about and choose the best options available for your kitten's well-being.

Take the time to evaluate your own expectations and abilities, and what you can and cannot offer to a kitten in the way of commitment. That, more than anything else, will help you choose the "perfect match" for the lifetime of that pet. That's the smart way to choose, and then raise your kitten.

Lots of fascinating tidbits of information about cats and kittens season our body of practical knowledge, the same way salt enhances the flavor of our food. It's fun to know how to describe your kitten's unique coloring or figure out what that tail-talk means, but issues such as choosing proper toys or healthful food can be a matter of life and death. And knowing why cats cover their waste or use scratch behavior provides the basis for preventing some of the biggest cat behavior problems before they ever develop.

I want you not only to understand your kitten, but also to appreciate her unique and odd and mysterious kittenness. In my experience, this understanding will prompt you to do the right thing for your kitten.

Kittens don't stay kittens forever. They grow up and develop into beautiful, amusing, affectionate adult cats with their own individual foibles and special needs. Even as a kitten's cute factor gives way to maturity, her love for you also matures and grows stronger. *Adoption is for the lifetime of the cat*—that can be thirteen, sixteen, even eighteen years or more when proper care is given. And just as the kitten changes during these years, our own lifestyle and home situations may also change.

I hope you'll keep *Complete Kitten Care* handy as your furry baby grows, because lots of the information in this book applies to adults, too. And, of course, kittens can be addictive and you may want another one before too long. Firsthand experience offers a great background for the proper way to bring up cat babies. You'll know better what to expect and how to react with subsequent kittens.

Organization of the Book

Complete Kitten Care is divided into five parts and contains all the must-knows of kitten care and behavior to ensure that your relationship remains a positive, rewarding one. You'll notice throughout the book that kittens are referred to as *he* or *she* (usually in alternating chapters, just to be fair). Each chapter also includes fascinating lore, fun facts, and insiders' training tricks. I expect you'll want to keep the book handy to find out why your kitten's favorite games include "gravity experiments," how she purrs, and how you can imitate Mom-cat to teach kitty some manners—and more!

Dozens of sidebars throughout the book flag fun, important, or more detailed information not otherwise covered in the regular text. In addition, several "theme boxes" repeatedly call out specific helpful information. For instance, "Kitten Purrs" point out many outstanding kitten products or services available, while "Tips" boxes highlight things that are particularly helpful for living with and caring for kittens, such as time-savers, healthy living ideas, "emotional" treats for your kitten (or you!), and even ways to save money. You'll also see a number of boxes marked "Technical Stuff," especially in the kitten care and behavior sections. You can skip over them if you're in a rush for information, and still get a good handle on what you need to know. But I hope at some point you will take the time to read these sections, because they'll help you better understand the subject. But whatever you do, don't skip over information marked "Warning." Warning text sections point out some of the most common and potentially dangerous mistakes made by kitten owners, along with tips to avoid them.

Part 1: Why a Kitten?

Kittens have traveled a long road to reach the special place they hold today in our hearts. In the past, kittens and cats have been not only celebrated as gods, as in ancient Egypt, but also reviled and persecuted as demons, as during the Middle Ages. Some myths about cats persist even today. You will understand and appreciate your kitten even more when you learn how and why she evolved the way she did and how this past helps her interact today with you and the world.

Although every kitten is deserving of your love, some may be more suited to your particular personality, lifestyle, or household situation. Are you a single, apartment-dwelling professional, or do you live with a spouse and children? Perhaps you are retired, have a large house, and will be home all day. Or maybe you need to integrate the kitten with other pets and won't have the time to provide daily grooming. I want you to know what to expect from the various kitten options available so you can make choices that best suit your needs. You can choose from a rainbow of colors and patterns, in shorthaired, longhaired, wavy coats—even bald! Picking the perfect kitten requires looking deeper than the outside package, but if you're drawn to a particular "look," there are many pedigreed cat breeds that can offer a bit more predictability in terms of appearance and sometimes attitude. For instance, you need to understand that the beautiful Somali cat will probably prefer leaping atop doors to sitting in your lap.

After you know what you want, you need to know all the best places to look for the kitten of your dreams—from breeders to shelters to the waif left on your doorstep. You'll want to choose a kitten that has the best chance of being physically and emotionally healthy. I've included some checklists for evaluating kitten potential to help you narrow your selection. And because I know our emotions don't always listen to logic, you'll also find helpful guidelines and suggestions to consider when dealing with the at-risk or less-than-perfect baby you're determined to rescue.

Part 2: Bringing Home Baby

After you've chosen your new family member, you'll need to figure out how to prepare for the little one. In this part there's a fun section on choosing a name. (Hint: Kittens often seem to name themselves!) You'll also find information about protecting the kitten from unexpected household dangers by kitten-proofing your home.

You'll need a list of all the must-haves to make your kitten feel at home—everything from food bowls and bathroom facilities to toys and grooming supplies. Today there are so many choices that selecting the "right" product for the kitten can be tough. I provide a discussion of the pros and cons of some of the most popular feline accoutrements so you can choose the one best suited to your kitten's needs.

In this part I also explain all about the feline social structure. Understanding how and why kittens act and react to other cats, as well as to strange animals, people, and places, lets you smooth relationships and speeds up the training process. That gives you the tools you'll need to introduce your kitten to the other adults, children, or pets in your life.

Part 3: Kitten Care 101

In this part, I address health issues, starting with proper nutrition. After all, kittens must eat to live—and establishing proper eating habits early can keep them from developing finicky or gluttonous habits that will damage their health. What food should you give? How much and how often should your kitten eat? Are treats okay? You'll find the answers to these and other questions in this section.

Kitten grooming is also addressed. You'll learn how to keep your kitten looking spiffy and feeling her best, what grooming supplies you need—from flea combs and shampoos to toothbrushes and nail trimmers—and most important of all, *how* to groom the baby so she enjoys the process.

Veterinarians agree that preventing health problems is much easier than treating illness once it develops. This part of the book tells you how to choose a veterinarian, the signs of good kitten health, and key preventive care such as vaccinations, parasite control, and elective surgeries (spay, neuter, and declaw procedures)—and the truth about what's involved. I'll also give you a list of the top kitten health concerns, and how to recognize possible health problems. Kittens often do need medicine, just like human babies, so you'll find step-by-step instructions on home medicating your kitten when needed. And because kittens do grow into adults, there's also information on what to expect as your baby grows up, from physical signs of maturity and behavior changes you'll see to recommended prevention care and some of the most common health concerns.

Chapter 11 covers the most common kitten emergencies and what to do. If the worst should happen—your kitten falls, eats the wrong medicine, or is bitten by a stray dog—you are the first line of defense. This chapter explains how to prevent danger and how to save your kitten's life. I pray you'll never need to do so.

Of course, no book can replace the expertise of a veterinarian. Never hesitate to call on the experts. Don't leave your kitten's welfare to chance. Better a false alarm than the kitten becoming sick (or worse).

Part 4: Kitten Sociability and Training

One of my favorite topics is feline behavior, and in this section you'll learn all about how your kitten sees, hears, smells the world, tastes her food, and feels when you pet her. That's important, because senses rule the why, when, and how of kitten behavior, from hisses and purrs to fluffed fur and furled whiskers.

This section also celebrates and explains the purpose behind kitten play. You'll learn how to make play sessions work for you as training tools and bonding therapy to bring out the best personality in your pet.

There is a common misconception that kittens—cats in general—cannot be trained. Nonsense! Kittens especially are eminently trainable, and I want you to know all the key elements for teaching your new baby the rules of the house, from crate training to leash walking. What kinds of rewards work? How can you stop "bad" behavior? You'll find step-by-step instructions on these issues as well as humane and effective cures for problem behaviors like biting, clawing furniture, and hit-or-miss bathroom use. So many people routinely travel these days that kittens often need to learn some rules of the road. You'll find information on keeping your kitten safe and comfortable during travel, whether she goes with you or stays at home.

Part 5: Feline Fascinations—Top Ten Lists

Cats have mystified humans for centuries, and I've had a great time compiling entertaining information about them. Fanciful legends offer explanations for everything from distinctive feline looks to how cats came to be.

You can discover even more fun legends, feline facts, kitty-care products, and cat chat communities by surfing the Internet. I've included a chapter listing some of my favorite kitten World Wide Web destinations.

We love cats because of their unique abilities and foibles. This part also celebrates and explains many of these fun feline facts. Why do cats love catnip, sleep so much, and hate the water? Find out in part 5, chapter 17.

How to Reach Me

I'd love to hear all about your kitten trials and tribulations, joys and successes, and I invite you to contact me. Many of my books and columns feature anecdotes about the special pets in people's lives. I often include stories about my own cat Seren in regular articles at the family health care Web site Peerlesshealth.com (www.peerlesshealth.com), and also in my weekly column "Way of Life—Emotional Health" that appears on the Purina Cat Chow Web site (www.catchow.com). I even have my own Web site these days—www.shojai.com—where you can learn about my latest books, my travel and appearance schedules, and other miscellaneous information.

You can send e-mail to me from my Web site or directly by writing to amy@shojai.com. Or you can post a letter. Here's the address: Amy D. Shojai, P.O. Box 1904, Sherman, TX 75091-1904.

PART 1

WHY A
KITTEN?

CONSIDERING YOUR OPTIONS

Rainbow Coalition

If you've purchased this book, you already *know* why you want a kitten. There is nothing quite so endearing as that furry imp, or as heartwarming as the trust embodied by this loving creature who is dependent upon you to shape his life. Kittens fill the empty places inside us that we didn't know were there. They make us laugh, offer us companionship, listen to our complaints and purr us out of bad moods, celebrate our successes, and are with us through setbacks. Kittens love us, and they never, ever lie.

There is a kitten to suit every taste and circumstance. Kittens come in a kaleidoscope of coat colors, patterns, and fur length. Each is a unique work of art formed by nature, and like snowflakes, there are no two exactly alike. In fact, the way a kitten looks often changes with the mere slant of the sun that may burnish a black coat with reddish hues or highlight the glint of a contrasting undercoat.

Early in their history, all cats looked alike. Then natural selection and environmental influences caused changes in their appearance. The first cats sported tabby stripes, short hair, and long, lithe bodies suited to hot desert regions. Long fur developed in the mountainous areas of ancient Persia, where cat bodies also became more compact for cold weather. And the first pattern mutation was solid color—black cats are most common, with orange-red colors most frequently found in Southeast Asia and Japan where the mutation may have first appeared.

The basic kitten coat can be categorized as either longhaired or shorthaired. A few kittens fall somewhere between these two with medium-length fur coats, or fur that's longer in certain areas, like the ruff. The fancy name for these categories—when kitty isn't a particular breed—is Domestic Shorthair (DSH), or Domestic Longhair (DLH). Shorthaired kittens have close-fitting almost slick-looking coats, while longhaired kittens can have fluffy to silky tresses, usually with a thicker, short undercoat beneath the long outer hairs. It's not unusual for a longhaired kitten to take many months or even a year to develop a full, plush coat.

Domestic Shorthair and Domestic Longhair kittens also boast every coat color and pattern available in purebred cats. There are five basic colors in the feline coat palette: black, gray, brown, red, and white. There are also shades of these colors—for instance, dark gray is referred to as *blue*, while light gray is called *lilac,* and the red color ranges from pale cream to yellow or an intense deep red. Anytime the kitten has all the same colored fur, from the root to the tip of each hair, the color and pattern is called *solid.*

Some kittens look as if they have solid color fur until you brush your hand against the coat's "grain" and see the contrasting undercoat. These kittens have a gradual variation in coat color—the root of the fur is different from the tip. That's called *shading*. There are three different shaded patterns. *Chinchilla* is bright, luminous white that has just the tiniest hint of another color on the very end of each hair. On *shaded* cats the outer ends of the hairs are a slightly different hue, so they seem lightly brushed with color. *Smoke* kittens have a striking white undercoat with a dark outer coat. Another pattern that affects the individual hairs is called *ticked* or *agouti*, and features bands of different colors all along each hair shaft. The agouti pattern looks wild, kind of like rabbit fur, and can come in a variety of hues.

Any kitten's coat that has some white on it is called *particolor*. Usually, the proportion is either one third white with two thirds color or pattern, or the opposite—and that pattern is called *bicolor*. Cats with one of the most striking bicolor combinations, black with white markings, are often referred to as *tuxedo cats*. Another common pattern with white is *van*—these kittens are nearly all white, but they have a cap of color on top of their head and along their tail. The third pattern, *harlequin*, is an all-white body with small patches of alternating colors or patterns all over.

If your kitten has a mostly solid color body that also has red or cream, you have a *tortoiseshell* pattern kitten. When the lighter color is mixed in, that's called *brindle tortoiseshell*. When the red or cream is in blocks of color, that's called *patched tortoiseshell*. A cat with a red, white, and black coat is *calico*. A cream, white, and gray kitten is a *dilute calico*. Calico cats are almost always females.

Many folks think the term *tabby* refers to a breed, or to girl kitties, but tabby is a coat pattern that features two contrasting colors. There are three kinds of tabby patterns. *Classic tabby* is the most familiar, with lots of darker stripes and circles on a lighter background. The *mackerel tabby* also boasts stripes and circles, but in a bolder form with typically a "bull's-eye" pattern on the kitten's sides.

(*Photo credit: Weems S. Hutto*)

These Turkish van kittens sport the characteristic contrasting color on their heads and tails. "Mutt" kittens can also display this distinctive pattern—no pedigree required. Although these babies look alike, kittens within the same purebred litter can often look quite different.

And the *spotted tabby* has spots in various sizes and shapes. If you get really fancy, a mixture of tabby markings on top of tortoiseshell colors is called a *patched tabby* or a *torbie*.

The final designation is *pointed* patterns. These kittens have color or pattern only on the ears, face, legs, feet, and tail, with the body a solid yet contrasting lighter shade. Siamese and Himalayan cats are known for their pointed coats, but DSH and DLH kittens can also develop this striking coloration. Solid points can be nearly any color, from deep brown or black to light gray or cream. When the points are tabby markings—that is, stripes and spots—the kitten is said to be a *lynx point*. Kittens can even have *tortie points* that appear as tortoiseshell colors. Very light points are sometimes called *sepia points* and can be hard to see, while *mink points* combine the delicate sepia with darker points. My cat Serendipity could be described as a seal point kitty.

It's interesting to note that Siamese and other "pointed" breeds are a solid light color at birth and their color develops as they get older. The darker colored "points" are related to temperature. The cooler the body, the darker the fur. In extremely cold weather, a Siamese kitten may turn completely dark!

Evolutionary Purr-spective

Your kitten won't want you to know this, but she is related to (ahem!) the dog. Starting about 220 million years ago, during the Jurassic and Cretaceous periods, the ancestor of your kitten was born. Miacids were the first meat-eating mammals, and they outlived the dinosaurs and ultimately founded all modern carnivores, from seals, walruses, weasels, and bears to cats and dogs.

But cats didn't really start to look much like modern cats until about 35 million years ago, in the early Oligocene era, when felids began to appear. There were a wide range of catlike creatures, from house-pet-size, to giant saber-toothed varieties. At the end of the Pleistocene era—2 million years ago—the last great Ice Age killed off many of the prey animals these prehistoric cats liked to eat. In order to survive, felids had to become faster and smarter. And they did, evolving into the two major cat groups we recognize today.

The *Panthera* genus includes all the modern lions, tigers, panthers, and jaguars. All smaller cats, from ocelots and lynx to wildcats and bobcats—and even that kitten purring on your lap right now!—are referred to as *Felis*. Today it is widely accepted that modern house cats evolved from one or more species of wildcat. The first historical evidence of feline domestication was found in Egypt and dates from 1600 B.C.

Boy Versus Girl

There are, of course, some differences between the sexes. It can be difficult to tell which is which with very young kittens, especially when they are very furry. Simply lift the kitten's tail to figure out the sex. A female kitten's anus and vulva looks something like a semicolon, while the boy cat's fuzzy bottom resembles an exclamation point. His testicles become more obvious the older he gets.

There are exceptions to every rule, but generally speaking, boy cats tend to be bigger at maturity than girl cats. As they reach sexual maturity, they can develop belligerent attitudes toward other males when they test their status. They can also wreak havoc when they spray strong-scented urine to mark their territory. Intact females become extremely obnoxious, noisy, and demanding when they go into heat—that period when they can get pregnant. Practically speaking, it usually costs a bit less to have a boy cat neutered than it does to have a girl cat spayed. You can read more detailed information about feline facts of life in chapter 9, on page 168.

During kittenhood, both boys and girls act very similarly. They eat the same, play the same, sleep the same, get into the same mischief, and generate the same amount of purrs and love.

Sex does matter when introducing your new kitten into a household that already has an adult cat. Unless the cats have grown up together, it's almost always better to introduce a kitten of the opposite sex to an adult resident cat, because the older cat tends not to feel quite so threatened by this arrangement.

Everything else being equal, the kitten's sex does matter in some specific circumstances, but should not be the defining issue when choosing the baby. Rather, the kitten's personality—that spark of recognition that says you were meant for each other—is much more important than its sex.

Aristo-Cat or the Cat Next Door?

I confess, I am an equal-opportunity pet lover. I fall in love with each kitten I meet, be it a random-bred beauty or pedigreed show kitten. There really is no right or wrong choice between these two groups. It comes down to a matter of taste. However, there are advantages and disadvantages to both options that you should consider before making your choice.

Pedigree Cats

Cats come in all shapes and sizes, and specific types are called *breeds*. Very generally, a cat is considered to belong to a particular breed when a mating between it and another cat of the same type produces kittens of identical type. In other words, mating two Persian cats produces Persian babies that will have the same long fur and large round eyes as their parents. And breeding two Russian Blue cats produces shorthaired dark-gray green-eyed kittens similar in type to their parents.

Some cat breeds arose naturally in certain parts of the world, while others were developed by the careful selection of dedicated cat fanciers. Meticulous records of these feline family trees, called pedigrees, are kept. Educated breeders use pedigrees to help predict what kind of offspring a particular mating may produce. They strive to preserve and improve the integrity of a given breed through carefully matchmaking prospective cat parents. Today there are more than one hundred different cat breeds recognized throughout the world.

Adopting a pedigree kitten from a reputable breeder offers the advantage of a known ancestry. You'll likely be able to meet at least one of the parents, which can help predict the future personality of your little one. Specific cat breeds are also known for certain personality traits, so you may be better able to choose a kitten that matches your own high-energy or laid-back demeanor. Purebred kittens also tend to have an above-average health-care history because good breeders are sticklers for preventive care, such as good nutrition, vaccinations, and worm medicine.

Finally, purebred kittens raised "underfoot"—that is, as members of the breeder's pet family—have the huge advantage of being properly socialized. Socialization refers to the period of time during early kitten life when the baby learns to accept people (and other animals) as safe, happy, and normal parts of his life.

There are some drawbacks to pedigree kittens. The most obvious is the cost—you can expect to spend much more on a purebred baby, in the hundreds or sometimes thousands of dollars. That's because some breeds are quite rare, and may not be available for "pet homes" because they are expected to compete in shows and contribute to their breed as future moms and dads. But the higher cost also often includes some sort of limited guarantee because of the investment the breeder has made in the health of the kittens.

After investing their time, money, and love producing high-quality kittens, breeders can be quite selective about who gets their babies. They also may limit your ability to breed the kittens, especially if they consider the kitten "pet quality" and not a show or breeding contender. After all, their reputation is at stake, and they want only folks who know what they're doing to breed their kittens.

Another potential downside of adopting purebred kittens is certain health problems that may be present in a given breed. Overall, cat breeds have many fewer of these kinds of inherited problems than do dogs, and reputable cat breeders are honest about these concerns.

The greatest drawback to adopting purebred kittens occurs when the breeder is not reputable. In these instances, both you and the kitten suffer the consequences. Paying lots of money does not guarantee a healthy, well-bred, and happy kitten. For more details about how to find and identify good breeders and quality purebred kittens, see chapter 2.

A Look at Cat Shows

Cats have been a part of human history for at least five thousand years, but cats were left pretty much to themselves until the mid–nineteenth century, when selective breeding became popular. That's when existing natural breeds began to be refined, and newer breeds were developed by dedicated hobby breeders. Cat shows offered a venue to showcase these successful efforts.

The first recorded cat show was in Saint Giles, Winchester, England, in 1598, and the first formal "benched" cat show was staged by Mr. Harrison Weir on July 13, 1871, at the Crystal Palace in London. About twenty-five years later, cat shows came to the United States when two hundred cats competed at Madison Square Garden in New York in 1895.

A cat show usually features pedigreed cats that are compared against a written "standard" of breed perfection. The cat that comes closest to this ideal wins the contest. Today, there are a number of national and international cat associations that register cats, keep records of pedigrees, publish breed standards, and sponsor cat shows. You can often find shows that include "household cat" competitions for nonpedigree kitties.

Each cat association has specific guidelines for showing, and it can get a bit complicated, but if you're interested, showing your kitten can be great fun! Contact information for the many cat associations can be found in the appendix on page 309 and will tell you exactly what to expect and how to get involved in the show fancy.

"Mutt" Cats

They are called mutt cats, random-bred kittens, or mixed-breed felines. Unlike their purebred brethren, nonpedigree cats do not produce predictable kittens from any given mating. The babies of a pair of Domestic Shorthair cats may sport a rainbow of colors and patterns, with some favoring long fur, others sporting short coats, and a random mix of eye colors and body types. But whatever they're called, our cat-next-door felines are without a doubt the most popular "type" of pet cat in the world.

The biggest advantage to "everyday" kitties is that they are always available, and for a reasonable cost. Be advised that no cat is free! Even the kitties that appear on your back porch require preventive and routine health care. The cost is the same whether he's a purebred kitten or shelter rescue.

Mutt kittens can be every bit as beautiful, healthy, and well socialized as their purebred counterparts. But they are at higher risk for health and behavior problems, because they may not have the advantages of being born to a healthy and pampered Mom-cat or handled by loving cat advocates.

Random bred or "mutt" kittens come in as many varieties as their pedigree cousins and are just as lovable. Siblings can look very different.

(*Photo credit: Ralston Purina Company*)

There are far more mutt cats than there are people to care for them. So when you adopt a random-bred kitten you are often saving his life. That's the biggest advantage of all.

Kitten Care Considerations

Other options to consider with choosing your kitten include personality, activity level, and care requirements. All kittens play and are active, and certainly every kitten needs to be groomed. But some kittens have no off switch, while others like to lap-snuggle after a romp, and a number of kittens—especially purebred cats—have very specific hygiene needs.

Cat breeds and types such as Maine Coon, Himalayan, and Domestic Longhair kittens need more coat care than do shorthaired varieties. That's because long fur gets matted and tangled very easily and should be combed regularly—kitten tongues just can't do the job by themselves. Longer fur also can catch bathroom deposits, so regular attention to the kitten's bottom helps keep problems from developing. Kittens that have very large, prominent eyes like Persians also need help keeping tears cleaned away.

Some kitten breeds are known to be particularly active, while others tend to be more sedate. The Abyssinian, an agouti-coated beauty, is one of the Tarzans of the feline world and loves to swing from drapes and scale the tallest perch. In contrast, the British Shorthair has been described as a calm, quiet, low-activity breed of cat. Persians often seem to know they are meant to be admired, and love to lap-sit and window-perch rather than leap about.

A few cat breeds are famous for their loud voices. Siamese-type cats have distinctive meows and love to hold long—and loud—conversations with their humans. If you adopt one of these kittens, they'll always get in the last word.

BREED TENDENCIES CHART

HIGHLY ACTIVE (In-your-face cats)	LOWER ACTIVITY (Tends more toward lap-sitting)	VERY VOCAL (Opinion about everything)	QUIET (Prefers watching)	HIGH-FASHION MODELS (Above-average grooming)
Abyssinian, Balinese, Bombay, Burmese, Colorpoint Shorthair, Cornish Rex, Devon Rex, Egyptian Mau, Javanese, Oriental Longhair, Oriental Shorthair, Russian Blue, Siamese, Somali, Tonkinese	American Wirehair, Birman, British Shorthair, Exotic, Himalayan, Persian, Ragdoll, Snowshoe	Balinese, Colorpoint Shorthair, Japanese Bobtail, Javanese, Oriental Longhair, Oriental Shorthair, Siamese, Tonkinese	American Wirehair, Birman, British Shorthair, Chartreux, Egyptian Mau, Exotic, Havana Brown, Korat, Scottish Fold, Snowshoe	Exotic, Himalayan, Maine Coon, Norwegian Forest Cat, Persian, Ragdoll, Scottish Fold (longhair)

2

LOOKING FOR YOUR DREAM KITTEN

Give Me Shelter

One of the best places to look for your dream kitten is the local animal shelter. These organizations often have kittens available by the armload, especially during the spring "kitten season."

Kittens from the best shelters have the advantage of being cared for by a knowledgeable staff and an army of caring volunteers. Animal welfare services often take great pains to handle and properly socialize these babies to ensure they will fit into your family and become the best pet possible.

Veterinary exams also screen shelter kittens for health problems, provide preventive care, and sometimes offer a discounted cost for future treatment. Often, a history of the cat's life is available, and may include any medical treatments, personality traits ("likes dogs"), and behavior foibles ("loves to climb"). Shelters want these adoptions to be permanent ones, and so may also offer counseling and support services to guide you through correcting or preventing any behavioral difficulties.

There is a wide range of shelters from which to choose. Nearly every part of the country has access to some type of facility that handles unwanted dogs and cats. They go by many names—Rescue Leagues, Animal Control, City Pound, Humane Society, and SPCA (Society for the Prevention of Cruelty to Animals).

Some shelters are very large and offer paid staff and a variety of services. Many are private facilities, others are city-run operations, and some are quite small. There are even shelters for cats only.

Shelters may be further divided into those that euthanize animals that are not adopted within a set time limit or are deemed unadoptable due to illness, injury, or temperament and no-kill facilities that rehabilitate and house the pet indefinitely. Euthanasia of unwanted pets is a sad fact of life at the majority of shelters, and until pet owners take responsibility and prevent the births of these unwanted animals, it will remain so. Unfortunately, all shelters (especially no-kill facilities) have limited space and aren't able to accept as many animals as they'd like.

The past few years, I've traveled a great deal and visited shelter facilities all across the country. Most are run by dedicated pet lovers who want to help the animals and the people they serve. Visit your local shelters to see how the kittens are housed, handled, and treated. The best situations will have clean, sanitary-appearing facilities with staff eager and willing to answer your questions.

At some facilities the cats and kittens are caged individually to help prevent illness, often in a room segregated from barking dogs. Others house pairs or litters of kittens together. Still others provide play areas or house groups of cats or kittens in cageless environments that allow them to interact with each other, climb cat trees, and play. This more natural setting can be healthier for the emotional life of the cats, but it does risk exposure to communicable illnesses if the animals don't receive proper health screenings.

Visit with the staff and find out their adoption policies. Although most shelters are not for profit, they must charge adoption fees to offset the cost of treating the animals and running the facility. Often, the adoption fee includes to-date vaccinations, veterinary health exams, worm treatments, and spaying or neutering surgeries. Some also microchip the adopted pet for identification purposes. Depending on the facility, kittens may be spayed or neutered prior to your taking them home, or you may be required to schedule an appointment at a later date. Often there will either be a veterinarian on staff, or a group of dedicated local veterinarians who offer lower-cost spaying and neutering services. And because kittens that are adopted together often do best, sometimes shelters offer incentives to adopt two littermates together at the same time.

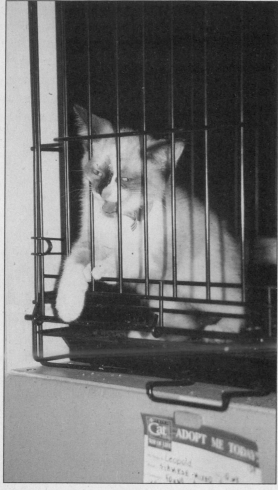

Shelters have hundreds of kittens available for adoption. This kitten, Leopold, was adopted on the day this photo was taken.

(Photo credit: Amy D. Shojai)

Shelter staff members often require you to complete a questionnaire or be interviewed about your pet history to determine what you want in a pet. That helps them match you to the perfect kitten. In some instances, a shelter may refuse to allow a person to adopt a pet if the staff members don't feel the home environment is appropriate or if the applicant's pet history is less than ideal.

For instance, some shelters require assurance that the kitten will remain exclusively inside or won't be declawed. They may also deny an application if the person plans to give the pet as a gift to a third party. An exception may be made for parents adopting for children—but even then, some shelters may not be comfortable allowing very young kittens into homes with youngsters who may not know how to properly and safely handle them. Finally, some shelters may actually require a home visit to be sure you have an adequate place for the kitten. In the case of apartment dwellers, shelters often require a letter from the landlord that grants permission to keep a pet.

Kitten-Keeping Trends

Prior to the 1960s, dogs won the pet popularity contest paws down. All that changed with the innovation of Kitty Litter brand cat box filler, which offered convenient indoor cat bathroom facilities. Once clay litter products became common (replacing sand), kittens traveled from the barnyard into the family room, and they've never left.

At about the same time, two-income families became more common, as did apartment living. Pet lovers unable to schedule time for dog walks or without room for the large dogs they'd loved as kids, discovered that cats suited their situations just fine. That resulted in an enormous surge in feline popularity during the 1970s. By the late 1980s cats had arguably surpassed dogs as the number one pet of choice among Americans.

Today, modern dogs and cats are nearly equal in their popularity. More households keep dogs, but because many people share their lives with multiple felines, there are more pet cats than dogs. Current surveys estimate that 72.6 million cats are kept as pets by Americans—that's about 34 percent of U.S. households.

Breeder Sources

Maybe you've got your heart set on a regal Russian Blue like Great Aunt Gretchen's or the Japanese Bobtail you saw at a cat show. Shelters rarely have purebred cats or kittens available. The only exceptions might be the nonregistered pointed-pattern Siamese look-alike, or the Persian that became too much of a grooming problem for an unprepared owner. There may be kittens that look similar to some of the purebred kitties, of course—but long fur doesn't make a cat a Persian, and a missing tail doesn't make him a Manx.

The best place to find a purebred kitten is from a reputable cattery in your area. Many of the specialty cat magazines, such as *Cat Fancy*, list cat breeders and catteries in the back of their publications. Not every breed will have a cattery near you, and not all catteries will be listed in these breeder directories, but this is a good place to start.

Another resource is Web sites that feature various breeds. Many of the cat registry association home pages offer a list of breeders and catteries that are available in different parts of the country. Some of the best purebred kitten sites are listed on page 309.

Purebred kittens are not cheap. You can expect to pay in the hundreds of dollars for one of these selectively bred babies. But unless you plan to compete in cat shows, a "pet quality" kitten can be the perfect and more economical choice for you. These are babies that for one reason or another—perhaps the kitten has eyes of the wrong color or less-than-perfect markings—are not judged by the breeder to be good show or breeding prospects. Often the cattery reduces the price on these pet-quality kittens.

Once you have narrowed your search to nearby catteries, call and talk with the owner or breeder, and arrange for a visit. Kittens won't be available all the time, and you may need to place your name on a waiting list. More important than cost or getting on a waiting list, you want to evaluate the cattery facilities where your potential new kitten family member is born and raised. It should be clean, the cats should look healthy and happy, and the breeder should be interested in you and willing to answer any questions you have.

In fact, you should expect to be interviewed thoroughly by the breeder. These folks invest a great deal of time, money, and emotion into their kittens, and they won't sell to just anybody. Just like you, they want the kittens to go to a home where they will be loved and taken care of in a responsible way for the rest of their lives. A good relationship with your kitten's breeder offers a good resource for answering any kitten questions that may arise down the road, and it can turn into a lasting friendship. And if you are at all interested in showing your kitten, you can't do better than the friendship and mentoring relationship offered by an experienced, responsible breeder.

At least some of the cats should have run of the household—"raised underfoot," in other words, which means they are treated and handled like pets and family members. The boy cats will likely be confined to certain areas to cut down on spraying, and very young kittens may also be segregated for their protection.

But if the facility isn't clean—the cats are all caged; the kittens and adults appear ill, unkempt, very shy or frightened; and the breeder seems more interested in getting your money than in the well-being of the kitten—*run, do not walk, away from this cattery!*

Sadly, there are bad apples in most any barrel, including cat breeders. Often, these establishments are referred to as "back-yard breeders" and the folks involved typically care more about making money on their furry livestock than furthering the welfare of the kittens.

It can be hard to tell the good from the bad or ugly simply from browsing an Internet or magazine listing. That's why it's so important to visit the site and personally choose your kitten with the breeder.

Breeders do, upon occasion, ship kittens across the country. That's not something I'd recommend, even from a reputable cattery. Kittens are easily stressed, and traveling as cargo on a plane puts them at risk. If your perfect breed isn't available locally, and you'd like to pursue this option, be sure to receive strong personal recommendations from people you trust about the cattery in question.

Pet Stores—Be Informed

Many years ago, when I still worked as a veterinary technician, a new client arrived, proud as punch over her brand-new four-hundred-dollar kitten purchased from a local pet store. As I filled out the history card, she corrected me from calling her kitten a DSH. "My kitten," she told me, "is a registered Patio Cat. I have the registration papers right here." I didn't argue with her—the four-hundred-dollar piece of paper made her happy—but there is no such breed as a Patio Cat. She was fortunate in that her baby was healthy, and her little random-bred kitten was lucky to have found a loving home. The message here is *buyer beware!*

Reputable breeders of purebred kittens—and of purebred puppies, for that matter—recognize the importance of screening new owners. Reputable breeders do not sell through pet stores. Period.

Warning: If reputable breeders won't supply them, then where do pet store purebred kittens come from? To be blunt, some come from the back-yard breeders mentioned above. They also come from establishments loosely described as kitten mills.

Termed "mills," these breeding facilities are better described as factories of horror. They are most common in the Midwest, Pennsylvania, and other farming regions of the United States. Adult animals spend their short, miserable lives in filthy wire cages with little to no human contact. They're often exposed to extremes of heat, cold, or other weather hazards, until untreated health problems and overbreeding wear them out. These animals' sole purpose in life is to breed and repeatedly give birth to kittens (and puppies) that are then supplied to unscrupulous pet stores. Animals no longer able to reproduce are killed and replaced. The pet industry, the U.S. Department of Agriculture, and cat breed registries condemn the practice and have instituted stricter regulations and inspection guidelines. Despite great efforts to better police these substandard commercial breeders, appalling kitten and puppy factories continue to churn out their tragic merchandise.

Some pet stores do offer purebred kittens for sale, and it can be hard to resist that big-eyed fuzzy face in the window. The store may even have legitimate registration papers. A few offer some type of health guarantee that could help defray veterinary costs in case the purchased kitten gets sick or dies shortly after you bring her home. Be aware that kittens generated by this industry have a much higher chance of developing health problems due to less-than-ideal breeding and hygiene practices. And as the kitten matures, behavior problems are also likely because they have not been socialized. Buying a kitten-mill kitten, no matter how altruistic the intention, supports the industry.

There is good news about pet stores, however. A number of the most progressive establishments, the superstore PetsMart for example, have taken steps to set a new standard for their industry. Instead of selling kittens and cats (or puppies and dogs), they have formed partnerships with local shelters to showcase adoptable animals in their facilities.

These liaisons offer a great opportunity for shelters, pet stores, and prospective owners to make educated choices. Of course, the kittens benefit the most.

Know the Score—Kitten Source Checklist

There are many places to find your dream kitten, and some are clearly better than others. Take a moment to ask the shelter staff, breeder, or other source these questions. That will give you an idea of the potential risk involved in adopting or buying from that establishment. For each question below, a yes answer receives one point, and a no response gets zero points. Tally the score when you finish to see how the kitten source rates—the higher the score, the better.

1. Can you tell me about the temperament of at least one parent (the mother)?

2. Can you tell me about the temperament of my kitten?

3. Has the kitten been "raised underfoot" and handled, so she's socialized to people?

4. Will you let me visit the facilities and see where my kitten has been raised?

5. If she's a purebred, is registration information available?

6. Can you provide a medical history of to-date vaccinations or other care given?

7. Does the purchase price or adoption fee include a health guarantee?

8. Do you provide a list of references or testimonials from satisfied adopters or purchasers?

9. Have you ever turned down a potential purchaser or adopter?

10. Will you be available to offer help and advice as my kitten grows?

Scores of 8 to 10 = IDEAL. Scores of 5 to 7 = FAIR to GOOD. Scores of 4 or less = PROCEED WITH CAUTION.

Friends and Neighbors

There are always neighbors, friends of friends, and family members who have rescued a pregnant cat or abandoned kittens—or have accidentally delayed spaying the family cat until she's in the family way.

When the kitten comes from someone you know, you have the advantage of finding out more about the baby and even making several visits to be sure which one strikes the chord in your heart. You also will know your family and friends' background and how well they've cared for your prospective pet. The history of the people raising the kittens—perhaps they've loved and successfully kept cats for the past thirty years—offers a great endorsement of how your new kitten will fit into your family.

Advertisements in newspapers may also offer good options. During the spring kitten season, your local newspaper will be filled with advertisements for kittens "free to good home." Here, too, you'll want to evaluate the environment just as you would a shelter or cattery. Are the animals clean? Well fed? Loved? Have the kittens been raised underfoot? Or do they live under the house with their feral mother, with no people contact?

Some folks will want to ask you questions and interview your potential as a prospective pet parent—that's a very positive sign. More often, though, people are simply eager to unburden themselves, and you will have free choice of the babies, no questions asked.

Remember, too, that such situations involve hidden costs. That "free kitten" has probably had no veterinary health care. That may mean extra expense down the road, in addition to routine vaccinations and other preventive attention. You'll find tips and information on how to evaluate kitten personality and health status in chapter 3—see "Pick of the Litter" on page 38.

(Photo credit: Amy D. Shojai)

Sometimes kittens show up at your door. These foundlings can become wonderful, rewarding pets despite their rough start in life.

The Waif on the Doorstep

In many instances, the kitten finds you rather than the other way around. A friend of mine has rescued, raised, and placed countless furry waifs who appear on her front porch. She says the cats have marked her house as a safe place, and they drop off their babies for her care.

That's what happened to me—Seren showed up in a flowerpot on the back porch. But I strongly suspect a human breeder, rather than her mom-cat, dumped her there after unsuccessful attempts to sell her.

I wouldn't trade Seren for anything. She has become an outstanding companion and family member—but the odds were against that happening. Adopting a stray kitten offers the most potential for problems.

These kittens have often been on their own for days to weeks at a time, without any type of preventive health care. They are often stressed or already sick when you find them. Seren, for instance, was about four months old and had been on her own for so long, she was severely dehydrated, infested with fleas and ear mites, and had the start of ringworm. Even so, she was far healthier than many strays.

Stray kittens have likely not had the benefit of handling by humans. That can make it difficult for the baby to bond closely with you. Behavior problems could develop down the road as a result of their missing this important socialization. Also, when you go in search of a kitten, you can prepare in advance before bringing home your furry wonder—not so with an unexpected bundle of joy.

Adopting an ill, needy kitten will require a much greater investment of your time, money, and emotion. You must be prepared for those sad instances when the best of intentions and veterinary care will not save the kitten's fragile life.

But when it works, it's magic. Rescuing a lost kitten and watching her thrive is incredibly rewarding.

History of Kitten-Keeping

When ancient people began to cultivate gardens that attracted vermin, wildcats suddenly became prized and were enticed to hang out near granaries. Rodent patrol—doing what kitty does naturally—was profitable for both the humans and the cats, and felines probably began to live nearby and alongside human populations from about 7000 to 4000 B.C. Along the way, the people and kittens fell in love with each other and started a partnership that has lasted thousands of years. The earliest documented evidence to support cat domestication dates from about 1600 B.C. in ancient Egypt.

In fact, the physical prowess of felines was greatly admired, and religious cults and beliefs that celebrated these abilities surrounded cats in many early cultures. By 950 B.C. cats of the Nile Delta in Egypt were celebrated as the earthly incarnations of gods. Kitties were so cherished, it became a crime for them to leave Egypt—but, of course, some were stolen and smuggled out, and by the tenth century, cats were widespread throughout most of Europe and Asia.

The Middle Ages of Europe brought a low point in kitten-keeping, when the religion of the day linked cats to the devil and turned them into scapegoats for all that was wrong with the era. By the sixteenth century, cats regained their reputation as loving companions. It's not clear when kitties first arrived in the New World, but very likely they traveled on ships with early settlers. These earliest cat pioneers were the founding feline fathers of the Domestic Shorthair and Domestic Longhair kittens we cherish today.

3

CHOOSING THE
PURR-FECT MATCH

Pick of the Litter

How do you choose a healthy, well-adjusted kitten? Choosing your kitten from a source that's above reproach will help ensure the baby is healthy and well socialized.

No matter where you find your kitten, you can use the same criteria to evaluate his health and emotional status. Not every furry baby will have stellar health or start out with the best socialization. You may choose him anyway, and that's fine—these babies are often the most needy and deserving of a loving home. But it's important that you recognize the problems so you know what to expect and can take steps to make up for any false starts, giving the kitten every opportunity to thrive.

Head-to-Toe Physical

The kitten's skin is the largest physical structure of his body, and along with fur, is a barometer of kitten health. Pet the kitten all over. Short fur should be shiny and clean, long fur fluffy and without tangles, and there should be no bald spots or sores anywhere on his body. Skin sores or lost fur can be a sign of parasites such as fleas, fungus infections like ringworm, or poor nutrition. All are treatable with prompt veterinary help.

The skin of the ears should be pink, clear, and clean. Any sort of discharge could indicate either an ear infection, or more commonly, parasites like ear mites. Ear mites are very contagious among pets, but are highly treatable.

Kitten eyes should be clear, have no squint, and show no discharge or crust. His nose should be clean, with only a small amount of clear discharge, if any. Runny eyes or nose, or both, could be a sign of an upper respiratory infection (URI)—a kitty cold. These are highly contagious among cats and can be devastating to young kittens. Again, veterinary attention and home nursing care are often necessary to help the baby recover.

Look inside the kitten's mouth. Sores inside also point to URI and can make it hard for the baby to eat. The gums above the teeth should be pink—if they're very pale, the baby may be anemic or dehydrated from fleas. If you suspect dehydration, check by grasping the loose skin at the baby's neck (scruff) and lifting; then release. When the baby is dehydrated, the skin will "tent" and stay elevated rather than springing back immediately.

Check the area beneath the kitten's tail to be sure it's clean and has no signs of diarrhea. Diarrhea can result from a wide range of health problems, from viruses to intestinal parasites. It can also cause dehydration very quickly in a tiny kitten. A healthy kitten has only one speed when not sleeping—*zoom!* Any time the youngster acts depressed or weak is cause for concern. Anemia, dehydration, fever, and a wide range of illnesses put a damper on kitten energy.

Warning: Many kitten conditions are quite contagious. Even if the one you choose appears healthy, if his mom or any of his siblings have signs of illness, your kitten may be incubating the disease and could become sick after you take him home.

Emotional Evaluation

Kittens in a litter can not only look very different, they can also have a wide range of personalities. It's a good idea to first evaluate all the babies together—with the mom present, when possible. There's security in numbers and the kittens will often show their true colors when they have other cats nearby.

To get a good read on personality, sit on the floor and let the kittens come to you. You're a huge creature compared to the baby, and you'll be more approachable once you're on his level.

The ideal kitten meets the world with curious eyes wide open, ready to explore, and with a courageous, take-no-prisoners curiosity. I call these kittens the Christopher Columbus kitties because they seem to thrive on new experiences.

Look for a baby who, after perhaps a brief hesitation, comes forward to meet you with his tail spiked straight up to the ceiling. That's a kitten greeting reserved for Mom and "superiors," and is a very good sign. He recognizes people as safe but all-powerful beings and defers to you.

A certain amount of caution is healthy, of course. But the shy, shrinking violet kitten that hides under the bed or cowers and shivers at your touch will need lots of help to become better adjusted. Others may actually be so terrified that they hiss, spit, or even try to attack and can require more attention than you have to give. For shy babies, try enticing from a distance with a feather toy or ribbon to see if they'll forget their reticence. Pick up the kitten—cup his furry bottom with one hand and support his chest with the other—and set him on your lap. Does he snuggle down and purr? Does he fight and bite your hands? Or does he leap off your lap and chase after another game? Each kitten type can become a great pet, and it depends on what you want out of the relationship. Keep in mind that kittens often change as they mature. But chances are the purr-baby will more likely grow up to be a lap kitty, while the game-minded kitten will more likely prefer ankle-rubbing and chase games. Try to match the kitten to your expectations rather than fight kitten nature and become disappointed when you fail to change him down the road.

The biting kitten could frankly go either way. He'll need a family who has the time to offer consistent training to help him learn to inhibit his bite and respect people. Otherwise, he's likely to become the ruler in your house—and you may not like his rules!

Is He Old Enough?

What age is best to adopt your new kitten? The majority of professional cat breeders and many well-respected cat behaviorists say that cat babies should stay with siblings and Mom-cat for *at*

It doesn't take long for kittens to fall in love with people—or vice versa! Here, cat advocate Libby Ottiger has found a power-kissing kitten.

(Photo credit: Amy D. Shojai)

least twelve to sixteen weeks. Of course, that's not always possible.

Maturity has as much to do with emotional development as it does with physical growth. Physically, kittens are able to eat and thrive on commercial food as early as three weeks of age and most are weaned by six to eight weeks of age. That's the most common age when kittens leave and go to new homes, primarily I believe for convenience's sake. Shelters often have limited space, so as soon as kittens reach that six- to eight-week mark, are able to eat on their own, and have had a set of preventive vaccines, they're out the door.

But by that age, kittens are just beginning to learn to be proper cats. And no matter how well intentioned, human caretakers aren't able to do as good a job as furry siblings and cat-parents in teaching them. Kittens learn from other cats how to use the litter box and cover their waste, groom themselves, play nicely, inhibit claws and bites, use and understand body language and verbal cues, and defer to dominant felines. They also take their cues from other cats about what's safe and what's scary and to be avoided. If, for example,

Mom-cat shows kittens a positive reaction to a friendly dog, they'll be more likely to get along in a multipet home.

Kittens adopted too early often bite and claw more than those who have been kitty-corrected by Mom and siblings. They also may be fearful or less tolerant of other cats because they don't understand all the proper feline etiquette of the social structure. And because cats tend to consider their human to be part of their family, it's important for the kitten to respect you and defer to your rules of the house, just as he would a cat in command.

Proper socialization includes not only interaction with other cats, but also positive handling by people during this critical period. That will ensure the baby is well adjusted, confident, and emotionally healthy.

We do not always have the luxury of adopting our kitten at the "ideal" age. So you, the human parent, must make your best effort to do Mom-cat's job and teach Junior how to be a proper cat. Each age has particular challenges, too. After all, a kitten is a kitten from birth until he reaches his first birthday—that's a lot of physical and emotional growth and development!

Technical Stuff: The intestinal tract provides a defensive barrier that keeps large, potentially dangerous molecules like viruses or toxins from being absorbed. The exception is antibodies found in the Mom-cat's milk. During the first twelve to eighteen hours of life, the newborn's gut allows these large antibody molecules to be absorbed into the body. That's how the kitten acquires protective immunity that helps keep him safe until he can begin to manufacture his own antibodies (starting at about four weeks of age).

Because the open gut closes after these first few hours, it's important that cat babies nurse very soon after birth. When the mother cat is unable to nurse her kittens (for whatever reason), professional breeders often place newborns with a foster Mom-cat. The antibody level of feline colostrum (first milk) is not significantly higher than milk produced later, so this arrangement helps ensure that the babies benefit from this natural immunity boost.

Kitten Growth Progression—What to Expect

Neonatal Period=Birth through week two
Transitional Period=End of Neonatal Period to week three
Socialization Period=Week three through week nine to ten
Juvenile Period=Week ten until sexual maturity

AT BIRTH

When your kitten was born, he measured four to six inches long and weighed only two to four ounces. He was blind, deaf, toothless, and unable to regulate his own body temperature to stay warm. Newborns are only able to maintain a 95-degree temperature (normal adult temp is 100 to 102.5 degrees) so they must be in contact with Mom or surrogate warmth to survive.

At this age, kittens depend on touch, the sense of smell, and thermal sensation to find Mom and food, and they move by wriggling their bodies from side to side. Babies purr as they nurse, and most return to the same nipple every time. That's because they scent-mark the nipple the first time they nurse and the smell acts as a beacon to draw them back thereafter.

WEEK ONE

After seven days, the kitten's birth weight doubles. Kittens spend four hours a day suckling, and more than sixteen hours sleeping. Instead of moving like little worms, their shoulders, pelvis, and legs develop enough so they can drag themselves along the ground. They look a bit like swimmers paddling across the bedding. By this age, the body's shiver reflex develops, which means they are better able to regulate temperature and keep themselves warm.

WEEK TWO

By the second week, kittens suckle up to three hours a day. Their eyes begin to open between nine to twelve days of age, and babies

<u>Tube Feeding</u>

Sometimes newborn kittens are so sick and weak, they aren't able to suck or swallow, and will starve without being helped to eat. Experienced breeders often tube feed these kittens. It only takes a couple minutes to do—a huge time-saver when feeding several babies—and you know each baby gets the correct amount. A flexible hollow tube is threaded down the baby's throat into the stomach and food is injected with a syringe. It's easy to do once you've been shown how by the veterinarian. Here's how breeders and veterinarians recommend tube feeding be done.

1. Buy a Number 5 French catheter with a 6 or 12 cc syringe from your drugstore. It's a good idea to lubricate the inside of the syringe and plunger with cooking oil before you begin, so there's no sticking. And after each use, be sure to wash everything in hot soapy water, rinse it, and keep it clean in a plastic bag.

2. Measure the distance between the kitten's mouth and his stomach, so the tube doesn't fall short of the target or go too far. Place the end of the tube at the baby's last rib—that's where the stomach lies—and measure from there to his mouth for the proper length. Mark the place on the tube with a piece of tape that can be moved as the baby grows.

3. Fill the syringe with the proper amount of commercial kitten formula. Warm it to body temperature—about 100 degrees—by floating the formula in a bowl of warm water while you place the feeding tube.

4. Hold the baby in an upright position to make it easier to pass the tube. Put the open end of the tube against the roof of his mouth, and thread it down the esophagus into the stomach. This tends to trigger the gag reflex, but that should stop once the tube has gone beyond the back of the throat, and the kitten will swallow to help it along. The trachea (airway) opens at the center of the throat, so aim for the sides to find the esophagus. Don't force the tube; it should slide down easily and if it doesn't, you may be in the airway by mistake—so withdraw the tube and start over.

5. Some kittens are so weak they may not cough or struggle even if the tube goes into the lungs, so check your placement before giving any food or you could drown them. If the kitten cries, the tube is in the right place (they can't vocalize with the tube in the airway). Put the end of the outside portion of the tube straight down in about an inch of water, so that no water runs into the tube—if you see a stream of air bubbles escape from the tube, that means you're in the lungs. Remove the tube and try again. Usually this isn't a problem because typically the tube is too large to pass through the windpipe and most easily goes down the esophagus as it should.

6. Connect the formula-filled syringe to the tube and slowly inject the kitten formula down the tube into the stomach. Then quickly remove the tube, and cuddle the baby for a moment to settle any bruised feelings. Usually, healthy kittens older than two weeks become strong enough to nurse on their own, and begin to struggle against the feeding tube.

learn to recognize Mom and others as friends or foes. Ears begin to unseal about this same time.

All kittens have blue eyes when they first open. The final, adult eye color develops as they mature, usually by three to four months. Some kitties, like the Korat breed, may not develop final eye color until they are four years old.

Kittens practice raising their chest with front legs, and strengthen their muscles by moving about more. The first deciduous (baby or milk) teeth start to appear at this age, the tiny incisors across the front of the mouth.

Week Three

Nursing time starts to decrease, but the babies still suckle about two hours a day. The rear legs gain strength and kittens start to stand and walk on wobbly legs.

A lot happens during this period. The sense of smell becomes fully developed, and the babies begin to catalogue the meaning of different scents. Kittens start to clumsily play with each other, follow Mom around, learn about the litter box, and are now able to retract their claws. They start to watch Mom and mimic her by grooming themselves. Body temperature control develops. Normal body temperature rises to between 97 to 99 degrees during this period.

The prime socialization period begins. What kittens experience beginning at this age will have a huge impact on how well adjusted they become as adults. Kittens handled a few minutes daily by people during their first month of life have an improved ability to learn.

WEEK FOUR

Kitten hearing is fully developed by week four, and the body weight has doubled again. Mom's milk production starts to decrease just as the kitten's energy needs grow. Curiosity and hunger spur the babies to sample Mom's solid food.

By this age, kittens understand the concept of the litter box from watching Mom. However, they still have a limited capacity for "holding it" and may have accidents when the box isn't close enough to accommodate their needs. They continue to develop physically. Needle-sharp canine teeth appear next to the incisors, and premolars grow behind the canines (three on the top, two on the bottom).

Social play with Mom and siblings begins now, and includes running, rolling, biting, wrestling, climbing, and jumping. The righting mechanism that allows cats to land on their feet is fully developed by week four—but kittens can still be injured by falls. Play helps them tone muscles and practice all the necessary cat moves they'll need as adults. Play is also fun. If you are the "mother figure," it's up to you to teach baby about the litter box, playing "nice," and eating grown-up food.

Take the little one to the litter box immediately after he's eaten—that's a prime time for elimination. Scratch your finger through the litter to give him the idea. It may help to plant one of his "deposits" in the box for a scent cue, too. Once he's been productive and urinated or defecated, praise him, and use the scooper to cover up the waste. Let the kitten leave the box and room under his own power, if possible, so he learns and remembers how he got there.

Mom-cat and siblings let the baby know if he bites or claws too hard, and they'll hiss at him or put an end to the game. As surrogate Mom, you should do the same. Avoid letting him play with your fingers or toes—that only encourages him to bite. And when he does accidentally nail you, don't put up with it. Hiss at him sharply, or say "No!" and end the game. He'll learn to play nicely and inhibit his bites and claws to continue playing.

WEEKS FIVE TO SEVEN

Finally, the body thermostat has matured enough so the kitten doesn't rely on Mom or siblings to stay warm. Kittens gain two to four ounces a week from birth to five to six months of age. The kitten immune system is also fully developed by six to twelve weeks of age, while the immune protection he gained from Mom begins to fade.

The last premolars erupt by six to eight weeks of age. The drive to copy Mom is very strong, and they learn what they should do by imitating her. Kittens spend nearly an hour a day eating solid food—but they'll still pester Mom to nurse, if she'll let them.

Play and interaction with others takes over. This is the period when kittens learn to recognize friends and enemies. Good experiences with people and other pets during this time ensures they'll be well-adjusted adult cats.

When you adopt a kitten at this age, it's up to you to expose him to a wide range of situations so he'll be willing to accept them as he ages. He should learn to accept being handled and groomed by you and strangers, so the veterinarian won't have to fight him for an examination. This is the best age to train him to accept the cat carrier and leash. That will allow him to travel with you when necessary, either to the vet or groomers, or across town to visit Grandma. And if you think another pet (dog or cat) or a child might be in your future, introduce him to positive experiences at this age. That way, he'll accept them as a normal part of his world, and you'll prevent behavior problems down the road.

WEEKS EIGHT TO NINE

By this age, kittens are fully weaned and eating a commercial kitten food. They spend up to an hour each day in play and switch from playing with each other to playing with objects—toys, feathers, and the like. Play strengthens their muscles, allows them to practice social skills, and teaches them life lessons. They learn to inhibit bites and claws, discover what rolls or bounces when patted with a forepaw, and what runs away or fights back.

MONTHS THREE TO SIX

Social play reaches its peak between week nine through week sixteen. Kittens continue to play after four months, but not to the same extent. Baby teeth start to fall out at twelve weeks and are replaced by permanent adult teeth. A total of thirty adult teeth are present in most cats by age seven months.

Female kittens may experience their first breeding season (heat) and may become pregnant as early as four months of age, but most reach this point at five to six months of age. "Oriental" breeds like Siamese tend to become fertile at an earlier age.

> **Tip:** Ask your veterinarian about early-age spays and neuters. Many shelters and some private practice veterinarians now routinely sterilize kittens (and puppies) as early as eight weeks of age or when they weigh at least two pounds. That prevents any possibility of an "accidental" litter.

MONTHS NINE TO TWELVE

Male kittens become sexually mature and are able to father babies as early as eight to nine months, and they develop male-cat behaviors like spraying as early as six to seven months (average age is nine months). Both sexes continue to fill out and gain weight. Coats on longhaired breeds like Maine Coon and Persian cats may not fully develop until they are fifteen to eighteen months old.

Matching Your Lifestyle

The kitten is only half the equation necessary to make this match work. Before you settle on your final choice, it's important to evaluate your personal situation, because not every kitten is right for each

Feeding an Orphan

Sometimes the mother can't or won't feed her babies. Perhaps she's too ill, injured, or doesn't have enough milk to feed a large brood. Or maybe the kittens were abandoned. Whatever the circumstance, when their mother can't do it, you must become the mom-cat and take care of the kitten's needs. That includes keeping him warm, fed, and clean and helping him eliminate waste.

When the baby is by himself, he'll need help staying warm. Wrap a hot water bottle in a heavy towel to provide a heat source. An empty plastic pop bottle filled with water works well, too, or fill a sock with dry uncooked rice and heat it in the microwave. Be sure to buffer the object with towels so the baby won't be burned.

For food, commercial preparations are the best. Just Born or KMR products are available at pet-supply stores or from your veterinarian. How much and how often to feed depends on the size and age of the babies and the product content; so, follow the directions on the package. Newborn kittens need feeding every two to four hours.

In a pinch, professional kitten breeders recommend a homemade formula called *glop*. Combine a twelve-ounce can of evaporated milk, two tablespoons mayonnaise, two tablespoons yogurt, two tablespoons Karo corn syrup, and two egg yolks, and mix well. Then dissolve one package of Knox gelatin in twelve ounces warm water (or Pedialyte), and combine into the mixture. Keep the glop in a refrigerator until needed. The mixture forms a custard and can be warmed until melted into a liquid to put in a bottle or syringe for feeding.

If you have nothing else, then regular cow's milk or diluted evaporated milk can be used on a temporary basis. Be sure to warm the formula to about 100 degrees so it doesn't upset the kitten's digestion. Nursing bottles are also available, or you can use an eye dropper or medicine syringe. Be sure to keep the baby in a normal nursing position—on its tummy—for best results. Most babies can begin eating solid food by three weeks of age.

Finally, be sure to wash the baby from head to toe with a dampened soft cloth. This mimics the feel of his mother's washing tongue, and also gets him used to being handled. You must also stimulate him to use the bathroom—his mother would lick him. You simply use a cloth or cotton ball dampened with warm water and gently wash the genitals to prompt urination and a bowel movement.

circumstance. Living with the baby will be much easier if you choose a kitten that fits your lifestyle, rather than one whose needs you can't meet. By knowing what to expect, you can avoid major heartache later.

Kitten Purrs: The SnuggleKittie is a wonderful surrogate "mom" for small kittens away from home for the first time. The soft stuffed animal includes a heart-shaped battery-powered capsule that fits inside the body to provide a "heartbeat" to soothe the youngster. It also includes two disposable heater packets that last up to twenty hours each to simulate Mom-cat body warmth. The tummy pouch on the stuffed cat also accommodates a kitten baby bottle for the full Mom-cat effect—perfect when you're feeding an orphan. The SnuggleKittie is available from www.snuggleme.com.

Apartment or House? City or Country?

Where do you live? Where will the kitten stay? Take into consideration the amount of space you have, not only for a tiny kitten but also for the adult-size cat he'll become in twelve months. Cats are very territorial and do best when they can "claim" some of the real estate as their own property. This is especially important if you consider adopting more than one kitten and want to avoid future squabbles. A good rule of thumb is to have no more cats than you have rooms—so a one-bedroom apartment is perfect for one kitten. But don't be surprised if the little kitten claims the bedroom and leaves the sofa for you!

Cats adapt well to apartment living, but city cats are not safe outside. Keep in mind that your kitten should be safe at home whether or not you're there to supervise his antics. If you rent your apartment or home, be sure to get permission from your landlord. Owning your own home eliminates the landlord question, and gives you more room to satisfy an active kitten—or even several. A home with an enclosed garden or yard may also offer the possibility of safe outdoor excursions.

Don't forget to take a look at your décor as well. Kittens and lots of fragile, expensive breakables within paw-reach are a recipe for disaster. All kittens play like nonstop whirligigs, and some may retain their high-octane antics even as adults. Decide whether you prefer a swing-from-the-drapes climbing fanatic, like one of the Rex kittens, or if a more placid Ragdoll kitten would suit you better.

Time Constraints

Every kitten takes time. Cuddling and playing with your new baby, building an unbreakable bond that lasts a lifetime, are part of the fun. You must consider how a young kitten will fit into your daily routine. Do you work outside the home for long hours, when the kitten must be left alone unattended? If you're lucky (like me!) you can take your kitten to work with you, or work at home. Even then he'll need a safe place to sleep, eat, play, and use the bathroom while you're distracted by business.

You'll also have to add training time (yes, kittens can be trained!), litter-box duty, and routine maintenance care to your schedule. All kittens need basic care like nail trims, but some like the lovely Scottish Fold breed, require more attention to ear care. Kittens with flat faces and big eyes, like the Exotic, need help keeping their eyes clean and healthy. While Domestic Shorthairs and their purebred short-furred cousins need only a lick and a promise for coat care, Persians and other kittens with luxurious long fur may need grooming every day. Before you choose your ideal kitten, be sure you'll have time to devote to keeping that fluffy big-eyed beauty in perfect condition.

Other Roommates?

Unless you live alone and own your own residence, you will need to consult with other people—the landlord or family members—and consider their concerns before choosing your kitten. Does your spouse or roommate support the decision to acquire a kitten? Are your children responsible enough to take part in the care of the new family member?

Discuss plans with your roommate or spouse and be sure you have his or her support. After all, he or she will have to make adjustments, too. The new kitten deserves to have a happy and stress-free environment, and be accepted by all the people he'll live with. It's not fair to him to be the target of tension or resentment.

Very young children can be taught to properly handle and respect a pet as a living creature—and not a stuffed toy to be dragged about by a leg or tail. Depending on age, children can also become involved in the care of the kitten by filling the food or water bowl and playing with the baby. But make no mistake—no matter what age your children may be, the ultimate responsibility for the kitten always falls on the child's parent. Always.

So if you choose to adopt a kitten and you have a toddler, then a pet several months old is the best choice. Very young kittens are incredibly fragile and can be injured unintentionally by your youngster simply by being dropped or held incorrectly. An older kitten is better able to stay out of the child's way and avoid being "loved" too hard; that also protects your child from an inadvertent scratch or nip when the kitten tries to defend himself. Young children beyond the toddler stage will also need supervision, but can help with some caregiving. Having a pet can, indeed, be a great way to teach a child responsibility—just be sure it's not at the expense of the kitten.

You must also consider the impact a new kitten may have on other pets. I often talk with people who already have an adult cat and want to adopt a kitten as a "gift" to their pet for a playmate or companion.

The age and sex of the new kitten can affect how well he'll be accepted by resident pets. A good rule of thumb is to introduce a younger animal of the opposite sex to the resident pet, because there's less chance for territorial challenges or threats to the older animal's social position.

Warning: Are you sure the resident cat really wants a companion? An additional pet rarely solves an existing cat behavior problem and may actually prompt new ones. Statistically, single-cat households have the fewest behavior problems. The potential for spraying and fighting increases with each cat added to the household.

When resident pets are involved, careful introductions are important to help the new kitten become part of one big happy family. That can take a great deal of patience, energy, and time. When you have a dog, it's certainly possible for the kitten and canine to become fast friends. There will be safety issues, though, because some dog breeds have tendencies to be aggressive toward small animals. Detailed information about how best to introduce your new kitten to children, cats, dogs, and other pets can be found in chapter 6.

Which Side of the Fence

The indoor-outdoor debate continues to polarize cat lovers around the world. The question is, should your kitten be allowed outdoors, or should he be confined to an indoor lifestyle?

There are pros and cons to both sides. One argument says that cats that spend time in the great outdoors may enjoy a more "natural" lifestyle. Some proponents believe this promotes the cat's emotional health. Others like the convenience of letting the cat take care of bathroom business and scratch-marking outside the house. In the best of all possible worlds, I'd agree.

However, the great outdoors has many risks for cats, and especially for kittens. Being hit by a car is the number one cause of pet injury and death. Kittens have no experience avoiding these dangers, and even savvy adult cats do not have the necessary vision to accurately dodge cars. They simply cannot judge how fast a car travels, or tell if it's coming toward them or speeding away.

Outdoor kittens are at high risk for bite wounds from other animals, because the neighbor dogs or cats, or even wild animals, may not take kindly to a curious baby trespassing on their turf. Contact with strange animals also exposes the baby to life-threatening diseases like rabies, feline leukemia, and feline immunodeficiency virus. Outdoor life opens the door to many parasites—from fleas to ticks to intestinal worms—that love to make a meal of your kitten and can make him sick besides. Cats allowed to roam outdoors are more likely to die at an earlier age, due to accident or illness.

Frankly, most kittens never offered the opportunity to go outside don't miss it or feel deprived. You can provide an interesting, stimulating indoor environment to keep your kitten emotionally and physically healthy. Offer lots of climbing opportunities, hiding places, kitten toys, secure sleeping places, scratch objects, and window perches to watch birds and other critters from the safety of the indoors. Some kittens get a huge rush out of videos of chipmunks,

Kittens given access to the great outdoors should always wear a collar and identification. That way, if the worst happens and he wanders too far, the tag will get him safely home to you. Tattoos or microchips are other forms of identification.

(Photo credit: Amy D. Shojai)

Kitten Purrs: Kali-Ko-Kathouses are one of my favorite cat condos. They are modular vinyl-covered cages that come in a variety of designs and sizes—and yes, they work outdoors. You can learn more about Kali-Ko-Kathouses at www.roverpet.com. Fencing the yard may provide a safety barrier for most dogs, but as the kitten grows, she'll likely be able to climb and vault out. A product called Cat Fence-In Systems can help. It is available by mail order and listed in the advertisement sections of cat specialty magazines. The system provides netting that attaches to an existing fence or other structures, and prevents the cat from climbing out. Cat Fence-In Systems can be one answer to safely containing a kitten within the boundaries of a yard. Learn more at www.catfencein.com.

birds, or fish designed for their entertainment. If you live in a high-rise apartment, there's really no other option.

I recognize that everybody has different circumstances, and that some older kittens can "insist" on going outdoors. At times it may indeed become a quality-of-life issue to keep him happy by providing some outdoor time. If you live in a more rural area, there are ways to offer your kitten the outdoors and still keep him safe.

I do not believe it is ever acceptable to simply open the back door and let kitty roam at will. Would you offer that freedom to your four-year-old human child? Any outdoor time should be supervised by you to make sure your kitten stays out of trouble. Training the baby to walk on a leash—what I call "liberation training"—gives him the ability to safely travel beyond the walls of your home.

You can also create safe outdoor playgrounds for your kitten, either by building a homemade enclosure or investing in a commercial cat condo. These can be set up in a shady section of the yard so the kitten has a chance to enjoy the tickle of grass between his toes, and can chase butterflies, but strange animals are kept out and kitty's ability to find cars is limited. You can even design these kitty playgrounds to have access through a window or pet door. Cat show professionals often invest in lovely "cat condos" that keep their beauties safely contained.

When the Heart Rules

Even when you know how to pick the healthiest and best socialized kitten from the ideal source, your heart may not listen to your head. Instead, it's that sickly kitten with bald spots, covered with fleas, and eyes barely open that captures your soul. These "challenged" kittens need lots of help and will require much time and energy.

It's important to ask yourself several questions. Will you have time to medicate a sick baby, or get up throughout the night for kitten feedings if he's an orphan? Special needs kittens can require your attention and help twenty-four hours a day. Be sure you can address these needs, either yourself or with help, before committing to such an adoption.

When the kitten starts out with strikes against him, it's a good idea to have your veterinarian evaluate his health so you know what to expect. Sadly, there are kitten illnesses like FIP (Feline Infectious Peritonitis) that cannot be cured. Rather than invest lots of time, money, and heartache, you'll both be better served by making the baby's life as happy and comfortable as possible. And perhaps, with the caring help of a veterinarian, humanely end the suffering.

With dedicated nursing and medication, some sickly kittens can survive, and even thrive. It may require weeks of added expense and time. When the condition is contagious (like ringworm), you'll need to consider how to protect your other pets and children.

I can't make that decision for you. Just be informed before you embark on your kitten-saving crusade. Success will forge a strong, unbreakable bond between you and your cat that can last all the years of his life.

PART 2

BRINGING HOME BABY

4

PUTTING YOUR
BEST PAW FORWARD

Kitten Central—A Room of Her Own

Every kitten deserves a room of her own. A private room offers several advantages, and more than anything else, helps your kitten more easily make the transition into becoming a part of your family.

Kittens are so small, they can become lost in a large home or apartment. Above all, you need to keep an eye on the baby, especially during the critical first several weeks. Because frankly, if there's trouble to be found, your new kitten will be in the middle of it.

By turning one room into "kitten central," you help divide the kitten's territory up into manageable chunks for her to explore and learn. Cats, by nature, are not interested in meeting new people or other animals, and making friends until they are familiar with their surroundings. A whole house overwhelms the new baby, but a single room allows her to explore, cheek-rub to leave her comforting scent, and find all the really good hiding places. This room becomes her safe haven, a place that's comforting, familiar, and stress-free, where she can retreat when the world becomes too much. This should be a place she can go to nap, play quietly by herself, or escape the hectic pestering of children or other pets.

It's easy to create your own kitten central. Choose a room that has little foot traffic. I chose the laundry room for my cat Seren, but a small second bathroom or guest bedroom could also work. Even a walk-in closet might be appropriate.

On one side of the room, place the kitten's litter box. Position her food and water dishes on the other side of the room, as far from the bathroom facilities as possible. Cats dislike eating near their bathroom—wouldn't you? When the kitten is old enough to manage jumping or climbing, you might decide to place the dishes on a countertop to add some distance.

Include a kitten bed—a cat carrier with a soft blanket works well—and a scratch object for her to use. Cats like to have a good scratch after they wake up or finish a meal. Finally, don't forget some favorite toys. Your kitten will spend many hours in her safe haven, and it should be the most pleasant room in the house for her.

Kitten-Proofing 101

You'll need to make the house safe for your kitten just as you would for your human baby. Kittens poke objects with their paws. They pick up and bite and taste everything. They climb and explore high perches and squirm into interesting dark empty areas. They have no experience of what's safe and what's not, and may not survive a mistake.

Besides protecting the baby, kitten-proofing also protects your valuables. For instance, kittens love to invent games I call "gravity experiments" where they tap-tap-tap the antique porcelain figurine to see if it will fall off the ledge. They'll "help" you by digging up freshly potted plants, using the soil as a toilet, or clawing the leaves to pieces—what fun! You want to *prevent* problems like these, so you can enjoy the baby and build on the bonding experience instead of yearning to retaliate.

Before anything else, kitten-proof kitten central and make sure that her safe haven really is safe. Then move on to the rest of the house, everywhere she'll have the opportunity to explore. Start first with kitten-level; invest in knee-pads and get down on all fours to see the house from her perspective. Then take into account the second-story kittens, because as she grows, you can be sure she'll graduate to vaulting onto tabletops and other high perches that hold dangers.

Once you've kitten-proofed the house, don't relax your vigilance. For the first couple of weeks, whenever she's not safely confined in her room, it's a good idea to follow her around. Kittens find danger you never imagined, so running after her will ensure her safety and ease your mind. Here are some common household hazards to address.

Electrical Cords

Kittens aren't nearly as mouth-oriented as puppies. But like all babies, young cats explore their world by mouthing and biting objects, and they love to attack moving objects—like electrical cords. A bite can cause terrible burns, or even death when the kitten stops breathing from the shock.

Eliminate as many electrical cords as you can and remove temptation. For those that are left, immobilize them with tape or run them through a length of PVC pipe to make them less attractive and accessible.

For a few kittens, a commercial spray called Bitter Apple that tastes nasty may deter mouthing and biting. But an offensive smell usually works better to act as a kitty deterrent. Most cats dislike citrus scents. They also tend to dislike menthol, so try smearing a bit of Vicks VapoRub on exposed cords to keep the kitten far away.

If the worst happens and your kitten is shocked, be sure to turn off the electricity before you try to help her, or you may become injured, too. More details on first aid for electrocution are found in chapter 11, page 204.

Hidey-Holes

Kittens adore finding hiding places and cubbyholes to sleep, or to lay in wait and leap out at unsuspecting human feet. In many instances, the dresser drawer, cupboard, or empty cardboard box doesn't sound dangerous. But you may not hear the baby's cries if she's accidentally trapped inside a hiding place, and a day or more

The motion of the spiral telephone cord can be endlessly attractive to a playful kitten, and can also shock and injure the baby if she bites it.

(Photo Credit: Amy D. Shojai)

without food or water can spell disaster. Make sure you check for a kitten inside before you shut doors.

More lethal places include appliances like dishwashers—the kitten may want to lick the soiled plates—or the warm clothes dryer. Even the open oven door can be attractive to a heat-seeking baby. Kittens die every day from being trapped inside appliances that are turned on. When Seren was a baby, she was once trapped *behind* the warm dryer. Luckily I heard her cries for help. And once I had to pull her out of the fireplace when she thought climbing above the flue would be exciting.

Block off dangerous kitten-size openings. Check every appliance before turning it on. Make it a habit to bang on the tops or sides of the clothes dryer as a safety check. And if you see your kitten venture into one of these deadly places, it might be worthwhile to temporarily shut the door and then bang like crazy on the thing before letting her out. That may be enough to scare the kitten away from the danger permanently.

Plants

To your kitten, a plant invites a walk—or climb—on the wild side, and an opportunity to play "jungle kitten." If she can't climb it, she'll shred it, bat the leaves into submission, or dump the pot for excavation. Oh, what fun!

Depending on the kind of plant, kitty may be in for more than a scolding. Dieffenbachia, philodendron, and English ivy are some of the most common houseplants that can cause toxic reactions when eaten. The kitten doesn't have to chew the plant to be poisoned, either. Clawing the plant and then licking her claws clean can have the same effect.

Make sure all plants are removed from the kitten's room, and place toxic plants out of reach or, better yet, get them out of the house. Give them to a petless friend. Kitten-safe houseplants like coleus, piggyback, jade plant, or others should be placed out of reach on high shelves, or hung from hooks.

String

Both kittens and adult cats adore string-type toys like ribbon and yarn. Supervised games are fine, but when you can't be there, keep them out of reach. If swallowed, thread or other similar string-type kitten lures (like fishing line) turn deadly.

Kittens can strangle if they become hung up in curtain cords, or choke on swallowed pieces of cord. When these materials reach the tummy or intestines, they can block the digestive system or cause cuts on the inside. Emergency surgery can be required to remove the string and repair the damage.

Tie up curtain cords out of reach, or buy the child-safe kind that have a breakaway feature. Keep sewing supplies and fishing tackle boxes in secure cupboards. And be sure that favorite yarn, ribbon, and fishing pole type toys are kept out of reach when you can't be there.

Warning: If you see a string-type object hanging from your kitten's mouth—or coming out the anus—*do not pull it!* Chances are, it's attached somewhere on the inside of the body and you could do irreparable harm. Get your kitten to the emergency veterinarian as soon as possible.

Swallowed Objects

There are no safety standards for cat toys, so it's up to you to ensure that no small objects—like eyes or tails—can come off the toy and be swallowed. Like all babies, kittens tend to swallow lots of nonfood objects. Besides the string-type hazards, sharp items like pins, paper clips, and needles are common targets. Coins, rubber bands, and rubber baby nipples can also cause problems because they react with the digestive acids.

Even objects you wouldn't consider dangerous can stop up the kitten's innards and cause life-threatening blockages. Anything that the kitten can put in her mouth could potentially be swallowed. Having a kitten around has forced me to become neat and keep the floor picked up.

Pay particular attention to human medicines, especially if the kitten's safe room is a bathroom. Pills are great fun to bat and chase, but most pet poisonings come from swallowed medicine not meant for them. Keep your medication secure and out of reach in the cabinet.

Cleaning supplies under the sink can also pose a hazard for kittens if they are spilled on them, or the baby walks through something and then licks it off. Some kitties, like my cat Seren, learn to open cupboard doors. In these instances, childproof latches on cabinets that contain dangerous substances are an excellent investment.

Growing kittens can have voracious appetites and may eat any food scraps left within reach. That can not only interfere with nutritional balance, but could also upset their tender tummies. Keep garbage covered and beyond kitten reach. Once the baby is able to leap to countertop level, you'll also need to put away sharp objects so she won't cut her tongue licking food off a knife or food processor blade.

Warning: The most tragic kitten poisonings occur when an owner gives the pet something on purpose, without recognizing the danger. Tylenol and aspirin are poisonous to cats. So are chocolate and onions. Stick to a commercial food, and only medicate on the advice of your veterinarian.

(*Photo credit: Amy D. Shojai*)

Sewing supplies lure kittens into dangerous play. Needles and thread are great fun to bat about, but if swallowed, they cause life-threatening emergencies.

Hot Stuff

Although all kittens believe they're hot stuff, they're particularly vulnerable to being burned for a couple of reasons. First, they have no experience with fire. Shy kittens may be fearful, but very bold kittens may want to play with a candle flame. They'll end up with singed whiskers or worse. It's best to keep candles out of reach and fire screens in place to protect these inquisitive babies.

Second, kittens aren't likely to realize the difference between the stovetop when it's off and safe, and when you've just cooked and the burners are still hot. Paw pads are the most sensitive part of the kitten's body, and take a long time to heal. Make countertops near stoves off-limits, and enforce this rule even when you aren't cooking. Physically remove the cat when you catch her in the act. A long-distance squirt gun can act as a surprise reminder. You can also cover the counter around the stove with tin foil—cats hate walking on this stuff, and it keeps most cats away.

A love of warmth prompts some cats to sleep too near heat sources. They can tolerate temperatures up to 126 degrees before registering discomfort. That means they can singe their tail by sleeping too near the fireplace or even suffer a burn before they realize they've been hurt.

Holiday Hazards

Many holidays throughout the year pose hazards to curious kittens. Halloween candy and scary strangers at the door (kittens can dash out) cause dangerous disruptions. Thanksgiving with lots of rich food and friends and family also offer risks. But the Christmas and Hanukkah season is the most dangerous of all, because often the holiday decorations offer hard-to-resist feline temptations.

The menorah and other holiday candles can burn kitten paws, gift ribbons can choke and strangle, Christmas plants and tree ornaments can prove deadly if swallowed, and the cord from twinkling lights can produce an electrical shock if bitten. Spray-on artificial "snow" that's lead-based is toxic if consumed, and icicles or tinsel are especially hazardous when swallowed. Tree water doctored with aspirin or other preservatives can kill the kitten that drinks from the reservoir. Even tree needles can hurt when swallowed.

Less dangerous, but no less irritating, the tree seems designed for kitten-climbing enjoyment. A toppled tree won't make your holiday particularly merry.

In most instances, you can apply kitten-proofing tips to the holiday season. Keep candles out of reach. Secure electrical cords. Hang breakable ornaments high up, and use only yarn or ribbon rather than wire hangers for ornaments. Avoid tinsel and snow-type decorations, and secure the tree so it won't topple. Some folks have luck placing the tree inside a baby playpen to keep the kitten out, or simply put it in a room that is blocked off from impetuous pets.

Some kittens and cats will leave the tree alone when it's sprinkled liberally with cinnamon. It's not the smell, but the dust they dislike. Or, look for the tacky sheets available at Home Depot and other stores designed to secure throw rugs. Place these beneath the tree branches—cats hate the sticky feel and avoid walking on the surface.

You might want to invest in a small second tree that's decorated with kitten-safe ornaments like catnip mice or dried flowers. That might satisfy the kitten's urge to play, and save your formal tree.

Crossing the Threshold

Welcome home, baby! There's nothing more exciting than bringing your new kitten home. The first few days—and especially the first night—can be a stressful time for both of you. After all, this budding partnership will change your lives. If at all possible, plan to bring her home at the beginning of a weekend, or take a few days off, so you have the time to devote to getting the relationship off to a good start.

It's a good idea to bring something the kitten is familiar with from her first home. Cats identify safe places and things by the way they smell, and the baby will certainly miss the scent of her mother and siblings. When possible, plan ahead to scent a small hand towel or baby blanket with the signature smell of Mom-cat and the babies. Simply rub or pet the mother and other kittens with the fabric; then bring it home with your kitten as a friendly reminder. Place the scented fabric in the kitten's new bed.

Of course, you'll transport your new kitten in a cat carrier—or if you don't have that, a cardboard "pet caddy" available from shelters. When you are in the car, driving is your priority. The kitten must be confined not only for the driver's peace of mind, but also for her own safety. An accident with a loose kitten in the car turns the baby into a furry projectile that probably won't survive.

Bring the baby into her safe room. It should be ready with food and water, litter box, scratch object, bed, and toys available. Set down the carrier, open the door, and let the kitten come out on her own. Some shy kittens may prefer to stay hidden and won't want to come out until you leave the room. That's fine. You can try sitting on the floor, which is less threatening to the baby. Give her ten minutes to come out on her own. If she doesn't, leave the room and come back in thirty minutes to check on her. Some kittens can't wait to explore their new home. That's fine, too.

She should not leave her room for at least the first day or so. That gives her time to scent mark her "home base" and build an allegiance to it and the litter box location. Confining your new kitten also eliminates the opportunity for mistakes. She's not a mind reader and should be given every opportunity to do the right thing, like scratch the right object (and not your sofa), use the litter box (not the rug), and sleep in her familiar bed.

After the first few days, you can open the door and allow her to explore the rest of the house, at her own pace. One room at a time works best, and usually it's preferable to let the kitten make her own way from kitten central rather than carrying her. That way, she will know the way back to find her food and litter box.

When you aren't able to supervise kitten antics, the best and safest place for her is her room. It takes only a few seconds for her to get into trouble. By the time you take the cookies out of the oven, or finish up that important phone conversation, she could be swinging from the drapes, knocking Grandma's collectibles off the mantel, or leaving you a fragrant pile under the piano bench.

Seren hasn't been a kitten for quite some time. As I write this, she is a little over three years old. And I still use her room as a safe, secure place to keep her comfortable when I'm out of the house. That's peace of mind for both of us.

Choosing a Name

Finding a proper name is serious business. Kitten names come to us in flashes of inspiration, and often seem to be chosen by the pet herself. For instance, my cat's name—Serendipity—describes how I felt about finding her. Lucky, indeed!

When you adopt a purebred kitten from a breeder, she will likely already have a name, at least in part. The "registered name" is the official identification for the purebred kitten, and can be a long tongue-twister that describes her ancestry. First names are usually the cattery where the kitten was born. These often describe the breed of cat as well. For instance, Earmark Cattery breeds Scottish Folds, Wegiekatt is home to Norwegian Forest cats, and CeltiCurl breeds American Curls. The second name often describes the looks or attitude of the kitten, and a final name may be added to cite the name of the new cattery owner. For instance, Kel-Lin Blazer Girl of Charlicats is a lovely Burmese female bred by Kel-Lin Cattery, now owned by Charlicats Cattery.

But kittens need not be registered to sport glorious, exotic, and imaginative names. Cats are named for appearance (Tiger), location where they were adopted (Dallas), personality (Lovey), and even for famous people (Elvis). They may have descriptive names—such as Six-Pack, who sports six toes on each foot. Rimshot got his name by paw-drumming his owner's head each morning to wake him.

There's only one rule to follow when it comes to naming your kitten. Make sure the name is a positive one. Kittens have egos, and she may not know the verbatim meaning of the word, but the emotional intent comes through loud and clear. That's why negative names all too often foster poor behavior, while a positive one promotes self-esteem.

Once you've found a name for your baby, try it on for size to be sure it fits. Kittens have a way of responding to and accepting the perfect name, and it may take you a while to find it. Take your time. Kitten christening celebrates the feline spirit and should complement the individual soul of your special friend.

5

KITTEN EQUIPMENT

A-Shopping You Must Go

What a world we live in, where all the proper kitten paraphernalia can be found nearly anywhere you look. In the past, only pet specialty stores carried certain items like scratching posts. Today, you'll find a selection in most comprehensive department stores, like Wal-Mart or Kmart, and even the neighborhood grocery store may have a pet-supply area.

The smaller independent mom-and-pop pet-supply stores often offer a range of products that satisfy kitten needs. Retail chains like Petco and PetsMart offer one-stop shopping with a variety of choices. Some of these stores even allow you to bring your pet along, and also provide care or training services from staff veterinarians or groomers.

Besides traditional walk-in stores, a huge number of mail order catalogues offer unique kitten equipment, from inexpensive to luxury items. Of course, your kitten won't care how much you spend, nor will he have an opinion about the color of his leash or bed. He'll be satisfied with simple, utilitarian equipment.

<u>On-line Pet Supply</u>

You can find nearly anything in the way of kitten equipment by surfing the Net. Some on-line stores even deliver food or litter to your door, as needed. Some of the fanciest and priciest products are available on specialty cat sites, while other on-line stores offer products for a wide range of pets, from kittens to dogs, birds, fish, and reptiles. Take a peek at some of the products for "small" dogs or ferrets, as well. Some of their toys or equipment (bowls, carriers, beds) may be the perfect choice for your kitten.

On-line sites may provide mailing lists and newsletters, pet-care articles, chat rooms, and bulletin boards where you can share stories about your new pet. Some of my favorite sites are listed below:

Care A Lot, www.carealot.org
Doctors Foster & Smith, www.drsfostersmith.com
That Pet Place, www.thatpetplace.com

Suppertime—Bowls and Dishes

Your kitten will need at least two bowls, one for water and another for food. If you offer him canned food, a third bowl or dish is a good idea. A variety of dish styles are available. Before making a fashion statement, it's most important to plan for the kitten's preferences and care requirements. Above all, choose something that's easy to keep clean.

Plastic bowls are inexpensive but can hold the odor of old food and be difficult to clean. Some kitties seem to develop allergic reactions to plastic dishes. Stainless steel bowls are the veterinarian's choice because they don't chip or break, and they're easy to keep clean. They may also be too lightweight, allowing the kitten to scoot them around the floor as he tries to eat. I like glass or ceramic because they are usually dishwasher safe and convenient to wash.

Kittens with long fur or flat faces, like Persians, do better eating from a saucer rather than a bowl. Many kittens (and adult cats) prefer these shallow dishes because it keeps them from bending their whiskers by dipping down into a deep bowl. One economical

(Photo credit: Ralston Purina Company)

A hungry kitten won't care what the bowl looks like, as long as the food suits him.

choice that some kittens prefer is to eat from a small paper plate. Rather than washing it when through, you can simply throw it away.

Once you've narrowed the practical choices, go wild. Goofy, whimsical, colorful, and elegant food and water dishes can be found. You can even have your kitten's name inscribed so there's no question who the bowls belong to.

Kittens are "occasional feeders." That means they don't eat a huge meal at one time, but nibble, go away, and come back several times a day. When you feed a dry commercial food, you can "free feed" and leave a quantity in the bowl available all day. But for wet foods that spoil if left out too long, an automatic food dish might be something to consider. There are several kinds, but all have a series of small, sometimes refrigerated compartments that hold the meal, and open on a timer, so the food stays fresh.

Kitten Purrs: When cats were wild, they obtained most of their water by eating prey animals. House kitties don't always drink as much water as they should, which can lead to urinary tract problems. Cat owners often notice their pets love running water, though, and may beg to lap water from the faucet. Veterinary Ventures found a way to promote feline drinking by using this natural urge. The Drinkwell Pet Fountain encourages cats to drink with a six-cup well that circulates the water and pours a constant adjustable stream. The Drinkwell Pet Fountain is available from many pet supply sources, or from www.vetventures.com.

The Kitty Commode

Bathroom facilities for your new kitten require special attention. Hit-or-miss litter-box behavior is the number one complaint of cat owners. Offering your kitten the proper equipment from the beginning will go a long way toward training him properly and preventing problems as he grows.

There are three components to the kitty commode: the pan, the filler, and accessories like the scoop.

Litter Pans, Plain and Fancy

The prime consideration when choosing the baby's first bathroom is that he is able to climb inside the litter box. When he is very small, it may be best to use a temporary facility until he grows up enough to manage commercial-size products. The cardboard lid from a shoe box or even a disposable foil cookie sheet from the grocery store may work fine. Don't invest in a nice but small commercial pan that he'll outgrow within several months. A too-small litter box is at the root of most kitty bathroom misbehaviors.

You'll need at least two litter pans. The rule of thumb is to have one pan per cat, plus one. That's because cats often don't want to share bathroom facilities, or may prefer to use one for urine and the other for feces. Also, tiny kittens need extra help reaching a distant box, so two located at either end of the house help prevent accidents.

Several commercial litter box styles are available. The standard plain-and-simple litter box measures about 5 × 12 × 18 inches and is made of an easily cleaned plastic. Like food bowls, these pans come in nearly any color you want. Larger litter pans are available, and unless your kitten is a breed that remains petite, like the Singapura, it's a good idea to go with the largest size available. When there's not enough room in the box, some cats become confused and obsessively scratch the *outside* of the box instead of covering their waste.

Plan for when your baby grows to full size. Average to large cats may have trouble maneuvering in the smallest boxes, and a covered model helps keep them from "hanging out" over the side. It also filters odor, offers kitty more privacy, and helps keep the litter from being flung out of the box during enthusiastic excavations.

The ultimate in kitten bathroom facilities are litter boxes "disguised" as attractive furniture, like the Purr-Fect Privy available at www.pfprivy.com and the Hidy-Tidy at www.hidytidy.com. Other models are hidden inside planters. The cat won't care, of course, but these may be more aesthetically pleasing for some folks.

There are also kits, like Feline Evolution CatSeat, said to do away with the litter box forever by training kitty to use the toilet. You can learn more about this product at www.catseat.com. Training kitty to flush isn't part of the package, though.

Warning: Tiny kittens can drown in a very small amount of water. I'd advise that the kitten be at least five months old before attempting to train him to use the toilet.

Kitten Purrs: Cats hate a dirty litter box and often find a better place—like under the dining room table—if it's not kept clean. Automatic litter boxes take care of that problem by scooping after every use. My cat Seren got a LitterMaid for Christmas 1999, and we both love it. She always has a clean box, even when I'm on the road and my husband isn't home all day to scoop. Ten minutes after Seren leaves the box, the cleaning comb rakes debris from the clumping litter and deposits it in a disposable container. Visit the company Web site at www.littermaid.com to see a demonstration and learn about the product.

Cat Box Filler

Once you choose the litter pan, decide what to put in the box. Clay-based products remain the most popular and economical choice, but there's a huge variety available to fit every preference. You can find what you need at most grocery stores, but pet specialty stores and on-line venues may offer more choice.

When choosing a litter, remember that kittens prefer sandy, soil-like textures for easy digging, and strong perfumes or dust may turn them off. Once you've found a product kitty likes, *don't change it!* A new litter might turn him off to the litter box.

Plain clay litters work very well, and often include odor-control technology that helps keep the bathroom smelling fresh to both you and the kitten. Clay litters absorb moisture and help contain the waste by drying it out. You'll need to clean out solid waste (and liquid, as much as possible) at least once a day, and once a week change the entire contents with fresh litter.

Clumping litters are composed of finer granules that are less abrasive on tender paws. They congeal liquid waste into a solid ball for easy removal. That prolongs the life of the rest of the litter. Clumping litters are one of the most convenient, popular products available. Clay-based clumping litters were the first to appear, and they are recommended for the automatic litter pans.

Warning: Small amounts of ingested litter aren't likely to be a problem with adult cats, but very young tiny kittens who taste everything can become ill if they swallow any amount of a clay clumping litter. Monitor your kittens to be sure they don't eat any litter—none of it is good for them. Litter made from biodegradable or digestible products like corn or paper are less likely to cause problems if they are eaten.

There are also new kinds of litter made from crystal-like "pearls" designed to trap odor and moisture. They do not clump, and you need to clean out solid waste, but they are designed to contain urine for up to a month without changing the box. An example is Tidy Cats Crystals. More information and a product demonstration are on-line at www.tidycats.com. Crystal Clear Litter Pearls is available through www.harvestventures.com.

Other products are made of paper, wheat, cedar shavings, pine pellets, and all sorts of environmentally friendly ingredients. Those that are biodegradable may be flushable, too—but that will vary depending on your septic system.

Cats and owners are raving about a product called World's Best Cat Litter. The texture is soft and easy on kitty feet, and it clumps like the older clay-based products. But it's made from corn, is biodegradable, and can be digested by an inquisitive baby. The product weighs less than comparable clay products, too. This is a great choice for cat owners who like "natural" products. Learn more about it at www.worldsbestcatlitter.com.

Toilet Accessories

Slotted scoops are designed to sift waste from the soiled box and allow clean litter to filter back into the pan. Commercial scoops are readily available, but even a large slotted spoon or spatula will work.

Plastic litter pan liners can help make cleaning the box more convenient. These go into the clean box, and the litter is poured on top. When you're ready to change the box, you lift out the soiled litter with the plastic liner, and throw the whole thing away.

Deodorants can be added to the box, but most commercial cat box fillers already have odor control properties. Simply keeping deposits cleaned out is the best answer, because cats tend to hate strong perfumes and may avoid the box when they are used. Charcoal filters designed to fit in some covered boxes do help absorb the strongest odors.

All cat litter will track out of the box to some extent. Clumping litters are the worst culprits. Litter "mats" designed to wipe kitty feet as he leaves the box can be helpful in containing the mess. It's also a good idea to keep a hand vacuum or broom handy. You'll also want to keep a covered wastebasket or other container nearby to deposit the kitten's waste as you clean the litter pan. A diaper pail works well. Or use the empty plastic jug that some commercial litters are packaged in, then throw away the whole thing.

Tip: The gallon-size resealable plastic freezer bags work well to contain kitty deposits. Keep a supply near the litter pan. For a tiny kitten, one bag can last many days. Sealing it contains any odor, until it's full enough to add to your garbage.

Cat Nappers and Beds

Nothing looks sweeter than a kitten curled up fast asleep in a bed of his choice. Kittens sleep a lot, and they tend to have specific preferences. A warm, cozy, and soft surface is best.

Lots of commercial cat beds, from pillowlike stuffed sculptures to hammocks, will please the most persnickety kitten. I've seen the best selection at cat shows, where you can color-coordinate a bed to match or highlight your kitten's markings. There are even miniature human-style sofas for the diva kitten!

Most kittens are perfectly happy to cuddle up on a soft blanket. A washable blanket is best.

A great idea is to let the cat carrier play double-duty and serve as the baby's bed. Take off the door or leave it open, put the blanket inside, and it makes a wonderful kitten cave for sleeping. That also gets your kitten accustomed to being in the carrier, so there's less stress when he must ride there for a trip to the vet.

Cat Toys

Kitten play inspires people to create wonderful, fun toys for their enjoyment. It's hard to say who has more fun—the kitten or the person watching his antics. Your kitten will tell you there's no such thing as too many toys. Playtime keeps the kitten brain stimulated, prompts exercise to keep him physically fit, and keeps him emotionally engaged and happy. A bored kitten will seek out entertainment, and you may not like his choices.

There are two basic categories of toys: solo toys for kitty alone and interactive toys for you to use together. Make sure you have some of both.

The best solo toys are lightweight, easily moved with a paw-swat, and have an interesting texture or make an intriguing noise. You'll need to experiment to see what your kitten likes best. Seren loves the soft sparkly fuzzy-ball toys she can bat and carry around, but she dislikes the fabric balls with bells or hard plastic toys. Other kitties have opposite tastes.

Any toy can become interactive, when you're involved. A fishing pole style toy works great to exercise energetic kittens. These often have a feather or other "lure" on the end of a long string, and you can sit in a chair and play with the baby from a distance. Please re-

(*Photo credit: Amy D. Shojai*)

A curious kitten can have hours of fun playing by himself. Cat track-style toys are great, and offer holes to poke and balls to chase.

member never to leave string-type toys out unattended. Kittens may inadvertently swallow the ribbon or string and end up in the emergency room.

Kitten Purrs: Two of the best lure-type toys available are the Galkie Kitty Tease and Da Bird. Both are fishing pole style toys. The Kitty Tease is nearly indestructible and has heavy string with a fabric lure that keeps cats chasing and running for hours. Da Bird has a feather lure on the end of the string that twirls and dips through the air, and inspires incredible kitten leaps.

There are stuffed animals, battery-powered bugs and mice, even puzzle toys that can be filled with treats for kitty to maneuver for a tasty tidbit. Modular fabric kitten tunnels can be designed for hideaways and play zones. Kittens often have loads of fun chasing the beam of a flashlight—and you'll never have to leave your chair to fish it out from under the sofa.

Warning: Avoid laser pointers. They can damage the eye.

Some of the best toys are homemade or found items your kitten discovers. I call these "cheap thrills" and some of the best include empty boxes or paper bags for hiding, wads of paper for playing chase and fetch, and hair scrunchies swiped by the baby. One of Seren's favorites is a Ping-Pong ball tossed into the empty bathtub. She can lie on her back in the tub and swat the ball in circles, but never lose it.

Feathers are a huge favorite with nearly all cats. A range of colorful, exotic feather "kitty teases" as well as single feathers are sold at cat shows. Peacock and pheasant feathers work well. If you can't make it to a cat show, hobby and craft supply stores often sell these feathers.

For Paws That Claw—Scratching Objects

Scratching objects and cat trees are vital to the emotional health of your kitten. Kittens—and adult cats—claw. Period. You will never, under any circumstances, stem the urge to claw and climb. If such urges don't have a legal outlet, the kitten will make do with what's available. You'll end up with damaged furniture and a strained relationship with the kitten—and he won't have a clue what he's done wrong. The answer is very simple. Provide your kitten with a legal scratch outlet, and train him to use it from day one.

As with other kitten equipment, there are many choices. Here, though, you need to be selective. The most readily available—and least expensive—cat scratching posts are pretty worthless. Forget about matching your color scheme and instead meet your kitten's needs. The scratching target should

- be stable under the kitten's assault. A tippy post that falls over may scare him so badly he'll never go near it again.
- accept the kitten's full-length stretch when he scratches. One purpose of scratching is to exercise the shoulder muscles, and an object that's not long enough falls short of this ideal and may be ignored.
- satisfy the kitten's texture preference. Every cat has different tastes, and while some may like carpet, others prefer upholstery or wood, and many like variety. Don't fight him. Give the kitten what he wants, and training him to use the object will be a breeze.
- accommodate the kitten's ideal scratch posture. As with texture preferences, different cats have different styles of scratching. Some reach up to scratch downwards. Others stretch out on their tummies and scratch. My cat Seren lies on her back and scratches overhead. Choose either a vertical or horizontal scratch object—or one that matches other preferences—based on your kitten's needs.

Kittens can outgrow a small scratch object very quickly—their reach will increase dramatically from age twelve weeks to twelve months. Get a scratch object that will still satisfy him when he's full-grown.

Some very effective scratch objects are quite inexpensive. Many cats love the sandpaper-textured horizontal scratch objects that are impregnated with catnip, and others are thrilled by sisal-wrapped objects you hang from the doorknobs. Your kitten won't care how much you spent, or what the scratch-target looks like, as long as you've satisfied his needs. In fact, you can make your own, if you like. One of Seren's favorite scratch objects is a two-foot-long cedar limb I salvaged from a dead tree. It's on the floor next to her automatic litter box. She also uses a plank wrapped with many layers of upholstery fabric that I bought from a remnant bin at the fabric shop. You could also use carpet remnants and mount them on a plywood sheet or wooden post wrong side out so the dense backing is exposed. It can be leaned against a wall, or left on the floor for horizontal scratching.

Fancier scratch objects often include perches for kitty's napping pleasure. These vary in style from simple to elaborate "trees" or colorful sculptured furniture in whimsical designs. When possible, it's a great idea to invest in a cat scratch object that has elevated perches, to satisfy your kitten's urge to climb and find lofty places from which to survey his kingdom—er, I mean, your home.

In fact, one of the most common complaints from owners is cats leaping onto high counters, lounging on tabletops, and climbing the furniture. The best cure for such antics is to give kitty his own jungle gym, the taller the better. Of course, you'll want to monitor the climbing when your baby is still small, to prevent falls that could injure him. But cats are drawn to the highest lookout in the house. If you make sure the highest perch is his own furniture, he'll leave your countertops alone.

Seren has a three-tier cat tree that's about four and a half feet tall, with carpeted half circles to nap in, and three rough cedar posts to claw. Fancier trees can reach to the ceiling, and look quite rustic with tree bark still attached, or have soft-stuffed hiding places for napping and play. One of my favorite on-line cat furniture sites is www.angelicalcat.com. But don't worry if you can't fit one of these fantasy creations into your home. Kitty would be satisfied with a stepladder with lots of toys tied to it—yep, Seren has one of those, too. Do you think she's spoiled?

Traveling Kittens

Every kitten must travel during his lifetime, if only to visit the veterinarian for preventive care. Confinement in a carrier keeps the baby safe while he's in the car. Halters and a leash control him when he's out of the safety of your house. Should the worst happen and your kitten is lost, identification will allow him to be returned to you.

Cat Carriers

Many styles are available, from disposable cardboard to hard plastic designed for airline travel. The plastic carriers have doors that open on the front or top, and come in several sizes.

Cats prefer carriers that offer enough room, but are snug enough that they feel secure and don't rattle around inside. Inexpensive cardboard carriers are available from pet stores, shelters, and veterinary offices. Both the cardboard boxes (set on their side) or plastic carriers with doors removed or left open can double as the kitten's bed, as well.

No matter what style carrier you choose, be sure you place it in the back seat of your car when traveling with your kitten—if possible, secure the carrier in place with a seat belt. Don't place the carrier on the front passenger seat. An airbag that deploys may crush even a rigid plastic carrier, and injure or even kill the kitten.

Soft-sided duffel-style carriers with zippers are also quite popular, especially with people who travel a great deal with their cats. They can be slung over your shoulder, and tend to fit easily under the airplane seat so kitty can accompany you as carry-on luggage.

Warning: Kittens and cats should always be confined during transportation in a car. Some pets become upset and interfere with the driver by getting underneath the pedals. Others become carsick and containment helps prevent a mess. Even well-behaved pets should be confined, for their own safety. If you are in an accident, a

(Illustration: Wendy Christensen)

Cat trees come in plain to fancy designs, and offer perches, napping platforms, and legal scratch opportunities. A jumbo-size tree accommodates multiple kittens.

loose pet inside the car could injure you or be hurt or killed from the impact, or he could get lost.

Leaving Him Behind

Many kittens and cats dislike traveling or spending time away from their familiar home surroundings. There are also occasions, like business trips, when it's not possible to take kitty with you. What are your options?

Leaving him alone is never the ideal choice. I wouldn't advise leaving a kitten younger than six months old alone for longer than the ten to fourteen hours of some workdays, especially when you're both still getting to know each other. A short period alone can work with older kittens—say, over a weekend. Confine him in his safe room with plenty of dry food and water (at least twice as much as you think he'll need!). Make sure the litter box is clean when you leave and that he has plenty of toys. Ask a friend to be on call during this period, in case your plane is canceled and return is delayed. Be sure your friend knows where kitty's food, litter, veterinarian's phone number, and medical history are located—just in case.

When you must be gone longer than that, ask friends to stop in once or twice a day to check on him. They can make sure he has food, hasn't spilled his water, and that the litter box is clean. And they can play with him and make sure he's not too lonely. Kittens don't have a good sense of time—he won't recognize whether you're gone one day or seven days, but gone is gone. He will miss human contact, especially you.

If twisting a friend's arm doesn't work, the best option is hiring a professional pet sitter. You can get a referral from Pet Sitters International at 1-336-983-9222 or www.petsit.com. These folks are bonded and come to your home to care for your kitten once or more times a day, as requested.

The last choice is to board your kitten. This may be a fine solution for confident kitties, but very shy ones handle the stress of your absence more easily if they can stay in familiar surroundings. The American Boarding Kennels Association in Colorado Springs can give you a referral to a facility in your area (call 1-719-667-1600).

The best facility will be for cats only, so he's not stressed by barking dogs. Ask your veterinarian for options, too. Some vet clinics offer a boarding service for their clients.

Collars and Identification

Collars come in every color, with rhinestones or plain and simple, but they are more than a fashion statement for your kitten. They provide identification should he ever stray from home. Even indoor-only kittens sometimes slip out the door, and a tag may be the only thing that brings him home. It's a sad truth that many kittens and cats picked up by shelters lose their lives because their owner can't be found. A collar is life insurance for your cat.

Choose a collar with an elastic insert that allows it to expand slightly. Cats have more fragile necks than dogs, and if the collar should get caught on something, it's important that the cat be able to escape without risk of strangulation. Collars must fit snugly with room to slip two fingers underneath.

Keep in mind that depending on his age, your kitten will likely outgrow his first collar. He's also likely to lose the collar once in a while, because the cat's head is rarely bigger around than his neck and the collar easily slips off. Find an inexpensive one, and keep several on hand just in case.

Once you've found the collar, either order or make an identification tag to attach to it. Include your address and a couple of phone numbers to make it as easy as possible for someone to contact you about your missing kitten. The rabies tag your veterinarian gives you, which says your kitten is current on his important vaccinations, can double as an ID, because the clinic is required by law to keep a record of that tag number. Several years ago I found a beautiful gray-and-white stray cat. I was able to call the vet's office, noted on the rabies tag that he wore. The staff looked up the tag number, and Bosco was reunited with his owner within two hours.

There are many styles of identification tags. The best provide the necessary information and don't bother the cat. If he's irked by the jingle of the tag, he's more likely to try and remove the collar. Some collars have plastic windows where you can insert identification information, and there's no dangling irritation.

Other identification systems can also be effective. Tattoos are more popular among the dog fancy, but may be used on kitties, too. Generally the pet's registration number or the owner's social security number is placed on the skin of the inner thigh. Of course, once the fur grows back, that's hidden—and whoever finds the cat must know to look there.

Many shelter-adopted kittens are microchipped. A tiny piece of surgical glass about the size of a grain of rice is injected beneath the skin, between the shoulders. The glass capsule contains identification information about the pet that can be scanned with the proper equipment—which, of course, the shelter has—so if your kitten is ever lost and returned to the shelter, he'll be identified as your lost waif, and returned.

Warning: Don't rely on microchipping alone. Usually a lost cat is found by neighbors who may not turn him in to the shelter. A tag on the collar remains one of the best ways to protect your kitten.

Halters and Leashes

Never attach a leash to the cat's collar. If he becomes frightened and fights it, he could injure his neck. Some savvy kitties learn to pull backwards so the collar simply slips off over their heads and voila—the great kitty escape!

Halters are the best choice for kittens and adult cats. They distribute the pressure more evenly, and when properly fitted, they are much less likely to peel off the cat. For larger kittens, an H-harness designed for either cats or small dogs may work fine. The harness is built like the letter H, and the top and bottom "feet" of the letter join to form two circles connected by the middle bridge portion. One circle goes around the chest behind Kitty's front legs, and the second fits around the base of his neck. The "bridge" of the H joins the two circles over his shoulders.

Most harnesses are adjustable and can be enlarged as the kitten grows. Go for quality with your halter choice; be sure the catches are secure and won't come loose in the middle of a jaunt across the back yard. A good harness will last the cat's entire life.

The "figure-eight" harness designed specifically for cats is the ideal choice. Cats have much more difficulty escaping them, and they fit any size animal from a tiny six-week-old baby to a twenty-pound adult cat. The leash and halter are all a single length of cord, with the "halter" end formed into a double loop. One goes over the cat's head, while the other goes under and behind his front legs and hooks to a metal or plastic capture device over his shoulders. The remaining loose end serves as the leash. Look for figure-eight cat harnesses at pet specialty stores.

Once the halter is fitted onto the kitten, the leash attaches to the metal or plastic ring set into the material at his shoulders. Look for a lightweight leash that won't weigh him down or be too cumbersome for a small kitten. Those designed for small dogs work well.

Some kittens never bat an eye when presented with the halter and leash, and others throw a hissy fit. Learning to accept leash-training opens up the world and allows your baby to accompany you—safely escorted—beyond the walls of your house. Learn all about "liberation training" and how to introduce your kitten to the halter and leash in chapter 14, on page 257.

Ins and Outs of Cat Doors

The cat flap—a small pet door—may be an option you want to consider. These doors can help keep your kitten's private space protected. Nosy dogs are kept away from kitten food, and other pets or inquisitive toddlers can't investigate the litter box—yuck!

Pet doors can be added to provide kitten access to an extra closet, the back porch, a small utility room, even to an outdoor playpen. Pet doors allow the kitten to come and go at will, so you aren't jumping up and down to let him in or out.

Pet doors can be installed in interior or exterior walls, doors, windows, or even sliding panels. The simplest offer a finished opening that's too small for other pets, and is used for access into interior rooms. The next level provides a vinyl flap that covers the opening, for the cat to push through, and protects against wind and wet.

More expensive models provide a hinged screen or window, which keeps the opening free from buggy intruders and seals heated or cooled air inside.

The ultimate in pet doors offer "keyed" access that lock so that only the cat wearing a special magnetic collar can get into the house, preventing strays or wild animals from invading your home. Some pet doors can be locked with security panels, when you aren't at home, and most of these doors can be locked to keep the cat in or out.

To determine the size door needed, measure the pet's height at his shoulders. Remember that your kitten may have some growing yet to do. If you have other pets, decide if you want them to have access, too, before deciding on the size of the door. One of the largest selections of cat doors is available through Doctors Foster & Smith, a mail-order pet-supply vendor available through catalogue sales at 1-800-381-7179 or their Web site at www.drsfostersmith.com.

On the Road

Cats love the status quo, and unless they begin to travel as babies, most will not be happy when you hit the road. Show cats travel all the time, of course. These cats do well because they've learned to accept being in their carrier for long periods of time—four to six hours or more at a stretch.

You probably won't need any special preparations to drive your kitten an hour or so away to visit friends or family. Most states require that pets carry a health certificate from a veterinarian if they cross state lines. It's a good idea to bring your cat's health records with you.

He'll be in his familiar, safe carrier, of course, strapped safely in the back seat. Take along a bottle of water from home to be sure strange water doesn't upset his digestion. Include his food bowls and food, favorite toys and blanket, litter, and a litter pan. Disposable pans work best when you're on the road—aluminium roasting pans from the grocery are perfect. If the trip is longer than a couple of hours, stop in a rest area, set up his litter pan (in the car!) and give him a break. Be sure he's safely back inside his carrier before you open the car doors.

If you want to travel by plane with your kitten, plan on spending at least an extra fifty dollars each way for his fare. Depending on the airline, small pets may be allowed to travel in the cabin of the plane with you as carry-on luggage, but the carrier must be no taller than nineteen inches to fit under the seat. The Vari-Kennel (size 100) will fit under most seats, and the soft-sided bags like Sherpa Bags also work well. You'll want to feed and water the kitten only small amounts before the flight, and give him an opportunity to use the bathroom. Most babies settle down and sleep during the trip. You must make a reservation and arrive early if you wish to carry on your kitten because airlines usually allow only two animals per cabin at a time, and it's first come, first served. Otherwise, your kitten will have to travel as cargo with the other luggage.

Most airlines restrict the time of year animals can travel as cargo, and disallow them if it's too hot or too cold. Frankly, cargo travel may not be safe and certainly can be scary or uncomfortable for the baby. To travel as cargo he must have a hard-plastic airline-approved crate. Call the airline and get their specific requirements. Be sure to check him as "excess baggage"—don't send him "freight," because freight may not travel on the same plane. Ask the flight crew to watch out for your kitten during the flight by monitoring the atmosphere in the cargo hold.

When you intend to stay in a hotel, plan ahead and be sure the management will accept a pet. Most do, particularly if you pay a refundable pet deposit in case of damage. If you need to leave the kitten in your room when you go out, confine him to the bathroom. Then make a sign for the door that warns housekeeping. Nothing spoils a trip faster than losing your kitten in a strange hotel.

6

COMPETABILITY:
KITTEN SOCIETY EXPLAINED

C'Attitudes—Understanding Feline
Social Structure

Imagine that an explorer searching the most hidden places on earth stumbles upon an unknown civilization never touched by the outside world. The inhabitants have never experienced strangers before. The explorer—a human being—is shocked at the strangeness of the other's language, culture, and social structure.

Science fiction? No, this is reality when it comes to the interaction of human and feline society and culture.

The social structure of cats is completely foreign to people because our social system is based on a "group" mentality and held together by vocal communication. Cats evolved to depend on themselves alone and on silent communication through body posture and scent signals. Each system works well for that particular group, but when you put the two together, there are bound to be misunderstandings. Unless you understand where your kitten is coming from, there will be a culture clash.

Human Society

To understand cat culture, you must first take a close look at the human equivalent to see how different they are. Social groups provide benefits that aren't available to the individual. Early people banded together to hunt and bring down big game that one person couldn't tackle alone. People built communities for safety, raised children together, and shared responsibilities. Working together offered great rewards in terms of food, safety, and companionship.

In order to work together, people needed to communicate. When disputes arose, people created ways to settle arguments so that the group didn't suffer and fall apart. In broad terms, human society chooses a "leader" to make the decisions for the entire group and settle disputes. The "followers" who bow to the leader's wise counsel benefit from this situation by gaining the protection of the group. When the leader is absent, a second in command takes over until the boss returns.

In a modern-day example, when you report to work a "boss" makes the decisions for you and your coworkers. When you follow the rules (do your job correctly), you receive your colleague's approval and respect, the boss's loyalty, and a paycheck reward. That's the way it's supposed to work, anyway.

People tend to understand dog behavior more easily because human society has great parallels with wild canids. The "pack society" of wolves allows the group to hunt together. One wolf can't bring down an elk, but a group can. The group also offers better protection—its members can take turns guarding territory and den, and communally raise the young. A wild dog that follows the rules gets to eat with the group and has earned the affection and loyalty and protection of his peers.

Cat Culture

Kitty culture, like the human equivalent, is based on individuals who make the rules and those who follow them. But feline society is not a democracy, has no set leader, and is marked by a fluid yet despotic rule. That is, one cat is the ruler, and there is no second in command when she's away. If she leaves, a free-for-all decides the new dominant cat of that territory.

That's because cats evolved to hunt alone. After all, there is no reward for group hunting when the prey is mouse-size and feeds only one. Therefore, cat society revolves around a "me first" attitude—each cat considers herself to be the center of the universe, and ruler of a particular territory she claims.

In fact, the only time wild cats come together is to breed. When the male Romeos wrangle over a feline, only one tomcat needs to win. Gaining runner-up status in the contest doesn't matter to the losers, because there's no benefit to hang around. They do better to find another mate and be number one in a different territory.

Similarly, once the mother cat gives birth, she is the absolute boss to her kittens. She decides the rules and enforces them. When she's away, the kittens wrangle amongst themselves until one is clearly established as the leader.

Technical Stuff: Lions are the only known feline to routinely live, hunt, and raise offspring together in a communal fashion. But recent evidence suggests that *felis libyca* of the Middle East, a likely ancestor of our pet cats, may also share this sociability and indulge in group living and shared feeding responsibility of kittens.

When enough food is available, our domestic kitties also can form stable, primarily matriarchal colonies. You'll see this in groups of "barn cats" or feral cat communities. Females (often related) help each other in the birthing process, and groom, nurse, and guard each other's babies. They often form strong affectionate attachments to each other. Serious aggression is uncommon and reserved more for nongroup members entering the group's territory or trying to join the colony.

To complicate matters, a particular cat doesn't necessarily rule in all instances. She may be queen in the house, but she bows to the whims of another cat that rules the back yard. Ownership of a particular territory rules feline society.

This arrangement isn't as foreign to people as it might seem at first. After all, your boss may be in charge at work, but you make the rules in your own house. When you think about it, this makes sense for your kitten.

Ownership of property defines the cat's status. The one who owns all the highest perches, the best resting spots, the prime "real estate" is the boss. That won't matter much when you have only one kitten—she can be queen of all she surveys! But it is particularly important to understand if you have more than one pet, especially when you're adding a kitten to a household that already has a cat.

Cats tend to practice a unique time-share mentality that allows each to feel like a ruler and not have her nose rubbed in the fact that another kitty rules. This goes back to the fluid structure of dominance and subordinance within a specific territory. One cat "owns" the bedroom and the prime sleeping areas there while a second cat claims the television room. A third is queen over the back yard. The other two cats make way for the ruler in that particular territory, but *only when she is present.* If she's nowhere around, then another cat feels perfectly within his rights to grab a nap on the best spot—after all, the queen isn't using it.

Time-share means the cats don't fight over property. They graciously make way for the ruler when she's present—often without deigning to admit they are doing so—and otherwise share when she's not around.

The time-share concept is particularly important when training your kitten. She may understand you don't want her to sleep on the dining-room table, and follow the rules when you—the Top Cat—are there to enforce them. But she'll "time-share" and use the table whenever you aren't using it. Often she'll get off the forbidden spot as soon as you walk into the room, following the kitty rules of property possession.

Kitty Poker

Cats are masters of the bluff. Rather than getting their tails in a twist over dominance issues, they play poker.

Each cat has certain cards she's been dealt in life—such as age, health, and personality. Instead of unfurling her claws and immediately launching an attack, each cat brags and postures to show the other cat what a great winning hand she owns. Fur rarely flies in these face-offs. Instead there may be lots of hissing and growls, fluffed fur and cat curses in a game of feline "chicken." The one who backs down first and turns tail and runs is the loser. The winner claims the territory.

It can be hard on you to see a longtime cat friend being "bullied" by a new kitten. Our inclination is to interfere and make them play nice. Refrain from this temptation. It only prolongs the sorting-out process, and makes the more dominant cat even more determined to put the other one in his place. Hard as it is, peace will reign more quickly if you accept the pecking order the pets have established for themselves. Reinforce the status of the "top cat" by feeding her first, and letting her claim the best sleeping spots, even if it means she chases the other kitty away. Once everybody "agrees" who rules, things generally calm down.

Sometimes, when two cats can't agree on who should be boss, they ignore each other altogether. That's the time-share mentality kicking in again. The subordinate cat may look the other way and get off the sofa when the dominant cat shows up, but never by so much as a whisker-flick will she acknowledge it wasn't her idea all along.

Crowning the "Ruler"

How do cats decide who will be the boss and who will be the follower in a particular territory? Several factors influence dominant and subordinant positions. There are exceptions to these rules, but basically four categories decide the status of a cat.

Sexual status plays a major role in the feline community. Cats that have not been spayed or neutered typically rank higher than sterilized ones. The mom-cat with kittens has the most power of all. Neutering all the cats helps level the playing field, and eliminates the potential for many squabbles.

Personality affects the way the kitten perceives herself, the world around her, and other pets. Every kitten is an individual, and early socialization—exposing kittens to positive experiences during their formative weeks of life—will prevent many cat hierarchy disputes later in life. Shrinking violets that hide under the bed may become the subordinate kittens in the household, but then act out with behavior problems to compensate. Bully kittens, the brash in-your-face youngsters, are more likely to become problem cats because they like to pester even the boss-cats, or may not be satisfied with a lower-ranking position. Confident kittens, those with the middle-of-the-road calm personalities, seem destined for leadership and handle it well.

Age defines who rules to a great extent. Kittens almost always bow to the rule of adult cats. A mature cat will usually be dominant over an elderly kitty. But a cat may be physically mature by twelve months, and not reach social maturity until two to four years of age. That means kittens raised together may get along fine until they reach their second or third birthday, and then they begin to jockey for social position.

Health status throws out everything else. A sick cat loses any status she has, and becomes subordinate to healthy ones. Even a young kitten may bully a sickly elder-statesman cat.

Most cats get along very well together, especially when all are spayed and neutered and they have been properly introduced to each other. Cats raised in litters of four or more, which remain together until they are twelve to sixteen weeks old, usually get along best with other cats. The feline dance of dominance is so subtle that it can be hard for anybody but the cats to know what's going on.

Nose-to-Nose at Last

Often we are so excited to have a new kitten, we want to share our joy—immediately!—with everybody in the household. We bring the new kitten into the living room, dump her on the carpet, and everybody crowds around to get a look at the newcomer.

In the best of all worlds, the rest of your family (furred and otherwise) will accept the kitten with no problem. It's love at first sight, and a peaceable kingdom is born. But more often, such an introduction backfires—everybody (including the new kitten) gets upset, and it can take days, weeks, or even months to smooth out the relationships.

The key to successful introductions is patience. One step at a time gets the job done, with the least trauma to everybody involved. Once your new kitten becomes a part of your human and pet family, she'll have a lifetime to get to know you better. Make sure everybody gets off to a good start. That not only prevents misunderstandings and potential behavior problems, but can also increase the chances that the new kitten and your existing family will fall in love, permanently.

Tip: If your new kitten and resident pet are acting up because they weren't properly introduced, it's worth starting from scratch and reintroducing them the right way. It doesn't matter if they've been together for several days or even weeks. If they don't get along, go back to the basics—pretend you've just brought the kitten home and begin fresh.

Resident pets—be they cats, dogs, or other animals—also have emotions that need to be considered. After all, how would you feel if a stranger suddenly appeared and wanted to share your food, your bed, your favorite belongings—even the affections of your loved one?

Whether your kitten is ten weeks old or ten months old, she is still a stranger in a strange land, and will be frightened of the change. Cats of any age dislike the unexpected, and they identify security with a known territory. That's one reason why kitties will not be anxious to meet anybody new until they become familiar with their surroundings.

That's why creating a room of her own is the first and most important step when introducing a new kitten into your home. It breaks up the enormous territory of a new home into a smaller, more manageable kitten-size piece of real estate. She can become familiar with her room first, and use that as a safe retreat and home base. That's important if she's an "only" pet, but it becomes vital when she will share the house with other animals.

This segregation keeps the new kitten quarantined until her health is assessed by your veterinarian. The last thing you want to do is to expose your resident feline to an illness from the new kitten.

Finally, segregating the kitten tells your resident pet that only a part of her territory is being invaded. The closed door may pique hercuriosity, rather than raise her hackles. Segregating the pets early on lets you control the introductions.

Some pets require more time than others to become used to the idea of meeting new animals. Resident pets that already get along well with other animals may accept the new kitten more quickly. A shy kitten may take days to weeks to feel comfortable in the new environment. You must also be prepared, though, for some pets to simply dislike each other. In these cases, you can help them learn to tolerate each other.

Meeting Other Cats

All else being equal, adult cats tend to more readily accept pets that are younger than themselves and of the opposite sex. That means, if you have a resident neutered adult male cat, a female kitten would make a good choice; a resident spayed female cat would likely do well with a boy kitten. Of course, pairs of girls or boys can also become lifelong buddies with the right introductions.

Remember to spay or neuter your kitten as early as possible. That will eliminate many potential behavior problems and also help smooth the pet relationships as the kitten reaches maturity.

The adult kitty will much more quickly learn to accept a new cat if exposed to them during early socialization. Be warned that a four-year-old (or older) feline who has never before lived with another cat may strenuously object to a newcomer. He may become antagonistic or hide. Oftentimes, owners adopt another cat to keep the resident cat company—and the cat's reaction typically is: "Nobody asked me! I like having all the attention to myself!" A set-in-his-ways older cat may take a long time to accept a new pet, so again, patience is key.

Have your "kitten central" room set up before you bring the baby home. Then, if at all possible, have a friend carry the kitten in his carrier into the house. That sends a subtle signal to your older, resident cat that you are not the one behind the invasion. Take the carrier into the kitten room, shut the door, and let the kitten come out at her own pace. She may prefer to spend some time in the carrier with her familiar-smelling blanket until she's alone in the room and can explore on her own.

Try not to make a big deal out of the little one's presence. If anything, give your resident kitty even more attention and praise; make sure he knows he's important and special. Spend time with the new

(*Photo credit: Amy D. Shojai*)

It often takes a bit of wrangling for new pets to work out their social status. Pairs of kittens adopted at about the same age often do well together—even though their play may look like fighting.

kitten when the older cat is otherwise occupied. At this point, you don't want him to feel neglected because of the attention you pay the new kitten.

The resident cat and kitten should meet for the first time via paw-pats under the door. There may be some hissing and posturing involved. That's normal. They're playing kitty poker, with each one boasting about the cards they hold. It may take several hours or days before they stop hissing and growling.

Even if they seem interested and happy about meeting under the door, delay the nose-to-nose meeting for at least three days. A week or more of segregation may be necessary, particularly with older resident cats.

Once they show more curiosity and interest than fear or antagonism, take the next step. Switch the cats. Bring the resident adult cat into the kitten's room, and shut the door. Meanwhile, allow the kitten to explore the world beyond kitten central. That will give the resident cat a chance to sniff and explore the baby's room and figure out what's going on behind that closed door. He'll become more familiar with the other cat's scent, too. The kitten will do the same thing on the other side of the door. Give the kitten a minimum of three hours' solo exploration. If your resident cat throws a fit, stay in the kitten room with him and have somebody else supervise the little guy's exploration. Or you can give the kitten the three-hour allotment in single-hour increments, if your resident cat has a fit.

Kittens will not be interested in meeting another animal until they have become familiar with the territory. To ensure the first whisker-to-whisker meeting goes well, the kitten must have time to cheek-rub the rest of the house, find the good hiding places, and feel comfortable with her surroundings.

> **Tip:** Use the vanilla trick to help ease the transition. Cats identify their family and friends by scent, and everything that's familiar and safe to them will smell like them. Cats scent-mark people and other friendly pets by cheek-rubbing against them, and by grooming them with their tongue. The new kitten won't smell like them at all, and so at first "sniff" will seem strange. To help everybody smell alike—so the resident cat thinks the baby is safe, and vice versa—dab a bit of vanilla extract onto the back of each cat's neck and at the base of each tail. Those are the prime "sniff" locations for cats. That can help take the edge off the first fearful face-to-face. The vanilla trick (or your favorite perfume) will work on dogs and other pets, too.

After the kitten has had time to explore outside of her room, it's time for the first meeting. If anything, this should be anticlimactic.

Simply open the door that separates them, and let them meet at their own pace. You should not make a big deal over the event.

It can help to give the kitten and the adult cat something other than each other to engage their attention—like food. You can feed both cats at the same time, but on opposite ends of the room. Believe me, they'll know the other critter is there. This distance gives them an excuse to ignore each other, and also helps convey the idea that good things happen when the other cat is present. For some cats, it works best to engage each one in a favorite game, at opposite ends of the room. Above all, you want to associate positive activities with the kitten's presence.

Some cats will ignore each other and go their separate ways. That's fine. Others will approach each other, posture a bit with fluffed fur, and hiss. That's fine, too. Of course, you should be prepared to cut the introduction short if hisses escalate to growls and flailing tails.

It may take only an hour or so, or several days or even weeks for the new kitten and resident cat to come to an understanding. Until you are satisfied that neither one poses a danger to the other, the kitten should be safely segregated in her own room whenever you are not there to supervise. You'll know that the pair accept each other when they begin to play together, groom each other, or sleep together.

"Play fighting" can sometimes look like the real thing, because the cats may fluff their fur and bat at each other, or wrestle. Usually you can tell the difference by listening—when spits, hisses, growls, or yowls are involved, call a time-out. Just toss a towel over the pair. That will generally break up the fight without your risking a scratch.

Meeting Dogs

Can cats and dogs live together? Get along? Even like each other? Of course! With the right introductions, your kitten and the family dog can become fast friends. According to the 2001–2002 American Pet Product Manufacturer's Association (APPMA) National Pet Owners Survey, 26 percent of people lucky enough to share their lives with a companion animal call at least one dog and at least one cat a part of their family.

There are inherent safety concerns when the kitten and the dog vary a great deal in size. After all, a well-meaning but bumbling big dog could squash a tiny kitten just by stepping on her. Besides this, certain dogs may view a scampering kitten as a tasty morsel. Fair play requires mention of the dangers of kitten claws to canine eyes as well, particularly in some of the dog breeds with more prominent eyes. In spite of these concerns, the vast majority of cat-dog relationships are positive ones. Many of the same kitten-to-cat techniques work just as well with kitten-to-dog introductions.

Remember, dogs and cats are very different creatures. They have different languages, different social systems, and want different things out of life. It's up to you, the owner, to understand them both and help them adjust to each other.

Understanding Canine Concerns

In terms of kitten and cat safety issues, as well as predicting if the pets will get along, canine personality is even more important than dog size. To a great degree, the dog's breed can offer clues as to what to expect. There are always exceptions, and because you live with your dog, you will be the best judge of his personality.

As with cats, canine society is defined by leaders and followers. However, most dogs are happy just to be a part of the group and aren't necessesarily driven to be the "top dog." Many are perfectly happy to pledge allegiance to a human—or even a feline—leader. When your dog looks to you for guidance, it may be enough that you like the cat and expect the dog to accept her.

Arguments over turf, which characterize feline disputes, rarely occur to the same extent between dogs and cats. That's because they have very different social needs. Your dog is a pack animal who is satisfied as long as he knows his place in the family group, while the kitten's first priority is to own territory. Dogs don't value "real estate" the same way cats do. Dogs can only lay claim to floor-level property. Meanwhile, kittens prefers high perches the dog can't reach. Both the kitten and the dog will think they have won the contest, and will be happy ruling their own little kingdoms.

Warning: Predatory behavior is very important when judging safety issues. All dogs and cats have predators inside their brains, waiting to pounce. That's what drives kittens to chase the fluttering ribbon, or the dog to fetch the ball—or to chase the cat. Certain dog breeds, like terriers and sighthounds, were developed to chase and kill prey. The instinct is hot-wired into them, and the dog may not be able to control the urge to chase and catch a tiny kitten. Extra care must be taken when introducing a kitten into a home with a resident dog that has such a heritage.

When introducing the new kitten to a canine companion, you should be the person who brings the baby into the house. That sends a message to the dog that his leader—you—have made this decision.

As with the kitten-to-cat introductions, the newcomer should remain in her own room for the first several days. Dogs that have been well socialized to cats when they were puppies will likely display some curiosity and want to sniff at the door. Whines and even a few barks are fine. Be sure to watch the dog's whole body to "read" his true intent. Be alert for raised hackles—the fur along the neck and shoulders stands up with excitement and potential aggression. He may growl or wag his high-held tail with excitement.

Let the dog sniff your hands and clothes after you've spent time with the kitten. He should have a good idea of what's inside the room long before a face-to-face introduction takes place. Dogs often consider you to be the most important part of their territory, and so take care that he doesn't feel neglected. Try to spend extra time with your dog, and interact with the kitten in her room when the dog is outside taking care of business or playing.

Once the kitten room has become old stuff, and any growls or raised hackles have subsided, it's time to let the kitten explore the house. You can send the dog outside to the yard with another person to play a game and keep him distracted.

Remember, the kitten won't care to meet your dog until she's familiar with the environment. It is paramount that she have the opportunity to explore the house, uninterrupted, prior to a face-to-face introduction.

With a kitten-to-dog introduction, even when you are positive the dog wouldn't hurt a fly, it's important that you place the dog under leash control. Only then should the kitten be allowed out of her room, to meet the dog at her own pace. The leash is a safety precaution in case the kitten proves irresistible to your normally obedient pooch. It also reminds him that you are in charge of the interaction.

Just as with the resident cat introductions, your goal is to have the dog associate the kitten's presence with good things for him. Talk to him, give him treats, and praise him when he reacts favorably to the kitten. In future, you can reinforce the notion that having a kitten around is a good thing by having a treat handy each time your dog acts "nice" to the new baby.

Be sure to segregate the kitten in her room whenever you are not there to supervise the two pets. Even friendly play can turn dangerous if either pet becomes overexcited or frightened. Kittens should always have a "safe place" available where they can climb—like a chair back or cat tree—that keeps them beyond the reach of the dog. Likewise, the dog must have a private place, like a crate, where he can go to escape unwanted attention.

Warning: Dog eyes can be damaged by a frightened kitten that lashes out in reaction to a nosy sniff. Before face-to-face meetings, be sure to clip the kitten's claws.

> **Tip:** Use a baby gate to keep the dog out of the kitten's room, but allow the baby to come and go as needed. That gives the kitten access to her litter box and food, and a safe haven for naps. And it keeps the dog from pestering her, or from snacking out of her bowl or toilet.

Meeting Other Pets

Kittens can become best friends with a wide range of animals. Remember, though, that kittens grow into cats and will have a predatory interest in creatures smaller than themselves.

For instance, an aquarium filled with fish or reptiles offers great feline entertainment. So do cages with birds or "pocket pets" like gerbils or hamsters. Remember, small pets—especially birds—may suffer severe stress and develop behavior problems if pestered by an inquisitive kitten, even when they remain safely sequestered inside a cage. If you have these types of pets, the cage or aquarium should

(Photo credit: Weems S. Hutto)

Dogs and kittens can become the best of friends.

be set out of the kittens reach, and doors or lids must be absolutely secure. You'd be surprised what a dexterous kitten paw can open.

The larger, more confident birds, like parrots, are at less risk for being traumatized by the presence of a kitten or cat. In fact, parrots are often so assertive they scare the cat, and she gives them a wide berth. Other times, the parrot learns to tease or treat the kitten by dropping toys or food within reach, or by calling to the kitten in a human "voice."

Direct contact between your kitten and any bird, or small rodent-type pets, is not recommended because the risk is just too great. Let them be friends from a distance, and with the benefit of bars or glass between them. The exception here is cats and rabbits, which can become the best of buddies with the proper introductions.

Before introducing your kitten and rabbit, be sure all the toenails on both have been trimmed. Bunnies pack a powerful paw-punch, and you don't want either pet to be injured. You'll also want to allow the kitten time to explore her surroundings, so she'll be more eager to meet new pets. When the rabbit is bigger than your kitten, place the bunny in a carrier or cage before allowing the kitten to approach for a sniff at her own pace.

When the kitten and the rabbit are the same size, or the kitten is larger than the rabbit, it's best to have both pets safely restrained on a halter and leash. Be ready to stop the interaction at the first sign of aggression from either pet. Usually, a confident rabbit will be quite interested in a kitten. And in fact, some experts say certain rabbits prefer the company and friendship of felines.

Eventually, cats and rabbits enjoy playing games of chase and hide and seek. Monitor the game to be sure nobody looks scared, and stop it before it gets out of hand. If they're taking turns being chased, it's a game.

Never leave the kitten alone with the rabbit until you are satisfied they get along. Once properly introduced, you can expect them to become fast friends, play together, and even sleep together.

Meeting Children

Children seem to have an affinity for kittens. You should know, however, that kittens may not see it that way—at least, at first. That's because even though the kitten may trust adult humans, children are so very different she may not recognize them as safe. Depending on their age, a child has a much higher pitched voice, often screams or cries, and moves very differently from adult people. Is it any wonder your kitten thinks the grandkids are from Mars?

Children need to understand that they can be scary to a tiny kitten. From a kitten's vantage, even a toddler looks like a giant. Running after her, reaching out with waving hands that might pull a tail or ear, making loud high-pitched squeals—all that's enough to send a kitten diving under the bed. Even the gentlest kitten will defend herself out of fear or anger if she's hurt or frightened.

Warning: Kitten bites and scratches can quickly become serious. Needle-sharp teeth cause painful puncture wounds that easily get infected. And kitten claws sometimes carry bacteria that can cause

CSD (cat scratch disease), which can cause mild to severe flulike symptoms. If you or your child are bitten or scratched by your kitten, wash the wound thoroughly with warm soapy water. Then call your doctor or pediatrician for further instructions.

When your children want to make friends with the new kitten, ask them first to sit on the floor. Chasing the kitten will at worst scare her, and at best force her to do something she doesn't like. The key here is to entice the kitten to come to the child on her own. Do that by making the experience positive and rewarding for the cat.

Sitting on the floor puts the child on the same level as the cat, which is much less threatening or frightening to the new pet. During the first session, let the kitten wander around the room exploring, and have the children pretend to be part of the furniture. This way, the kitten learns that having them there is a normal part of her environment. Ask the children to not pick her up yet. If she comes near enough, and lets them, a quick gentle stroke along her back is fine.

Very small children might first practice petting their own arm, so they know the best way to stroke the kitten without making her un

How Old Is Old Enough?

Pet owners are often eager to share their affection for animals with their children. Parents often tell me they want to get a pet to teach their kids about responsibility. Certainly, children raised to appreciate and properly care for pets will carry that love with them for the rest of their lives. But what age is best? And how much can you expect from your children—or from a new kitten?

Obviously, an infant is in no position to care for a kitten, although babies certainly may appreciate watching kitty play, or touching her soft fur. Both infants and toddlers may aggravate a kitten to death, poking fingers into her eyes or pulling fistfuls of fur. You will need to supervise all interactions between the new kitten and your infant or toddler. After all, when babies get together, anything can happen. You don't want the kitten to be dragged about like a stuffed toy, nor do you want your child to be scratched when he corners the frightened pet. Kittens old enough to outrun a toddler soon learn to avoid them.

By the time your children are six to seven years old, they can start to become part of the kitty care team. Perhaps they can make sure the kitten always has fresh water, or can help "exercise" the baby each evening by playing with her. Young children will need direction in how to properly hold or pet a kitten—no poking or tail-pulling allowed! Of course, the ultimate responsibility will be yours, and so be sure to supervise and follow up to make sure the kitten's needs are never overlooked.

comfortable. Perhaps you and your child can take turns "pretending" to be the kitten.

Another great way for children to interact with the new kitten is by playing with a long ribbon, feather, or fishing pole toy. This is particularly helpful with shy kittens who fear getting too close. They can play safely from a distance, and learn that your child is fun to be around. Also, once the kitten has been worn out with play, she'll be much more likely to want to cuddle on a lap.

Whenever the children want to interact with the kitten, make it a rule that they should sit down on the floor nearby and let her approach them. That will also help them control their excited, loud voices. Explain that kitty prefers soft-pitched talk, and that yells and screams and high-pitched voices are scary to cats.

After several successful sessions of play with the fishing pole toy, your kitten should learn that the children are fun, and they don't grab at her and make her feel scared. Once she starts to venture closer, make sure the children have a couple of scrumptious cat treats ready to offer her. If she can learn to associate your child with playtime and treats, she'll more readily accept them.

Warning: Never let your kitten play with fingers, hands, or feet. It's great fun for her to bite and pounce on these moving objects, but she can hurt or frighten you (or your children) if she gets too excited. A kitten grabbing your ankles as you walk down the stairs could, in fact, be dangerous. Instead, give her suitable toys to bite and toss, like stuffed animals.

Tip: The best way to pick up a kitten is with one hand beneath her chest, and the other cupping her furry bottom. That supports the whole cat so no feet dangle. It also makes her feel more secure and less likely to struggle.

PART 3

KITTEN CARE 101

7

FEEDING FOR HEALTH

Building Health from the Inside

Good nutrition is the foundation of kitten health. A shiny coat, strong bones, boundless energy, and a loving personality all begin with the proper diet.

A mother cat, called a "queen," produces nutrient-rich milk especially designed for the needs of kittens. Mom-cat takes care of the kitten's hunger pangs from birth to about six to eight weeks of age. A good diet for Mom ensures her milk will also provide optimum nutrition for her growing babies.

As the kitten grows, he becomes interested in what Mom eats and will sample food from her dish. Mother cats that hunt may bring their kittens mice or other prey animals, and begin the process of teaching them to hunt. Kittens allowed outside may supplement their diets with the occasional varmint, or buggy snack, but that won't be enough to fulfill the growing baby's needs. In days gone by, many kittens did not survive to adulthood, simply because adequate nutrition wasn't available. Today, pet kittens are fortunate because they only need to stalk the bowl to obtain a complete and balanced diet.

You should be aware that cats are "obligate carnivores." That means they require certain nutrients that can only be obtained from meat. They cannot survive on a vegetarian diet.

Part of your responsibility is choosing the proper diet for the

(Photo credit: Ralston Purina Company)

The first milk that kittens nurse, called colostrum, contains protective antibodies from the mother that help keep them healthy until their own immune system matures.

kitten. Today, there are literally hundreds of commercial kitten foods available. That makes feeding kittens simpler—and more confusing—than ever before.

Partly, that's because nutrition is an evolving science. We know more about feline nutrition today than we did yesterday, and brand-new information will be uncovered tomorrow. There are also differences of opinion among the experts. On top of that, kittens are not identical. These differences make one food better for this kitten, and another food ideal for that one.

How do you choose the best food for your new baby? First, ask for advice from a kitten expert you know and trust. Talk with the kitten's breeder or the shelter staff to learn what he's used to eating. Get a recommendation from his veterinarian. And read the rest of this chapter, so you know what to expect, what questions to ask, and how to evaluate your choices.

Kitten Food Ingredient List

Every food label you look at will be different, but some generalities apply to all. Because kittens *are* carnivores and require that certain nutrients come from meat, it's important that a food contain the right types of ingredients.

The food label must, by law, include a list of all ingredients used in the food. They are listed in decreasing order of the amount present, by weight. That is, the first listed ingredients are present in the greatest amount, and the last listed ingredients are present in the tiniest amounts.

In general, the ingredient list for your kitten's food should have:

- *one or more protein sources*, listed as one of the first several ingredients;
- *carbohydrate source*, such as cereals;
- *fat sources*; and
- *large numbers of minerals and vitamins*, toward the bottom of the list.

Unfortunately, the label won't tell you anything about the quality of the ingredients. Also, pet food manufacturers may get "creative" when listing ingredients, and include "fractions" of a food type rather than calculate the total amount. For instance, they may list "*corn, corn gluten meal, corn by-products*" separately, which places them further down the list—when, if listed together, they would be noted nearer the top of the list because they make up a large percentage of the total volume.

Kitten Nutritional Needs

Food scientists spend years researching the specific nutritional needs of kittens. Because your new pet is a baby and growing so quickly, he has very different requirements than those of adult cats. It's important that you choose a food designed to support and promote kitten growth and health.

Kittens need a food that's "complete" and "balanced." That means the food contains all the necessary components, called nutrients, in the proper amounts in relation to one another. Nutrients benefit the kitten both individually and by interacting with each other in the proper ratios. Kittens need a combination of six different classes of nutrients for good health: proteins, carbohydrates, fats, vitamins, minerals, and water.

PROTEIN

When we talk about protein, our first thoughts turn to meat. In fact, proteins are made up of twenty-three different chemical compounds called amino acids. Some are available in nonmeat sources, like corn or soy. That's why many commercial kitten foods include a large percentage of cereal grains in the formulation.

> **Technical Stuff:** Some amino acids cannot be produced by the body in sufficient amounts and are called "essential" because they must be provided in the diet. Kittens—and adult cats—require dietary histidine, isoleucine, leucine, arginine, methionine, phenylalanine, threonine, tryptophan, valine, and lysine. Unlike dogs, cats also need dietary taurine which is found in meat. A deficiency of taurine may result in blindness or heart disease.

Neither meat alone nor a vegetarian diet will give your kitten complete and balanced nutrition. He needs the right balance of both. Protein builds and maintains bone, blood, tissue, and even the kitten's immune system. Cats are carnivores and require much higher levels of dietary protein than dogs do—about five to six times more per pound of body weight. Your kitten should never be allowed to eat dog food. Besides aggravating the dog, the practice could make kitty sick.

CARBOHYDRATES

You don't think of kittens needing starches and grains, and they truly don't need a lot. But carbohydrates provide energy, and the fiber helps regulates the bowels and can help the body absorb some of the other nutrients.

FATS

Fat may be what your kitten most loves about his food, because it provides the strongest flavor. That's important. After all, the best diet in the world is worthless if you can't get your kitten to eat it.

Fats also are the number one energy source in food. They provide two and a quarter times the energy of a comparable amount of carbohydrates or proteins. That's important when the kitten has high-energy needs for play and growth.

Fats and fatty acids give your kitten's fur coat that healthy sheen. A deficiency causes a wide range of symptoms, from greasy fur and dandruff to weight loss and slow-healing sores.

MINERALS

Minerals are needed in relatively tiny amounts, but in the proper proportions. Minerals are essential for nerve conduction, muscle contraction, fluid stability inside the cells, and a wide range of other functions.

Minerals work together, and the balance is as important as the amount. Too much is as dangerous as too little. Necessary minerals include calcium, phosphorus, magnesium, potassium, sodium, chloride, and the trace minerals cobalt, copper, iodine, iron, manganese, selenium, and zinc. An imbalance of minerals can cause bone deformities, anemia, muscle weakness, heart or kidney disease, and countless other problems.

Technical Stuff. Many cat and kitten owners become confused about the term *ash*. Pet food manufacturers use this word to define the total mineral content of a particular food. The food is burned, and what's left—ash—is measured to determine the ash content. In other words, ash includes *all* the minerals in the food that won't burn.

VITAMINS

Vitamins are used in biochemical processes inside the cells. They are divided into two groups. Vitamin C and the B-complex vitamins are water soluble and not stored in the body and so must be replaced every day. Fat-soluble vitamins are stored in the body and include vitamins A, D, E, and K. Fat-soluble vitamins can only be absorbed by the body when fatty acids are also present.

Only small amounts, in the right combinations, are necessary for good health. Too much or too little of certain vitamins can cause health problems, from skin disease and rickets, to bleeding and nervous system disorders.

WATER

I've saved the most important nutrient for last. A kitten's body weight is 84 percent water. Water is necessary for the body to run smoothly. It lubricates the tissues and makes it possible for the blood to carry nutrients throughout the body. Water is vital to keeping the kitten's body temperature regulated. It is used in digestion of the food, and it carries away waste products in the urine and feces. Water is so important to health that only a 15 percent loss of body water causes dehydration that can kill the kitten.

There is no clear-cut answer to the question "How much water does a kitten need each day?" As a general rule, healthy kittens and cats living in a comfortable environment (not too hot or too cold) need about 2.5 times as much water as the amount of dry food they eat.

When a commercial food is complete and balanced, all the nutrients have been calculated to the proper proportions. Special "therapeutic diets" are available from veterinarians for specific health problems. Every kitten is different, but most healthy kittens do well when they eat a quality brand commercial kitten food.

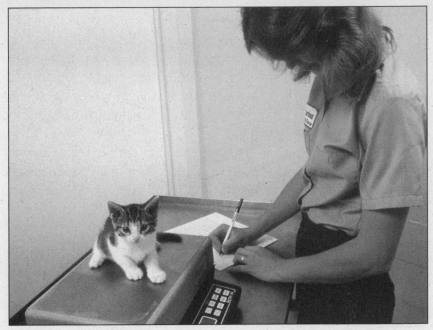

(Photo credit: Ralston Purina Company)

The growth rate and overall health of a kitten is carefully evaluated during feeding trials, to make sure the food supports normal kitten development.

Reading Food Labels

The labels on commercial diets will tell you everything you need to know—once you learn how to read them. They can be misleading when the manufacturer gets creative in describing the ingredients and benefits. To simplify the confusion, here are some basics to look for.

Kitten food. That sounds like a no-brainer, right? But seriously, the product should be labeled for use by kittens, not just "cats." Your kitten's nutritional needs differ from those of an adult feline. Typically, commercial pet foods are formulated for "life stages" of the pet. You want the one designed for "kittens," not for adult cats, senior cats, or other designations.

Complete and balanced. Some foods, believe it or not, are designed just for snacking or for supplemental feeding. Those may be fine for an adult that isn't growing so fast and gets the rest of his nutrition in another form. But kittens can only eat tiny bits at a time, so whatever they eat should be complete and balanced to ensure they're getting enough of everything. If the food does not say it is complete and balanced for growing kittens, choose another food.

Feeding trials. Look for a statement on the label that tells you the food has been tested by feeding it to other kittens. That's the only way you'll know that your baby will actually benefit from the food.

Warning: Some labels may say the food was tested or formulated to meet established nutrient profiles—but it has not been tested in feeding trials. This means a chemical analysis or calculation method was used to validate the food. It's perfectly legal—but it does not actually prove the food can be digested or used in a real live kitten.

AAFCO Guidelines. The Association of Animal Feed Control Officials (AAFCO) has established cat and kitten food nutrient profiles, and feeding trial protocols, that are used as the industry standard.

Recognizable company. There are countless pet food companies and even more brands available. The really good ones have been around for many years, and their reputations have stood the test of time. Reputable companies spend millions of dollars on research and feeding trials, and include information on the label that allows you to contact them with questions. Look for a familiar name or ask your veterinarian to recommend one.

A Matter of Taste

What is it that makes your kitten say, "Mmmmmm, yum"? The technical word for it is *palatability*. With kittens—and cats in general—the taste of the food is only a small part of what tickles their fancy. Pet food manufactures go to extremes to make their brands palatable so that kittens beg to eat them, and return to the bowl time after time.

Palatability means not only taste, but also smell. Kittens care much more about the smell of a food, and the more pungent, the better. Texture is also a deciding factor. Kitten food is available in several different forms—dry, canned, semimoist. Each has advantages and disadvantages, and every kitten has his own preferences.

Canned Varieties

Canned kitten foods are extremely tasty and most kittens readily accept them. That's because the moisture releases the odor that kitties love. Canned diets may be perfect for youngsters that are just learning to eat solid food. They come in a variety of flavors, and are packed with calories so kittens don't have to eat a lot. Because of the high water content, a canned diet partially fulfills the kitten's water requirement.

Canned kitten food is processed exactly the same way as human canned foods. Canning preserves the food, and as long as the can remains closed, it will stay fresh indefinitely.

Canned foods are the most expensive, though, because they are up to 70 percent water. That also means kittens fed canned food may have a softer stool than those that are fed dry food. Also, once the can has been opened, the food must be refrigerated or it will spoil. When feeding a canned product, you must pick up the leftovers after about 30 minutes. That can mean some waste if your kitten refuses to eat leftovers. Soft diets tend to stick to the teeth and can predispose the kitten to dental problems. Some of these diets are so tasty, they can actually promote "food addictions" in some susceptible kittens.

Dry Diets

Dry foods are relatively inexpensive. They come in bags, boxes, or plastic jugs, can be purchased in larger quantities, and do not require refrigeration. They are considered the most convenient diet, and can be left out at all times for the kitten to snack on at leisure. They are thought to help reduce the chance of tartar buildup and dental problems.

Some kittens prefer crunchy diets, but very young kittens may not be able to chew the food until they grow enough teeth. Because of processing constraints, dry foods also tend to rely more heavily on grain-source protein rather than meat. Called extrusion, this high-pressure cooking process dries the kibble and gelatinizes the starches in the grain ingredients to make them more digestible. Dry foods are typically preserved with additives that keep them fresh for several months.

Technical Stuff: Fats added to dry food makes them taste good. However, fats tend to spoil—oxidize—which is a kind of biological rust process. Antioxidants help preserve the dry food and keep it tasting fresh and the nutrients viable. Common antioxidants include chemicals like BHA and BHT; or "natural" additives like mixed tocopherols (a kind of vitamin E mixture), vitamin C, and vitamin E.

Semimoist Meals

Semimoist foods are often packaged as individual servings. They are kept moist by ingredients like corn syrup that keep the food from drying out. These foods are convenient to use, especially for travel, because they don't need refrigeration. They tend to be more expensive than dry foods.

Remember, no matter which type of food you serve, kittens need something to drink along with it. Keep a bowl of water available for your kitten at all times. Set the water bowl next to his food, so he always knows where to find it.

Also, you should be aware that kittens—and adult cats—don't tend to drink as much water as they should. It's a good idea to have several bowls of water available for your baby, located around the house, so that when the urge strikes, he can take a sip. For instance, my cat Seren has a water bowl next to the sink in every bathroom. She also enjoys sipping from the dribbling faucet in the mornings, while I get ready for work.

"Quality" Categories

As more and more pet foods appear on store shelves, companies look for new ways to make their brand stand out of the crowd. Category designations have long been a way to differentiate products, but today the lines tend to blur.

First there were plain old "pet foods." They were typically inexpensive, and often available in grocery stores. Some were actually labeled as the generic store brand. In the past these diets used less expensive ingredients, and the pet needed to eat more of the product to obtain proper nutrition. Consequently, these diets typically filled up the litter box more quickly, when the output increased with input.

Next, "premium" foods came onto the market. They used higher quality ingredients that were more expensive, and so the product cost more. Often, they were sold only through licensed dealers—like pet products stores or veterinary offices. The better ingredients meant pets needed to eat less volume, so although the foods were more expensive, there was also more bang for the buck. The litter box volume decreased as well.

Lately, a surge in "superpremium" foods has hit the market. These claim to use the best quality ingredients, and command the highest prices. They tend to be calorie-dense foods so the pet requires a small amount to fill his nutritional requirements. They are so highly palatable, though, they can be very easy to overfeed. Again, the superpremium diets are offered through veterinarians or specialty outlets.

Today, with the advent of the "super" pet supply stores, grocery chains, and warehouse clubs like Costco and Sam's Club—not to mention the Internet—a wide variety of low-cost, premium, and superpremium diets are available anytime, anyplace.

It may be true that you get what you pay for. Certainly, the cheapest no-name food out there isn't a smart choice. Conversely, not every kitten will require the equivalent of rocket fuel, especially if he spends his life playing quietly in your living room. The average kitten does quite well on the midrange diets.

Ringing the Dinner Bell

Once you have figured out what kind of food to offer your kitten, you must set up a feeding schedule. How often you feed your little one depends to a degree on the form of the food, but more important, on your kitten's age.

Kittens are "intermittent feeders." That means they nibble a little throughout the day rather than gulping down huge meals all at once. There are a couple of factors behind this behavior. Small kittens simply don't have the physical capacity to consume all the nutrition they need at one sitting. Their tummies just can't hold enough. Even adult cats tend to eat in spurts and stops, which makes sense. Cats evolved to eat mouse-size meals, unlike dogs, which tend to be gorgers and fill themselves to bursting. That's why I recommend several meals a day—three to four until the kitten is six months old, and twice a day thereafter, even after they've become adults.

Warning: It is dangerous to "starve" your kitten into eating something. Felines get sick very quickly if they stop eating and can develop liver problems. As long as your kitten is otherwise healthy, it won't hurt him to miss one meal. But kittens should never go longer than twelve to eighteen hours without eating (adult cats shouldn't exceed about forty-eight hours without a meal). Lost appetite points to a health problem, so see your vet immediately.

Scheduled meals have several benefits. Certainly, a canned diet must be meal-fed anyway, to prevent your kitten from snacking on spoiled food. But meal-feeding dry diets works well because it allows you to monitor the kitten's eating habits. Does he finish all of the meal? Only part of it? Snub the bowl altogether? That can be an early warning of health problems.

Kittens thrive on routine, so feed your kitten in the same place every day, and at the same times. Locate the feeding station some distance away from the litter box. Kittens have an aversion to eating next to their toilet—wouldn't you? A low-traffic area works well, such as one end of the kitchen or the laundry room. A specific area of his private room is ideal. When you have more than one pet, that gives the kitten privacy to eat so that he isn't pestered. It also keeps older pets from swiping the baby's food; kitten formulas have more calories, and adult pets can gain weight on these diets.

Remember, obesity is the number one nutritional problem of adult cats, often due to the never-empty food bowl. Free-feeding dry food is more convenient, no doubt about that, but it's much healthier in the long run to start kittens out right, and continue meal feeding throughout their lives.

> **Tip:** Meal-feeding offers a great training advantage, too. It trains the kitten to expect when food is served, so he doesn't constantly pester you. Otherwise, kittens become very good at training the unknowing owner to jump to fill the bowl at each meow. You may find yourself being awakened at 3:00 A.M. to satisfy the baby's whims.

How much should you feed? That depends on the individual kitten, his age, and the specific diet you choose. Usually, kittens will self-regulate the amount they need to eat—that is, they'll eat just the right amount of a given food to fulfill their energy requirements. That could be more of one food, and less of another, depending on the calorie content.

Although obesity is a problem of adult cats, don't worry about restricting food for a growing kitten. He should be given as much food as he wants to eat. Use the guidelines on the package as a starting point. But every kitten is different, and some high-energy breeds may need more food than a placid kitten. Set out the food at mealtime, and give your kitten about thirty minutes to finish eating. Then pick up the food until the next meal.

Measure the amount of food you put in his bowl. Then measure the amount left after he finishes eating. Do this for two or three days to get an average amount kitty eats during the day, and that will give you a ballpark range of how to divide up the amount he needs per meal.

Kittens younger than ten weeks old may have trouble eating dry food, and you'll need to soften the kibble or use a canned diet. To soften dry kitten formulas, use warm water (about an ounce per 1½ cups of food). The warm liquid also tends to unlock odor, which triggers feline appetite.

Warning: Cow's milk can be hard on kitten digestion and cause diarrhea. That's because kittens past the age of weaning often don't have enough of the enzyme lactase needed to properly process the milk sugar lactose. Use warm water to soften food, or a commercial kitten milk replacer.

Once the baby is happily eating the softened kibble, begin to reduce the amount of liquid gradually. By ten weeks of age, kittens generally have enough teeth and the ability to eat dry diets, and won't need water added.

Kitten digestion can be delicate, so once you find a food the baby likes, try not to change it. Sometimes, of course, you'll need to make a switch perhaps on the advice of your veterinarian. When changing his food, always do so a little bit at a time and start out by mixing half the old food with the same amount of the new. Gradually increase the percentage of the new diet over a week's time until finally he's eating only the new kitten formula.

When your baby is younger than three to four weeks old, you'll need to take over nursing duties and provide a commercial kitten milk replacer until Junior grows enough to eat solid food. See "Feeding an Orphan" on page 49 for tips on feeding a tiny kitten.

Treats, Supplements, and Homemade Diets

Today it has become popular to offer our pets the same kinds of "natural" foods and supplements that health-conscious people choose for themselves. Some of these products are very good. Others are of questionable value at best. The difficulty arises in trying to tell the difference.

Do kittens and cats benefit from natural foods and nutritional supplements? Without a doubt, some benefit a great deal, particularly those that have less than ideal health status. In these instances, the kitten may actually need the extra nutritional help of a special diet, or a therapeutic food supplement. For instance, a kitten suffering from anemia would benefit from extra B vitamins, or food sources like beef or organ meats because the extra protein builds red blood cells.

Kitten Purrs: If you are interested in learning more about safe natural foods for your kitten, choose a veterinarian who specializes in holistic care. You can find a variety of alternative-practice veterinarians in your neck of the woods by browsing the Web site www.altvetmed.com.

The vast majority of kittens that are otherwise healthy will thrive on commercial kitten foods. Adding supplements, especially extra vitamins and minerals, to a complete and balanced commercial product can throw off the delicate formula. Dangerous toxicities can result when too much or too little of certain nutrients end up in the kitten.

Making your own homemade kitten food can be even more dangerous, again because of the necessity of carefully balancing all those nutrients. Be very cautious about taking the advice of the self-proclaimed experts. Lately there has been an explosion of "natural" diets promoting everything from feeding raw diets to cooked recipes to bones. When it comes down to it, frankly, the most natural diet would be offering your kitten live mice or birds, with all the attendant parasite concerns and bone obstruction dangers—not to mention the mess!

Yes, home-prepared foods are possible. Many reputable holistic veterinarians recommend these diets, and will offer good advice on how to prepare them safely. Practically speaking, though, it takes a great deal of time and effort to cook for your kitten—and it's very easy to make mistakes. I personally don't have the time, the patience, or the confidence that I could do it right—consistently—to ensure good health for my cat. There are just too many things that can go wrong, even when the recipe comes from a true veterinary nutrition expert.

When your kitten's health is at stake, I believe it's best to take the safest road. Choose a complete and balanced commercial kitten formula—there are products touted to be "natural" and that may be an option you prefer. Use this as a base, and then with the advice of your holistic veterinarian, perhaps you can offer appropriate kinds and amounts of fresh foods as treats.

Supplements tend to be regarded as therapeutic—that is, they are designed to act on your kitten's physical health in a positive manner. However, by definition, anything fed to your kitten in addition to his regular diet is considered a supplement—and that would include treats.

Treats are legal. They are, in fact, a great benefit to the bonding process and can be instrumental when used as rewards to train your kitten to be good. They work best, though, if reserved for special times—like rewarding good behavior. They'll lose their punch if fed too often, or for no reason. Also remember that small kittens get filled up very quickly, so keep treats to a minimum so they don't take the place of the meal your kitten needs to eat. Commercial treats often have the "complete and balanced" notice on the label, so you know they won't upset the baby's nutrition.

What about table scraps? I'll probably surprise you here, but I believe table food can be perfectly fine—it just depends on what's on your table! Junk food that's bad for people is no better for our pets; healthy foods like lean meats, fish, fruits (cats often love melon!), fresh vegetables, cheese, even yogurt are often relished as treats. Again, any treating from your plate must be done within reason. Nutritionists typically say that such tidbits shouldn't make up more than 10 percent of the pet's total diet.

Warning: Cats adore tuna. But the flavor is so strong, tuna can be addictive. Even worse, feeding a great deal of tuna has been linked to a health problem called steatitis, a painful skin condition thought to result from excessive dietary fish oil fatty acids. Tuna-flavored commercial foods are fine—but it's best not to serve the real thing.

Tip: Several times a month, I give my cat Seren a small piece of cooked lean meat like steak or chicken to help keep her teeth clean. Kittens and cats rarely chew dry food enough to scrub their teeth, and canned foods are no help at all. But a chunk of meat requires chewing, and that helps clean off the hard-to-clean molars at the back of the cat's mouth. Seren rarely finishes the piece—just chewing for the flavor seems to be enough to satisfy her.

Eating Habits

Every kitten develops his own eating style. Many crouch above the plate and munch. Others take one bite at a time, and carry it to another room to eat. Some want you to watch, or, purr so loudly when they chew that you fear they'll choke. A few kitties use their paws to eat or drink, dipping into the dish and scooping up mouthfuls as though with furry utensils.

Cartoons and advertising have celebrated two common kitty types—the finicky feline and the glutton. Both, of course, are extremes you hope to avoid.

The gluttons eat anything that doesn't move faster than they do. You'll need to keep an eye on the waistline of these kittens as they mature, and ensure they exercise enough to burn off the calories. They may also be at risk for "garbage gut syndrome." Such kittens think anything left unattended is fair game, and can even raid the garbage—and end up with predictable results (vomiting, diarrhea, or both). Oftentimes, it's the stray kitten, the waif you've rescued from the streets, that turns into a bottomless pit. That's likely because these babies have truly known hunger when they were on their own. They remember. And they don't want to take the chance of ever being hungry again.

The other extreme, the finicky kitten, is usually a product of the way a kitten is fed early in life. In other words, most finicky cats are taught to be finicky. Owners understandably grow concerned when the cat doesn't immediately eat the offered food—so they try another flavor or brand. Kittens can be just like children, and hold out for a favorite flavor, especially when they know you will offer them a choice. Kittens (and especially adult cats) may not be hungry for every meal. Just because they don't gobble it up all at once doesn't necessarily mean they dislike that food. Give them a bit of time.

In fact, when food is available for too long, too often, the hunger centers in the feline brain can temporarily shut off. Kitty appetite is better tempted by offering the food for fifteen to thirty minutes and then removing the food for an hour or so before trying again.

Many cats enjoy variety in their diet—and canned foods cater to this urge, as well as our own desire to treat and please our kittens.

Many cat owners offer a different canned food every meal. Others may provide a dry diet for one meal and a smorgasbord of canned varieties as treats for the second meal. This decision is up to you—kittens and cats can do well on such a plan.

However, you should know that kittens and cats do not *require* variety in the diet. People do—because we do not have available to us a complete and balanced "people ration."

As long as the kitten's diet is complete and balanced for a growing kitten, he will do fine on the same food every single day. After all, in the wild a cat eats mice or grasshoppers or voles every single day, if they're available to him. He won't know any different, and won't crave variety and become finicky, unless you teach him otherwise.

One last thing to remember is that pet food companies design kitten foods to tempt you first and your kitten second. After all, you are the one with the wallet. Kittens don't care about the color of the food, if it has gravy, or looks like luncheon meat—that's aimed to get you to buy the product. Commercial pet foods often develop products that appeal to human tastes first by looking like something we'd want to eat ourselves. To make the best choices, consider your kitten's nutritional needs above all else.

8

GROOMING CONSIDERATIONS

Crowning Glory—All About Kitten Coats

Oh, that soft, luxurious kitten coat—it feels so good to stroke, and to cuddle with your new furry wonder. The colors and patterns kittens sport are gloriously intricate, and help make them individuals as much as does the unique way they mew for attention.

The kitten coat goes beyond turning your kitten into one of the loveliest, most striking creatures on the planet. Fur has very practical applications for the cat. All cats have fur. Nature designed the fur coat to have very specific benefits.

The length of individual hairs varies widely. A longhaired kitten may have hair up to four inches long. Even the so-called "bald" Sphynx breed has fur. She's covered in downy, velvetlike fuzz that grows about ⅛ inch. She may have a bit of longer fur on her lower legs or tail.

Fur Function

The fur coat is made up of thousands of individual hairs. Each is a threadlike, multicolored filament made from keratin, a kind of fibrous horny protein that grows from the skin. This is the same material that makes up the claws. Hair is 95 percent protein. That's why one sign of kitten malnutrition is dull, lifeless fur.

The hair collectively serves as a protective barrier between your

Fur is the kitten's crowning glory. The longer the fur, though, the more you'll need to help with grooming.

(Photo credit: Amy D. Shojai)

kitten's skin and the outside world. Fur shields the kitten from extremes in temperature. It keeps tender skin from burning in the sun and protects the body from cold weather. It even helps shed water to keep the baby dry.

Muscles in the skin near where the hairs grow allow kittens to "fluff" their fur to offer ventilation to the skin on hot days. On cold days, the fluffed fur traps warm air between the hairs, and creates an insulating blanket of warmth next to the skin.

Fur, especially the whiskers, also serves as a communication tool. Fluffing the fur denotes fear or excitement, while whisker position signals a variety of emotions and intentions.

Most cats have three kinds of hairs that make up the fur coat.

The guard hairs are the longest, straight and coarse, and make up the outer coat. In some breeds they may be a bit oily, to offer weather-resistance and shed rain. The intermediate coat is composed of medium length awn hairs. Finally, the undercoat is short, downy, and curly or crimped. Rex breeds of cat have curly fur made up of this undercoat. Sinus hairs, also called whiskers, are specialized thick hairs set extra-deep in the skin adjacent to nerve endings, and are extremely sensitive.

Shedding

All cats and kittens shed. That's because hair grows in cycles, from the root within the skin, outward in a continuous pattern of rapid growth, slower growth, and a resting period. When new hair begins to grow, it pushes out the old hair, which is shed.

Shedding is normal, and is ruled by the kitten's exposure to daylight or artificial light. Warm weather has nothing to do with it. Daylight hours are longer during the late spring and early summer months, so that's typically when the fur flies.

Warning: Shedding does not involve the loss of hunks of fur that leave bald or sore spots on the skin. That might be a sign of a fungal infection of the skin called ringworm, which needs veterinary treatment.

The more your kitten is exposed to light, the greater amount she will shed. Indoor cats often shed year-round, because artificial light stimulates hair growth. Hair grows rapidly for several weeks in the spring, and the new growth pushes out the old, which is shed. That's followed by a more moderate growth period. The hairs typically grow between ¼ and ⅓ inch each day. As fur grows, the average adult cat generates a total of about sixty feet worth of new hair each day. Finally, the hairs stop growing during the "resting" period during the winter.

Mature hairs loosen in the follicles during the resting phase of winter and are more easily pulled out during this period. Any sudden fright or stress can cause a sudden shed. That's because such emotions activate "piloerection," specialized muscles along the cat's back and tail that are attached to the hairs and make them stand on end when the kitten is upset. If the hair is already loose, this muscle reflex literally pulls the hair out.

Your kitten's fur is grown and shed in an irregular pattern. Long-haired kittens especially may begin to look a bit moth-eaten as the woolly undercoat falls out. It can take eighteen months to two years for some longhaired cats to fully develop their mature coat.

All kittens need help grooming themselves, particularly long-haired beauties. When shedding, the coat is more prone to tangles—called *mats*—because the undercoat can get caught in the guard hairs and turn into a wad.

Even though kittens groom themselves every day, they all benefit from some human help. Combing or brushing your kitten every day not only helps you bond more closely with her, it also helps prevent skin problems, painful mats, and health problems like hairballs.

A Lick and a Promise—Kitten Self-Grooming

Cats are the neatniks of the pet world. Kittens start licking themselves clean as early as two weeks of age, and learn by copycat behavior—they watch Mom and imitate her technique. If Mom is a neatness freak, chances are Junior will follow suit. But when Mom has a haphazard approach to keeping clean, her babies may let themselves get quite grubby before they clean up their act.

For regular maintenance, cats tend to groom themselves at predictable times throughout the day. An after-meal cleanup is nearly universal, as is the wake-up wash after a nap. Beyond that, kittens develop their own individual grooming schedules. By the time she's a grown-up cat, your kitten will spend up to 50 percent of her time awake in some form of grooming behavior. In fact, grooming is so ingrained in the kitty psyche that it can be used as a barometer of kitten health. Cats that feel sick often stop grooming themselves altogether.

Cat Tongues

Cats use a number of techniques to clean themselves. The tongue is the number one tool and could be compared to a kitty washcloth. The saliva helps dissolve and wash away dirt, and the rough surface of the tongue doubles as a comb to scrub away debris. Cats pretzel themselves into all sorts of contortions to reach different areas of the body with the tongue. The grooming ritual often follows the same pattern, but individual kittens may develop their own habits. Usually the kitten begins by licking clean her mouth, chin, and whiskers, followed by each shoulder and foreleg. From there, the kitten licks clean each flank, rear leg, and finally her genitals. She'll stick her rear legs straight up into the air in a ludicrous position to reach every place she can. Then she cleans her tail, from end to end. Finally she washes her back, tummy, and chest, as much as her tongue can reach.

Paw Swipes

For the regions the kitten can't reach directly with her tongue, a paw swipe does the job. She dampens the paw with her tongue after every few swipes, and switches paws as needed to reach better. Kittens use paw swipes to scrub clean the face, head and ears. She may also use both paws to hold down her tail while she gets that elusive twitching tip clean.

A right-pawed kitten begins with that paw, while a left-pawed kitten starts with the opposite. Usually the kitty has a preferred or dominant paw, just like right- and left-handed people.

Nibbling Nails

Kittens use an additional technique to keep their claws in shape, aside from nailing your sofa. The rear claws especially benefit from nibbling, but kittens will also bite and pull at the nails on the front paws. It almost looks painful, but kitty is not picking her teeth or pulling out the claws by the root. This is a normal behavior designed to help get rid of the old outside layer of nail. Cats also use their teeth to nibble away burrs or clumps of dirt caught in the fur.

Scratching

Cats also use their claws—especially the rear ones—to scratch themselves and comb out the fur. Rear claws are particularly effec-

(Photo credit: Amy D. Shojai)

Kittens use their teeth to scratch itches and work out dirty spots in the fur. Seren has found something in her fur that needs attention.

tive at reaching and grooming the back of the cat's neck and her ears, where she can't otherwise reach. Along with other licking and nibbling behavior, scratching can also dislodge bugs, like fleas or ticks that have managed to hitch a ride. Kitten grooming offers a kind of parasite patrol that keeps the skin healthy.

Cool Cats

Grooming goes beyond making the cat look good. It also keeps cats cool. Cats don't often loll their tongue out and pant to cool themselves off the way dogs do. More often, cats lick themselves all over, and the evaporation of saliva helps cool them off. Grooming spreads skin oils to help waterproof the hairs, so the coat falls in insulating layers that keep the cat warm and dry.

Kitty Cologne

Licking also spreads the kitten's own personal scent all over her body. Scent is used by cats to identify territory and ownership, so self-scent is a very comforting, safe smell for a kitten. That's one reason your kitten may lick herself after you've petted her, or even lick you—to spread that kitty cologne around.

Stress Busters

An added benefit to grooming is the feline massage—it just plain feels good to the cat. Massage has been shown to lower blood pressure and reduce stress, and in fact this self-grooming helps upset kittens calm themselves. You may notice your kitten run around like a crazy critter, then accidentally slip or fall, or do something that's sure to make her feel silly. Other times kittens may be confronted with a scary situation—like a ferocious adult cat or strange human. Nearly always, such situations prompt a groom-like-mad session to help her calm down while she collects her thoughts. Feline behavior experts call this "displacement grooming." It may look a bit silly, but it's perfectly normal.

Kitten Comfort

Besides keeping cats clean, cool, and collected, mutual grooming—kittens grooming each other—offers two additional benefits. First of all, a buddy can clean up all those hard-to-reach areas like the back of the neck. And second, mutual grooming forms a social bond between the kittens and strengthens the trust and affection they have toward each other. It spreads that communal scent that identifies "home" and "safety" to the baby. That's one reason why your kitten loves to be petted and groomed by you. It makes her feel the way she did when Mom used to lick and take care of her. And that association helps increase the trusting bond between you and your kitten.

Hairy Situation—Why Kittens Need Grooming Help

Kittens are so clean, licking and nibbling themselves, that they never need a comb or brush, or (gasp!) a bath. Besides, they'd turn into Tasmanian devils and take your face off, should you even try. . . .

Wrong! Kittens actually do need your help, especially the long-haired babies. There's only so much a tiny tongue and scratching paw can do. One of the biggest dangers of abdicating your grooming responsibilities is painful mats that can develop in the fur of medium- to longhaired kittens.

What's the Mat-ter

Mats are hard, messy knots of fur that typically form behind the ears, beneath the tail, and in the creases of the legs of longer-furred kittens and cats. It's not just unsightly. Mats hurt, because they pull the tender skin and cause massive bruising when the baby tries to move.

Mats also create the perfect breeding environment for parasites such as fleas. The wads of fur prevent normal air circulation, and moisture that collects can prompt skin infections, as well.

Like many kitten ailments, mats are much easier to prevent than to fix. Simply make a habit of combing your kitten. Breeds like Persians need attention every single day, while some other medium- to longhaired babies may do fine with help only once or twice a week. Pay particular attention to the prime spots—under the "armpits" and behind the ears.

Dematting Kitty

Because mats are so painful, it can be difficult for a kitten to hold still while you untangle the mess. After all, pulling a comb through the mat just tugs at the bruised skin, and hurts even worse. Whatever you do, *don't* get the mat wet. That simply sets the tangle like cement. The key to detangling mats is to work with them dry.

Use a comb to help take some of that painful tension off kitty's skin. Thread the teeth of the comb through the mat, close to the skin. Then use another wide-toothed comb or a slicker brush, and brush on top of the buffer comb. That keeps the fur from being pulled as you work at the tangle. Start at the very ends of the mat, and comb it out a tiny bit at a time, layer by layer.

You may want to invest in a product called T*H*E Stuff made by The Lab Inc. It comes in a sixteen-ounce spray bottle for about seven dollars, and is used by professional groomers as a detangler for long cat fur. Spray the product into the mat and work in well with your fingers before picking out the mat. If you don't have a professional product handy, rub some dry cornstarch into the matted fur before you begin to comb. That helps separate the individual hairs and makes it easier to unravel the mess.

If your kitten will not hold still, the mats will likely need to be shaved out with electric clippers. Your veterinarian or a groomer can do this for you. Usually, a number 10 clipper blade is best because it doesn't tend to cut the skin. Ask your veterinarian or groomer for a demonstration before you attempt to demat your kitten yourself with electric shavers.

Remember, it's best to prevent mats altogether by grooming your kitten appropriately. Shaving or even combing out mats tends to leave bald patches that are unattractive. Turn grooming into an extension of petting so your kitten will welcome the attention—and prevent painful mats down the road.

Warning: Never use scissors to cut out a mat on your kitten—or any other pet, for that matter. Scissors are a recipe for disaster. Kitten skin is incredibly thin, and it stretches so you may nick the baby without realizing you've cut beyond the mat. Nine times out of ten you will cut kitten skin so seriously that she needs stitches. When the mat is so bad you think scissors are required, see your groomer or veterinarian so they can safely deal with the problem.

Hairballs

Your kitten's tongue works great as a do-it-yourself comb and brush. But as she licks herself clean, shed fur sticks to the tongue and is swallowed. Most of this fur passes through kitty's digestive system and ends up in the litter box, and causes no problems. But when the hair doesn't pass, it collects in the kitten's tummy. Eventually, enough collects that it irritates the stomach, and is expelled by vomiting.

The cigar-shaped nasty mass of wet fur you usually find, barefoot in the middle of the night, is called a hairball. You may see your kitten retch or hack before producing one of these prizes.

It is normal for kittens to occasionally experience a hairball. But if very large amounts of fur are swallowed, it becomes impossible for the kitten to pass them in either direction. That can cause impaction that results in constipation. Fifty percent of all constipation in cats is due to impaction from hairballs.

Commercial hairball products are available to keep kitty cleaned out. But frankly, preventing the hair from being swallowed in the first place is the best option. You can greatly reduce how often your kitten has a hairball simply by grooming her regularly. The fur you comb or brush off her is hair that she won't swallow later when she grooms herself.

Hairball Treatments

A wide range of commercial products is available. Usually they are made of nondigestible fat-type ingredients that slick down the wad of fur and help it pass out of the body more efficiently. Take care not to overuse commercial treatments. If used in excess, some can interfere with the way your kitten's body uses fat-soluble vitamins.

Home remedies work well, too, when used sparingly. Butter or other digestible fats aren't the best choice because they're absorbed before they have an effect—they may also cause some kitten diarrhea. But plain nonmedicated petroleum jelly can help. Spread a bit of the jelly on your kitten's paw, so she'll lick it off when she cleans herself.

Another home-remedy favorite is simply adding fiber to the kitten's diet. The fiber grabs the hair along the way and takes it to the litter box—naturally. Canned pumpkin appeals to many cats. Add just ½ teaspoon to the kitten's regular food, once a day, until she's regular again.

One of the newest options is hairball-preventive diets. Many such products are available. Be sure that the food you choose is also formulated for a growing kitten.

Grooming Supplies

Invest in some quality grooming tools. That way you'll have them for the lifetime of your cat, even after baby has grown to adulthood. The higher quality products not only last longer, but also tend to do a better job. For instance, cheaper nail trimmers become dull more quickly, and may end up crushing rather than snipping off the nail. And a Teflon-coated comb, or one with "rolling" teeth, is more comfortable for the kitten because it glides more easily through fur.

You don't need anything fancy for routine grooming. Basic grooming tools are available in most pet supply stores, your veterinarian's office, or over the Internet. If you have a purebred kitten and want to show her, there may be special grooming provisions you'll need to learn. Visit a couple of cat shows, and ask questions to get the answers you need for your special kitten. Your breeder is also a great resource for this information.

Kitten and adult cat skin are very sensitive. That means any comb or brush teeth must never be sharply pointed. They are designed to be smooth and rounded so the grooming experience is pleasant, and there's no chance of injury.

Kitten Purrs: Untangler combs are designed with stainless steel rotating teeth that glide through tangles and remove loose hair. The five-inch Kitty Kat Komb version costs about three dollars and is available at pet supply stores or mail-order catalogues.

FOR FUR

To take good care of your kitten's fur, you'll need at least one comb. The "teeth" of the comb will be set together in a fine, medium, or coarse fashion. The closer together, the finer the teeth are said to be. Medium to coarse combs are good for longhaired kittens, while medium to fine combs work best for shorthaired breeds.

Shorthaired kittens may do fine with regular sessions using "cat gloves." These are special gloves with inset rubber nubs in the palm that smooth the fur and remove any loose hair. Cat gloves are a kitten favorite because the action duplicates the experience of being petted.

You may also want to invest in a second fine-toothed comb to finish the coat once all the tangles are smoothed. A flea comb works great, and will also capture any stray bugs that set up housekeeping on your kitten. Or, there are combs designed that have medium-spaced teeth on one side and coarse or fine teeth on the other. Most handles on cat combs are short, for easier and more efficient handling. A flea comb works well to remove caked or crusty material from the kitten's fur.

When looking for a brush, be sure the bristles or nubs are soft enough not to scratch tender kitten skin, but firm enough to reach through the fur and brush efficiently. A curry brush is rubber or plastic with short nubs that work to smooth fur and remove loose hair on shorthaired cats. Some are designed to work on longhaired kittens, too.

A slicker brush is designed for the final finishing touch. It is made up of closely arranged fine wires that smooth the coat. You must be careful not to brush the skin, though, or you could cause "brush burns."

Warning: Use a slicker brush only after combing or currying out any tangles. A gentle touch works best.

Besides a brush and comb, you need a quality shampoo. Unless you see a problem with fleas, there's no need to choose a flea product—a grooming shampoo works fine. Often you can find one that includes some sort of conditioner, or can purchase a coat conditioner separately. Conditioner helps reduce static, tangles, and dry skin. I particularly like the cat bathing products that include oatmeal, which is a natural skin-soothing ingredient.

> **Kitten Purrs:** The Purrfect Pin Palm Brush from Aaronco is designed for brushing the longhaired kitty. Wire pins mounted in a soft, flexible rubber pad have protective round plastic tips on the end to ensure a comfortable brushing. Another option is a rubber curry-style brush called the Cat Zoom Groom. The tips are ultrasoft, and the brush is in a fun kitty shape. Cat Zoom Groom costs about four dollars at pet stores.

Warning: Kittens are highly sensitive to substances put on their skin. Bathing products that are safe for dogs—and sometimes for adult cats—may be too harsh for your kitten. Be especially careful of flea products, or you may accidentally poison your pet. Look for the words "safe for kittens" before buying the product.

There are "dry" shampoos available for cats. These are typically wipe-on, foam, or spray products that are worked into the dingy fur, wiped off, and left on. They may do a good job in between the more thorough dunking.

FOR CLAWS

You'd think that kittens would take care of their claws all by themselves. You got her a great scratch post, after all. However, kittens still benefit from manicures. If claws grow too long, they tend to get caught in the upholstery or carpet, can tear or split, and develop painful infections. I began trimming Seren's claws every week while she was still a kitten. That not only prevents potential problems, it also gives me peace of mind when she occasionally "forgets herself" and flexes those talons while sitting on my fine furniture.

There are three options for nail trimmers. All work well, and the choice is really up to you.

Tiny kittens have tiny claws. For them, human nail trimmers work very well. In fact, I still use human nail trimmers on Seren's claws, because even as an adult, she's small and her nails are dainty.

Scissors-style nippers are also a good choice. They may take the least getting used to, if you are new to pet nail trimming.

Guillotine-style nail trimmers are a popular choice. They come in a couple of sizes, with the smallest ones designated for cats. But even the dog-size guillotine clippers will work for kitty. You don't need to invest in species-specific grooming tools when it comes to the claws.

Two considerations are important when choosing a nail trimmer for your kitten. First, whatever the style, it must be very sharp so it cuts and doesn't crush or tear the claw. Second, you must be comfortable using it.

FOR EYES AND EARS

Kittens can develop small amounts of sleepy-crusts in their eyes, or a bit of light yellow wax in their ears. That's normal. Regular ear and eye checks are needed as much to monitor kitten health as to groom them. Any kind of discharge should prompt a visit to your veterinarian.

Normal eye secretions are clear and liquid, just like human tears. And the inside of a healthy kitten's ear is pink and clean. Dark crumbly gunk in the ears, or thick discharge from the eyes can be signs of a health problem. The most common causes of these signs are discussed in chapter 10.

Even normal tears can turn crusty in the fur and irritate the tender skin around the kitten's eyes. Flat-faced babies like Persians are particularly prone to this problem because their eyes are so large and prominent, and they tend to water.

Commercial preparations are available at pet stores that help remove tearstains safely from the kitten's fur. But you don't really need any special supplies for eye and ear care; what you have in your own medicine chest will work fine. Cotton balls, cotton swabs, mineral oil or baby oil, and plain water—even the saline solution used for contact lenses—are more than adequate.

FOR TEETH

We can't train cats to brush their own teeth. It's something we must do for them. Veterinarians provide dentistry services, including routine teeth cleaning to scour away collected plaque. But kittens—and adult cats—won't "open wide and say ahhhhhh," so veterinary dentists must first anesthetize the cat to clean their teeth.

That's not necessary if you train your kitten from an early age to accept your help brushing her teeth. You can greatly reduce or even eliminate the need for professional teeth cleaning simply by brushing kitty's teeth at home.

You'll need kitty toothpaste. Your veterinarian and pet supply stores carry special nonfoaming products designed for cats that are flavored with chicken or malt. Some cats (my Seren is one) actually consider kitty toothpaste to be a treat.

Never use human toothpaste products in pets. The foaming action is terribly unpleasant for them, and the fluoride is much too strong. Since kittens and cats can't spit, they swallow the paste and the fluoride can upset their tummies. Over time, the fluoride can damage their livers.

Choose a toothbrush designed for your kitten's small mouth. A child's baby toothbrush may work fine, but commercial products work better and aren't as intrusive as the large plastic brushes we use on ourselves.

You might want to try a "finger toothbrush" made especially for the small mouths of kittens and cats. The rubber product slips over your finger and has tiny soft bristles. Many cats that object to having a toothbrush stuck into their mouth will more readily accept a finger brush, because it's an extension of a human they love and trust.

Head-to-Tail Grooming Tips

Grooming not only feels good to the cat, it also doubles as a home health check. You can make sure your kitten is healthy, from whiskers to tail, simply by paying attention to her skin, fur, eyes, claws, ears, and teeth on a regular basis.

Combing and Brushing

Cats groomed daily as kittens learn to expect and relish the experience. Combing and brushing become an extension of petting.

Kittens thrive on routine, so decide on a regimen and stick to it. Choose not only a time, but also a place such as a tabletop, your lap, or other platform that's convenient for you. The top of the washer and dryer works great, and gives you space to set out all your combs and brushes. As mentioned before, shorthaired kittens can get by on a weekly once-over with a comb or slicker brush. Longhaired kittens, especially Persians, need daily attention to prevent painful mats.

Several days before you begin the lifetime grooming schedule, help your kitten get used to the idea. She'll want to sniff and investigate these strange items. Leave the comb and brush out with her toys—make them part of the furniture, an unthreatening addition to her usual territory. You may be surprised to see her play with the brush, or even rub her cheeks against it to mark it with her scent.

Always begin your grooming session with petting. Feel kitty all over, from head to neck, under her chin, down her back, in her armpits, along the length of her tail. Petting gets her purr a-rumbling and will tell you in advance if any problem areas have developed. That way you won't run the comb into a mat unexpectedly. Petting helps relax the kitten in preparation for grooming.

Kittens have very tender skin. Start with a light touch, and let your baby "tell" you how to proceed. Think of grooming as gently scratching the kitten's skin rather than brushing. She'll often arch her back into the brush when she wants a heavier stroke.

Begin and end your combing or brushing session by paying attention to the kitten's "sweet spots." These are her favorite places to be rubbed, and include her cheeks, chin and throat, and the spot right above the base of her tail. Attention to the sweet spots causes her eyes to shut, purr to rumble, and butt to elevate toward the ceiling.

After carefully combing her face—pay particular attention to the mat-prone areas around her ears—progress down both of her sides. Be careful not to brush or comb too hard, especially against her spine or nipples. Then cover her flanks, inside and out, and the area beneath the tail. The tummy can be tough. Kitties often dislike attention here, so take your time. There is no law that says you must groom the entire kitten at one sitting. If your kitten becomes upset, stop—finish at a later time.

For those hard-to-reach undersides, try lifting one rear foot off the ground while grooming the other side. That takes away kitty's balance, and distracts her into thinking about something other than grooming, while still giving you access to her nether regions.

Finish the grooming session as you began it—with the sweet spots. Also, offer your kitten a favorite game, or a treat once you've finished. That will help her associate the grooming session with positive sensations and make her look forward to the next time.

> **Tip:** Try petting your kitten with a clean electrostatic-charged dust cloth like Swiffer to remove surface grime and loose fur. Stroking your kitten with a dryer sheet helps reduce the static in her fur that can give you both an unpleasant shock. It also leaves her smelling fresh.

Bath Time

A bath stimulates the skin and removes excess oil, dander, and loose fur. It also gets rid of dingy spots your furry dust-mop has collected by playing under the bed. Too often, though, bathing can dry out the skin. So unless she gets really dirty, kitty probably won't need a bath more than once every six weeks. Shorthaired kittens may be fine with two or three times a year during shedding season, but longhaired kittens benefit from more frequent baths. Show kitties tend to get bathed before every show—conditioners help prevent any dry skin problems.

Warning: Very young kittens have trouble regulating their body temperature and can become dangerously chilled if bathed and not kept warm. As a rule, kittens should not be bathed until they are at least four weeks old—twelve to sixteen weeks of age is a much better age for a first bath, if they need it.

It's best to have clipped kitty's nails and thoroughly combed out any tangles prior to getting her wet. Water cements mats into place, so they'll probably need to be shaved off. You want the baby to have blunt nails, in case she tries to climb onto you to escape the bath.

Assemble all your bathing supplies ahead of time—towels, wash-cloth, shampoo, conditioner. Kittens are small enough to be bathed in the kitchen sink. A double sink with a spray attachment is the ideal setup.

Place a rubber mat or towel in the bottom of the sink to give the kitten something to claw rather than you. Kittens are scared of slip-pery surfaces. Also run the water before you bring in the kitten. It should be about cat body temperature—102 degrees—for the great-est comfort. Fill both sides of the sink with water up to kitten chest-level. A couple of buckets or roasting pans will also work with this "dunk" method.

Insert a portion of a cotton ball into each of the kitten's ears be-fore you suds her up. That protects the delicate ears from getting water or soap inside. Some veterinarians recommend you put a drop of mineral oil in both eyes, to protect them from soap.

If you use the spray attachment, remember to keep the nozzle close to the kitten's body. Cats dislike the surprise and sound of the sprayer, so it's best if they don't see the water coming at them. I pre-fer using the "dunk" method to initially wet and suds the cat, and reserve the sprayer if necessary to rinse.

Gently lower your kitten into the first sink of warm water and thoroughly wet her. Leave her face dry—you'll do that later with the washcloth. Kittens get upset when water splashes their faces, so this method helps keep her calm. Once she's soaked, lift her out onto the towel and soap her up. Use the washcloth to gently wash her face, taking care to avoid her eyes.

Again lower your soapy baby back into the first sink, and rinse off as much soap as possible. Use the cloth to clean her face. Then move her to the second sink filled with clean warm water, and rinse her there to be sure all the soap is gone. Any suds left in the fur tend to dry the skin. When the water runs clear, rinse once more just for good measure.

Lift the baby out, and wrap her in a warm, dry towel. Don't forget to remove the cotton from her ears. It may take a couple of towels to blot up all the water on an extra-furry baby. Some kittens will toler-ate a blow dryer on a low setting. Combing as you blow-dry the fur of longhaired babies will give them a more finished look. Use only the lowest setting on blow dryers, or you risk burning your kitten.

Tip: If bathing for fleas, you don't need a flea shampoo. Any shampoo will work, since water drowns the bugs. Just lather up the suds around the kitten's neck the very first thing. That creates a barrier the fleas won't cross, so they won't try to climb onto her head to breathe.

Trimming Nails

Claws grow at different rates depending on the kitten. Once a week or every other week is a good schedule for trimming. Choose a time when kitty is relaxed and cuddled for a nap on your lap. It's a great idea to get her used to having her paws handled, so she won't be startled when you need to trim her nails. Pet her paws, and handle them gently, several times a week—not just when you plan to snip the claws.

Trimming kitten claws is easy. Simply pick up the paw, gently squeeze to reveal the nail, and snip off the sharp hooked end. Trim only the end, which is usually white, and avoid the pink section that's nearest the toe. That pink section contains the blood vessels, and though it won't be terribly dangerous if you "quick" the kitten and cut into this area, it will bleed and be painful. Above all, you want nail clipping to be a ho-hum, not scary, and certainly not painful activity. Still, it's not the end of the world if you do "quick" the kitten claw and it bleeds. There are commercial products like Kwik-Stop powder that stop the bleeding. Or you can rake the claw through a bar of soap—that often works just as well.

Don't forget to trim the dewclaw, too. It's a bit hidden up the inside of the kitten's legs, kind of like a "thumb." Work quickly and efficiently. Be sure to avoid catching the long fur in the clipper blades. That pulls and can make the experience just as unpleasant as quicking the nail.

Once you've finished, be sure to give kitty a fabulous treat. She should soon understand that if she puts up with the procedure, she'll get a tasty reward.

Remember, nobody will think less of you if not all the claws are trimmed at one sitting. It's best to stop before your kitten gets

(Illustration: Wendy Christensen)

Take your time trimming the nails. No rule says you must do them all at once—one or two a day is fine. Clip off only the sharp hooked end (avoid the pink).

peeved, so be satisfied with clipping one or two claws each day. In a week, you'll be done.

Cleaning Ears and Eyes

Most kitten eyes and ears need minimal care, though Persian kittens and other flat-faced breeds require more eye attention. For eyes, soak a cotton ball with warm water or with saline solution used for contact lenses. Soften the secretions at the corners of the kitten's eyes with the wet cotton; then wipe them away. Daily attention to her eyes will prevent skin irritation.

Commercial ear cleaning solutions are available from your veterinarian or pet-supply store. For routine cleaning, you can use mineral oil or baby oil on the cotton ball or swab. Gently wipe out the visible areas. You can use cotton swabs to clean out the little whorls and indentations, but never go down farther into the ear than you can see. You can very easily damage your kitten's hearing without meaning to. Even liquid solutions can be dangerous, so don't drip mineral oil, baby oil, or other cleaners directly into the ear unless your veterinarian says to. Scottish Fold kittens need particular attention to their ears. This endearing breed has ears that fold forward like a cap on her head. That makes the inside of the ears more difficult to see, so you must make a point of being vigilant.

Brushing Teeth

Veterinary dentists say that ideally you should brush your kitten's teeth every single day. But if you can manage two or three times a week, you'll be doing better than most folks. Even once a week is better than nothing.

Introduce your kitten to dental care one step at a time. Begin by stroking and scratching her cheeks and chin, progress to rubbing her lips, and finally gently slip one finger into her mouth. Don't force her to open wide, just gently rub her gums for a very brief moment. Reward these sessions with a tasty treat—perhaps a lick of the flavored kitty toothpaste, to help her associate that flavor with handling her mouth.

Warning: Kittens begin to lose baby teeth at about three to four months of age. Be aware that your kitten's mouth may be a bit tender at times, as these new teeth erupt.

To start, flavor your finger with the toothpaste. Then wrap your finger with a soft cloth, add a bit of the paste, and massage your kitten's teeth and gums. Stop when she protests too much. Be satisfied if you can do one side—you simply want to build up her tolerance level.

Once kitty accepts your finger, it's a short step to the finger toothbrush. After kitty becomes used to you handling her mouth, graduate to a pet toothbrush or a human baby toothbrush. Dab the toothpaste on the toothbrush and use that to treat the kitten so she associates the brush with pleasant things. To keep her mouth slightly opened during brushing, try flavoring a wooden pencil and placing that in her mouth right behind the canines—those needle-sharp "fang" teeth. Be satisfied if you can brush one side of her mouth at a time. Kittens tend to tolerate brushing pretty well when you start them young. You'll be building a healthy habit that will last a lifetime.

9

PREVENTING KITTEN
HEALTH PROBLEMS

Bright-Eyed and Bushy-Tailed

A healthy kitten is happy and just plain fun to be around. Good health goes beyond physical considerations and includes emotional well-being. Emotional and physical health are two sides of the same coin and cannot be separated. Each influences the other. Physical illness affects the baby's attitude, and a positive or negative personality will influence physical health. Negative emotions, collectively referred to as stress, can depress the kitten's immune system. Stress makes the cat more prone to physical illness and delays recovery.

Body and Soul—Signs of Good Health

Your kitten shows he's healthy by the way he looks, acts, and reacts to the world around him. It's very easy to monitor kitty's health simply by paying attention to him. In most cases, signs of good health are very obvious. Once you become familiar with what is normal, you'll be better able to recognize signs of problems, both physical and emotional.

This kitten is the purrfect picture of health.

(Photo credit: Amy D. Shojai)

HEALTHY FUR

The fur on a shorthaired kitten should be shiny, smooth, and feel like silk against your hand. Longhaired kittens have fluffy, silky, or cottonlike hair.

FUR PROBLEMS

Dry, lifeless or brittle fur, bald patches, mats and tangles, and a dirty coat are all signs of a health problem. One of the first signs of illness shows up in the fur coat. It may point to problems with nutrition, or parasites like intestinal worms or fleas.

HEALTHY SKIN

In normal kittens, you won't see much bare skin. The inside of the ears, the nose, and paw pads are bare, and the fur is naturally a bit thinner on the shorthaired kitten's temples above and beside his eyes. When you pet your kitten, his skin underneath the fur should feel smooth and without blemish.

SKIN PROBLEMS

Any lump, bump, scab, or sore should alert you to a problem. Bald places, red or rough skin, or discoloration can be a warning sign of a variety of health problems. For instance, very pale skin on the inside of his ears may indicate anemia, while a yellow tinge—called jaundice—points to a liver problem.

HEALTHY EYES

Kitten eyes come in all shapes, colors, and sizes. The one universal is that healthy eyes are bright, clear, and have only a small amount of clear tearlike discharge (if any). Kittens meet the world with their eyes wide open.

EYE PROBLEMS

A squinting eye points to discomfort or pain. Kittens can scratch their eyes or get dust in them, and end up with a watery, squinty, or cloudy eye. Any discharge from the eyes, other than moderate clear tearlike secretions, is cause for concern. The causes range from simple irritation to a viral or bacterial infection like upper respiratory diseases that can be life-threatening to young kittens.

HEALTHY EARS

Normal kitten ears are clean. The visible skin is a healthy pink. There may be a bit of amber-colored waxy substance that's easily wiped out. Your new youngster will also be alert to interesting sounds.

EAR PROBLEMS

Shaking his head or pawing and scratching at his ears alerts you to problems with your kitten's ears. Ear infections or parasite infestations can cause these symptoms and make your baby miserable. Any sort of discharge points to a health problem. For instance, a crumbly dark material inside the ears is often due to an infestation of ear mites.

HEALTHY NOSE

Kittens are literally led around by the nose, so a healthy one is important for both physical and emotional health. The nose can be different colors, from light pink to black, or even freckled. Usually the nose stays moist, from the kitten licking his nose and from minimal clear discharge.

NOSE PROBLEMS

A stopped-up nose can have catastrophic consequences for your kitten. That's because baby's appetite is ruled by the smell of his food. If his nose is plugged, he won't eat, and that can make him even sicker. A gummy or crusty nose or sneezing are signs he needs help.

HEALTHY GUMS

The gums are naturally pink. Some kitties have a bit of pigment in the gums that makes them darker. Depending on his age, kitty may have a few teeth missing or new ones coming in. Those places can be a bit sore.

GUM PROBLEMS

Sores on the gums, on the tongue, or on the roof of the mouth can be a sign of an upper respiratory infection. The kitten may refuse to eat because his mouth is so sore.

HEALTHY CLAWS AND PAWS

Paw pads are soft and smooth, while the claws grow cleanly from the ends of each toe.

PROBLEM CLAWS AND PAWS

Kittens are so stoic that they rarely limp when a paw hurts. They may instead simply stop moving around as much. Torn or split claws are painful and need attention. Also, any crusty material at the base of the nail bed (where the claw grows out) could indicate a more serious whole-body health problem with the kitten's immune system.

HEALTHY ELIMINATION

The kitten's anus should be clean. Check the furry bottom area beneath his tail. Kitten elimination is a barometer of his health. The consistency of feces varies a bit depending on his diet, but should be well formed and not liquid. Normal urine is yellow to amber colored. Monitor your kitten's litter box to keep track of his normal bathroom habits.

PROBLEM ELIMINATION

An occasional soft stool probably isn't cause to worry, but diarrhea is serious, especially in tiny kittens. They can become dehydrated very quickly. Diarrhea can be a sign of a wide range of health problems, from intestinal parasites to viral infections. Straining in the litter box is just as serious, and may indicate such conditions as constipation or urinary tract problems. Blood in the urine or feces is always a sign of a health problem.

HEALTHY APPETITE

Kittens are intermittent feeders, which means your baby may not always gulp down his food when it's first presented. Kittens tend to nibble, go away, and come back to nibble some more.

PROBLEM APPETITE

Refusing to eat (anorexia) can be a dangerous problem in cats, and especially kittens. Loss of appetite can be gradual or sudden, and either can point to a health problem. Missing one meal probably won't hurt him if there are no other signs of ill health. But kittens should never go longer than twelve to eighteen hours without eating. Vomiting that is not associated with hairballs is another warning sign you should take very seriously. Like diarrhea, vomiting can dehydrate the kitten very quickly and make him even sicker.

HEALTHY ATTITUDE

By nature, a kitten has nonstop energy and loves to play. The emotionally healthy kitten meets the world with in-your-face curiosity. He is active when awake, grooms himself vigorously, and sleeps up to sixteen hours a day.

PROBLEM ATTITUDE

A red alert to a health problem in kittens is lethargy. Kittens that act depressed may be running a fever or brewing an illness that makes them feel icky. Any kind of personality change or alteration in normal behavior could point to a health problem. In other words, an energetic kitten that acts depressed, a friendly kitten that becomes aggressive or shy, or a laid-back kitten that turns hyperactive are all cause for concern.

Picking the Best Veterinarian

People become veterinarians because they like and care about animals. Your kitten deserves to be cared for by a professional whom you trust. Every kitten needs routine health care, and as kitty matures, some extra health care may be needed.

Some individual veterinary practices or doctors may suit your needs better than others. It's best to choose a veterinarian who is conveniently located, available when you need him, and willing to answer any questions you have. Mutual respect helps ensure that your relationship will best benefit your kitten's health, over his entire lifetime.

Veterinary medicine is in constant evolution, with advances made every day. Today, veterinarians can specialize in different areas of pet care, including feline medicine. You may prefer a veterinarian who specializes in cat care. You can find a cats-only practice by contacting the American Association of Feline Practitioners at www.aafponline.org.

One of the best ways to find a veterinarian is to ask people you trust for a recommendation. When your kitten comes from a local breeder, there may be a nearby veterinarian who is already familiar with your kitten's relatives. Shelters often have staff veterinarians who offer services to adopted pets and their owners. Don't forget to ask your family and friends whom they trust to care for their special pets.

Multiveterinary practices offer a wide range of services all under one roof. In such places you'll likely have one primary care doctor for your kitten but you'll also benefit from other veterinarians who offer specialized care in specific areas. For instance, a board-certified internist offers expertise in diagnosis of certain health problems above and beyond what a general practice veterinarian may be able to provide.

It's a good idea to make an appointment to visit a potential veterinary clinic ahead of time. The doctor's office is a busy place; call to schedule a time when the staff isn't tied up with surgery or appointments. Chat with the office manager, technicians, and the veterinarian when possible, and ask for a brief tour of the facilities. Some things to consider include the following:

- Does the practice have separate waiting rooms for dogs and cats? That can ease your kitten's stress.
- Are boarding facilities available? If you need to go out of town, you may feel more comfortable leaving baby in the expert care of the hospital staff.
- What about emergency and referral services? If the worst happens, you want to have access to lifesaving care. Practices often partner with other vet clinics to offer rotating twenty-four-hour emergency services. Veterinarians should always be willing to confer with their colleagues and other specialists to determine the best care options for your kitten.
- Are the hospital's hours convenient and is the facility located nearby? Many veterinary hospitals offer drop-off services in the morning before you go to work. The closer the clinic, the more apt you will be to seek necessary care promptly rather than putting it off for several days until it's more convenient to travel a long distance.
- Is the cost manageable? Kitten care can be expensive, and specialty practices typically cost more than general practices. Of course, when it comes to your kitten's health, cheaper isn't

necessarily better. The expertise of the veterinarian and staff should come first.

- Do you like the veterinarian—does he or she like you? Trust is a huge issue, and you must feel comfortable with the person who's responsible for your kitten's care. The veterinarian you choose should be willing to answer your questions in an understandable fashion, without jargon, and without making you feel embarrassed for asking. After all, you both want the best for the kitten.

A Partnership for Kitten Health

The veterinarian is your partner in health care for the lifetime of your kitten. In the best of situations, the veterinarian sees kitty only a couple of times a year. Meanwhile, you live with him, and that means you know your kitten better than anybody. You are in the best position to sound the alarm if your kitten feels under the weather, and get him to the veterinarian for the proper care. That's a dynamic and effective health care partnership.

The Doctor's Role

Your veterinarian will examine the kitten for general health, from head to tail. A technician usually takes kitty's temperature first and makes notes about the kitten's health history and any concerns you have.

Then the veterinarian listens to the baby's heart and breathing, feels him all over, and looks in his mouth, eyes, and ears for telltale signs of problems. She may ask the technician to run screening tests—to diagnose, for instance, any intestinal parasites. It's up to the veterinarian to keep an accurate record of the kitten's preventive treatments such as vaccinations, the status of his health, and any prescribed therapies.

Your Responsibility

Since you live with your kitten and know him best, it's up to you to learn what is "normal" kitten behavior and appearance. That way,

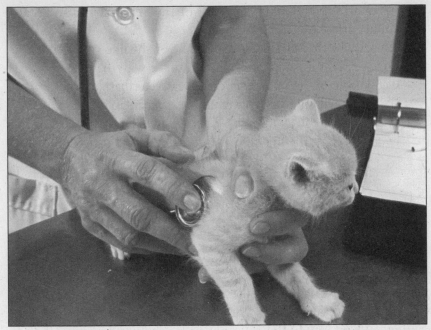

(Photo credit: Ralston Purina Company)

The veterinarian will examine your kitten from head to tail, including listening to his heart and lungs.

you'll easily recognize something that's out of the ordinary, in time to get help from your veterinarian.

The veterinarian relies on your information about the kitten to provide the best care possible. Does your kitten eat well? Play with enthusiasm? Use the litter box regularly, or have intermittent diarrhea where he misses the mark? Perhaps he pants or wheezes after a game of chase-the-feather. Or maybe kitty is the healthiest, best-behaved and prime example of kittenhood ever to grace the examining table.

When you take your kitten for his veterinary visit, be prepared to answer questions, offer information, and ask pointed questions of your own. Don't wait to get home to wonder what the doctor meant by something she said—there are *no* stupid questions when it comes to caring for your kitten. Be sure to get all the information you need to make informed decisions about properly caring for your kitten.

> **Tip:** When you call to make an appointment with a veterinarian, ask what, if anything, you should bring to the visit. For example, kittens are routinely checked for worms by testing a sample of their stool. It's much less upsetting for the kitten if you bring a fresh deposit from his litter box rather than having the veterinary technician obtain a sample on the end of a thermometer (or in some other rude fashion).

Preventive Treatments

Veterinarians agree that preventing health problems is much easier to do than treating the kitten once he becomes sick. It's also much less expensive. Preventive care has made an incredible difference in the lives of kittens. In the past, a large percentage of furry babies never reached adulthood because they became ill and died while in infancy.

Kittens are much more susceptible to illness because their immune system is still maturing. That's why it is vital to have your new kitten not only examined right away, but also protected against the most common kitty illnesses.

Preventive veterinary care, such as vaccinations, has increased the life span of cats. In the 1960s a cat could expect to live to seven to ten years of age. Today, it's not unusual for well-cared-for cats to live into their mid- to late teens, and beyond.

Vaccinations

Kittens are susceptible to a variety of diseases caused by viruses, bacteria, or both. To a large degree, they can be avoided with a series of preventive vaccinations—the shots every kitten should receive.

Vaccines work by "waking up" the immune system. Imagine that the immune system is the sheriff, but he's new to the job and doesn't know what the villains look like. Vaccinations offer the sheriff a description of the suspects, so he can deputize helpers who protect the body from attack in case a villain shows his face.

Technical Stuff: Vaccines contain harmless but recognizable parts of the disease-causing virus or bacterium. By presenting these to the body through shots—or sometimes through nose or eye drops—the immune system learns to recognize them as foreign. In response, the body creates antibodies that circulate in the bloodstream, and other components that work at the cellular level—for instance, inside the kitten's nose. These immune soldiers are like smart bombs, programmed to search out and destroy anything that looks like the disease-causing agent. Adult cats have a mature immune system that's ready and able to create these immune-protectors. Kitten immunity takes a bit more coaxing for a couple of reasons. First, their immune systems aren't quite up to speed until they're about eight weeks old—and every kitten is different, so it's hard to predict the timing. Development of the kitten's immune system takes several weeks and continues until at least twelve weeks of age. And second, all the good immune protection they got from nursing Mom-cat tends to sabotage vaccines by misrecognizing them as bad guys and making them ineffective. This "passive immunity" from their mother can last until the kitten is about fourteen weeks old. That's why it's so important for kittens to receive not just one, but a series of protective vaccinations over a period of time. This better ensures that as Mom's immunity fades and Junior's takes over, he'll be protected by some or most of the shots that he's given during that critical period.

Recently questions have been raised about how often vaccinations should be given. In the past, shots were given every single year as a matter of course, even though no studies had been conducted to show the duration of vaccination protection. Also, kittens and adult cats were often vaccinated against a wide range of illnesses, even when the risk for getting the disease was slim. Today, veterinarians agree that kittens should be protected against only those conditions for which they are at risk.

Most kittens are inoculated with a series of protective shots as maternal protection fades away. First vaccinations are typically given between six to nine weeks of age, with "boosters" repeated every three to four weeks until the kitten reaches fourteen to sixteen weeks of age. The exception is the rabies shot, which typically is given at twelve to sixteen weeks for the first time, and then either yearly or every three years, depending on local law. Because rabies has human health risks, many states require that cats be vaccinated for this disease.

Today, a number of veterinarians also recommend that after the initial kitten shots and first-year booster, cats be revaccinated every three years rather than annually. Follow your own veterinarian's recommendation. She'll know best what will work for your individual situation.

Warning: Preventive vaccinations are important to protect your kitten from life-threatening illnesses. However, even the best vaccine will not provide 100 percent protection. Your vaccinated kitten will still be at risk for disease, especially if he's repeatedly exposed.

Remember, every kitten is different. Some are "only" kittens that live exclusively indoors. Others share the house with many cats or run outside where they're exposed to extra risks. Therefore, no one vaccination program works for every kitten; it must be custom-designed for your baby, based on his individual needs. Your veterinarian will know what illnesses may be prevalent in your neck of the woods, and how the kitten's lifestyle may affect the risk of exposure to disease.

Some kittens and cats experience a "vaccine reaction." The pet acts a bit lethargic for a day or two, and sometimes has a small swollen or sore place near the injection site. It's a good idea to monitor the site of the injection to make sure any swelling goes away within several days. If it doesn't, a trip back to the vet is in order. A very small percentage of cats (about 1 in 10,000) may develop a tumor at the injection site, and early attention is important.

Warning: No vaccine is 100 percent effective. Most are designed to prevent disease, but some will only reduce the severity of the illness but not keep kitty from getting sick. The effectiveness of the shots depends on many things: age of the kitten, individual immune system, exposure risk, and other health problems. In the case of shelter adoptions, and of back-door waifs, the kitten may look perfectly healthy but be "incubating" an illness he was exposed to before you found him. The stress of a visit to the veterinarian may prompt him to come down with something—it's rarely the shot that causes such a problem.

Core Vaccinations

Just because a vaccination against sleeping sickness is available doesn't mean all people should get it. In the same way, veterinarians agree that just because a vaccine is available doesn't mean your kitten should automatically receive it. Generally, it is recommended that all kittens receive protection with "core" vaccinations—that is, the most common and dangerous illnesses for which the kitten will likely have the greatest risk of exposure.

Core vaccines include feline panleukopenia (sometimes called cat distemper), feline rhinotracheitis and feline calicivirus (collectively called upper respiratory infections, or URI), and rabies virus. Oftentimes, these vaccinations are given in combination as an FVRCP shot—that stands for feline viral rhinotracheitis, calicivirus, and panleukopenia. Rabies is given as a separate injection. The risk of your kitten getting deathly sick by skipping protective shots far outweighs the chance of a vaccine failure or problem reaction. All kittens need core vaccines to protect themselves—and you—from devastating illness.

Noncore vaccines are any other preventive shots that may benefit kittens and cats at risk for that particular disease. They may include vaccinations against chlamydia, another URI agent; feline leukemia virus (FeLV); feline infectious peritonitis (FIP); ringworm, a fungal skin infection; or giardia, a type of intestinal parasite.

FeLV requires a test that shows your kitten is clear of the disease before giving the vaccination. Kittens at low risk for FeLV—indoor, solo kitties never exposed to other cats—may not need this shot. However, FeLV is deadly and incurable, so discuss the options with your veterinarian.

FIP is also incurable. However, most of the veterinarians I've talked with at the major teaching universities currently do not recommend this vaccine except in extraordinary situations. Again, your veterinarian can advise you here.

The ringworm vaccine is said to reduce the symptoms of the

disease and speed healing. It may be recommended if your kitten is exposed to an afflicted cat, or if he comes down with the disease. Giardia can be difficult to cure, so if your veterinarian knows the parasite is a problem in your geographic area, she may advise a preventive vaccination.

Because of the recent concern over injection-site tumors, today veterinarians keep track of what shot is given, and the body location of the injection. In standard procedure, the FVRCP is given on the kitten's right shoulder; rabies as far down the right rear leg as possible; and FeLV as far down the left rear leg as possible. Most of these tumors have been associated with the FeLV or rabies shots, so pay particular attention to any bump or swelling after these vaccinations.

Warning: Vaccination reactions like lethargy or soreness are much more likely to occur when multiple shots are given at the same time. Ask your veterinarian about spreading the vaccinations out over several visits. Rather than the combination FVRCP, for instance, separate inoculations of one or two at a time may be more appropriate.

Warning: Cornell Feline Health Center reported in September 2001 that kittens and adult cats in several animal shelters and veterinary hospitals in Pennsylvania, Massachusetts, and New York have been infected by a highly virulent new kind of calicivirus. The existing FCV vaccines don't appear to provide protection against this particular strain. Affected kittens and cats develop swelling (edema) in the face, ear, and/or the extremities such as the paws. Chronic cases can develop ulcers or tissue death in these areas, and infection can also cause nose and eye inflammation, loss of appetite, and death. This virus is considered extremely contagious between cats. A 1:32 dilution of bleach in water (one part bleach to thirty-two parts water) is the recommended disinfectant. If you suspect your kitten may be affected, your veterinarian should contact Dr. James Richards, Director of the Cornell Feline Health Center (jrr1@cornell.edu).

Biting Back at Parasites

Kittens naturally attract all kinds of buggy freeloaders. They may be on the inside where you don't see them, such as worms that wreak havoc in the tummy or heart. Others, such as fleas, ticks, and ear mites, live on the outside of the body.

Internal parasites are best addressed by your veterinarian. Sure, there are "worm medicines" you can buy at the supermarket, but these are rarely effective against the particular kind of worm your kitten has. You'll waste your money or, worse, make the kitten sick by using home remedies.

Today, a variety of preventive therapies are available that keep kittens free of both external and internal parasites—some with a single product application. For instance, Heartgard for Cats not only prevents heartworms, but also prevents the intestinal hookworm.

In the past, flea control was complicated by the fact that the chemicals used to kill the bugs were often extremely toxic to kittens. Also, fleas lay eggs that mature into larvae, spin cocoons, and emerge as adults—and not all products will kill the fleas at each of these life stages. That means the flea war must be waged year-round in many parts of the world.

One of the best ways to control fleas is a two-pronged attack that protects your home and the pet. Adult fleas prefer to stay on your kitten, but the other life stages (eggs, for instance) end up in your carpet.

FOR THE HOUSE

Sprays and foggers cover every square inch of the home, creep into the crevices and delve into the carpet to treat hidden eggs and larvae. Choose one designed to kill the adult fleas on contact, which also contains an insect growth regulator (IGR) to stop immature fleas from developing. That zaps the babies as they emerge from the cocoon and stops eggs from hatching.

More "natural" premise control products that may help include borate-containing powders that dry out the fleas and kill them by dehydration. Diatomaceous earth (pet grade) does the same thing. Both can be a bit messy. Mint-type sprays have some repellent effect, but they don't kill fleas.

The best natural technique for fighting fleas in the house is daily vacuuming that sucks up flea eggs, larvae, and cocoons. Be sure to throw out the vacuum bag, though, or you'll risk having the bugs hatch inside and spread them the next time you vacuum.

Just because a product is "natural" does not automatically mean it's effective or safe. After all, poisonous mushrooms are natural, too. Kittens are incredibly sensitive to flea products, even natural ones like citronella, so follow your veterinarian's advice to avoid dangerous reactions.

Warning: Be sure to read and follow product directions very carefully. Many of the premise sprays and foggers are toxic to kittens and other pets (especially birds and fish). It may be best to take your kitten for a weekend vacation and have the house bug-bombed while you are away. Flea products used on the pet also have the potential for harming your kitten, especially if the product directions aren't followed. Read the label. Be sure it's labeled safe for kittens—flea products designed for dogs are not always safe for cats. Never combine products unless advised to do so by your veterinarian. What's safe when used alone may become deadly when combined with another product.

FOR THE PET

The safest, most effective flea products were developed in just the past several years. Program is a monthly pill or liquid that will "sterilize" biting fleas so they can't lay viable eggs. It won't kill adult fleas, but does help break the life cycle and gets rid of the bugs in the house. Frontline and Advantage are applied once a month as drops to the back of the kitten's neck, and kill adult fleas when they bite the pet. Frontline also kills ticks. These products are available only from your veterinarian.

Don't be fooled by copycat "spot on" products. Cheaper versions are available at some grocery stores or pet products sources, but veterinarians warn that these aren't always as safe or effective as Program, Frontline, and Advantage.

Other flea products for kittens include sprays, shampoos, collars, and powders. All can be effective when used as specified.

> **Technical Stuff:** Revolution is another "spot on" topical product that's recently been released. The active ingredient, selamectin, targets several kinds of parasites, including heartworms. It works by paralyzing the bugs. Revolution drops are applied once a month to the pet's skin, and kill ticks, ear mites, and adult fleas. Revolution also prevents flea eggs from hatching. It also kills hookworms and roundworms in cats.

I am a great believer in using the least possible amount of chemicals on my pet. Seren isn't exposed to ticks—she's outside on a leash only once or twice a week—so I prefer the flea-only control of Advantage. Also, I use the product every six weeks, rather than every month as recommended, and that seems to do the job as well. It also saves a bit of money. However, outdoor kitties regularly exposed to fleas will likely need the every-month schedule. Always rely on your veterinarian's advice for your kitten's particular circumstances.

Natural flea control gets mixed reviews. Stories abound regarding the benefits of supplementing kitty's diet with garlic or brewer's yeast, which has lots of vitamin B. There is no scientific evidence that these work to control fleas but some owners swear by them. Such supplements may not help, but they probably won't hurt, and in individual kittens, they may make a difference. The amount you give, though, should be determined by your holistic veterinarian to ensure you don't throw off the nutritional balance of the kitten's diet. You should be aware, too, that too much garlic can be dangerous for cats. It can cause a blood disorder called Heinz-body anemia, so always check amounts with a veterinarian before home-treating your kitten.

Basically, keeping the kitten as healthy as possible will help control fleas naturally, because sick or immune-compromised animals seem to attract more fleas than healthy ones. Fleas like to kick kitty when she's down.

Electronic devices touted to use ultrasonic emissions to "repel" fleas don't work. Save your money and your kitten's peace of mind. In controlled studies, these products have been shown to bother the hearing of the pet more than that of the bugs.

Breeding Babies

Take a look at the furry wonder sleeping on your lap. If he came from a shelter, consider that he is the lucky one who found a home. Four kittens out of every litter of five will draw the short straws and not survive to live the good life on some loving person's lap. There are just not enough good homes to go around.

Feline Facts of Life—Breeding Pros and Cons

Unless you are an experienced breeder and your kitten has the purebred qualities that would benefit his breed, there is no reason to mate him—or her. Responsible professional cat breeders spend a great deal of time and money on their animals. They research and study family trees. They learn about genetics to better predict what type of kittens they can expect from a particular match. And when kittens are born, they celebrate the joys of a successful breeding, and suffer the agonies of disaster when babies die. In any case, they fund their hobby with love and money, and take responsibility for bringing kittens into the world.

Breeding purebred cats can be incredibly rewarding but it's not easy to do right. If you are interested in this hobby, take time to learn about what's involved. There are some good books that provide guidance, but learning from a book alone isn't the best idea. A better place to start is your kitten's breeder. Ask him or her about the process, visit cat shows, and become involved in these fun family events.

Realize that cat breeders do not make money. After the expense of proper kitten vaccinations, parasite treatments, Mom-cat's veterinary visits and prenatal care, and feeding the whole crew, they do well to break even. The best-known catteries that demand the highest prices for their kittens tend to be those who invest lots of time, money, and energy into "campaigning" their cats to championships by traveling across the country and competing in many shows.

If you do decide to breed your kitten, be prepared to endure some unpleasant behaviors as he—or she—matures. Girl cats go into "heat" when they become receptive to the male's attention. Heat behavior can be quite obnoxious, with the female crying loudly, rolling about on the floor, and doing her best to get out of the house. Some inexperienced cat owners seeing this behavior for the first time think the cat is in pain. The behavior won't go away, either. It comes and goes about every three weeks during breeding season (about February through October), until she becomes pregnant. Depending on when your kitten was born, she may go into heat as early as four months of age.

Boy cats also want to get outside, to meet all those lovely girl kitties. To make sure there's no mistake about their intentions, intact male cats spray strong-smelling urine as an advertisement. That means your walls, furniture, carpet, and other household "landmarks" will become prime targets for this feline baptism. Intact male cats are also more prone to health problems such as abscesses from fight wounds. Spraying behavior can start as early as seven months of age, but more typically begins at nine to ten months of age.

Technical Stuff: Unlike conformation dog shows where the animals must be "intact" to be shown, cat shows have a championship category for spayed and neutered animals. Some cats first attain championship as intact kitties, then undergo the surgery and compete in the "premier" category where they win second championships. Household Pet categories offer competition for cats that are not registered at all, but are outstanding examples of loving, healthy pet cats.

Professional catteries tend to limit house access of their stud cats. Some are kept confined in easily cleaned kennel-like areas where plastic sheets placed partway up the walls protect them from urine marking. Once the stud cat has achieved his championship or otherwise fulfilled his fatherhood potential, breeders often "retire" the cat by neutering him. That way, he can enjoy the rest of his life as a pet and freely roam the house.

The Gift of Spay and Neuter

I guess you can tell I'm a huge proponent of responsibly "fixing" your kitten, the earlier the better. It's a personal issue with me. My cat, Seren, was a dumped kitten and very likely the product of a back-yard breeder who couldn't find a likely buyer. If I hadn't found Seren, she'd be dead. When I travel across the country, I see hundreds of kittens in shelters, each as lovely and loving and full of as much potential as my Seren. Few will find a home. It's not the shelters' fault; it's the fault of people who allowed the kitten's parents to breed. It's so simple to protect our pets from perpetuating this tragedy.

In the past, it was recommended that girl cats be spayed at six months of age, and boy cats neutered at nine months of age. However, these ages were arbitrary and no studies have been done to support the benefit of waiting until these ages. In fact, some kittens become sexually mature and can reproduce before these benchmark ages. In recent years, ongoing studies have investigated the benefits of "early-age" neutering. Today the American Veterinary Medical Association endorses spaying and neutering shelter kittens at four months of age. Many shelters surgically sterilize kittens (and puppies) as early as eight weeks old, using modern safe anesthesia and procedures developed in these studies.

Remember, the best time to perform spay and neuter surgeries is before your kitten reaches sexual maturity and starts to exhibit objectionable behaviors. Your veterinarian will advise you about the timing.

Spay surgery involves surgically removing both ovaries and the uterus from the female cat. It is a procedure performed under general anesthesia—that is, the kitty is asleep and doesn't experience pain during the operation. A small incision is made in the shaved abdomen, the organs are removed, and stitches or sometimes staples close the opening. These will be removed in about seven to ten days.

It's important to prevent your kitten from licking or chewing at her tummy stitches until the incision has healed. A wonderfully effective deterrent is Vick's VapoRub. Veterinarians tell me that cats hate the smell and will almost always ignore the stitches if you spread a tiny amount on either side (not on top) of the suture line.

Warning: Never give pain medicine to your kitten without veterinary advice. Aspirin and Tylenol can kill your baby! If kitty is uncomfortable after surgery, safe pain medicine is now available by prescription from your veterinarian.

Neuter surgery removes the testes from the boy kitten's scrotum. The kitten is anesthetized, fur is removed from the scrotal sac under his tail, and an incision is made through which the testes are removed. Usually the incision is so small that no stitches are needed.

Technical Stuff: Occasionally a boy kitten's testicles do not descend. The testicles are often in the scrotum at birth, but may move in and out of the scrotum for the first few months. *Cryptorchid* occurs when both testicles are involved and *monorchid* when one testicle is retained. In these cases the veterinarian will need to make a small incision in the kitten's abdomen to find and remove the testicle(s). Stitches and recovery are similar to a spay procedure.

Kittens usually spend one night in the hospital. They may be admitted the evening before, have the surgery the next morning, and be released later that afternoon or evening. Every kitten reacts differently to the surgery. Many want to sleep and lie around for a day or two, but most bounce back very quickly and act as though nothing has happened. Your veterinarian may ask you to restrict the kitten's activity until the incision has healed and stitches are removed.

Spay and neuter surgery offer several health benefits to kittens and cats. First, it eliminates the sex-related objectionable behaviors. That can prevent abscesses or diseases like FIV which are spread via bite wounds, and roaming behavior that puts cats at risk for being hit by cars. It also eliminates or reduces the possibility of some kinds of cancer, such as testicular or breast tumors.

These surgeries also relieve your kitten of the bother, nuisance, and stress of worrying about breeding issues. It frees them to become pets. Cats do not yearn to be "fulfilled" by parenthood—they simply won't miss what they've never experienced. Spayed and neutered kittens get to enjoy life by concentrating on bonding with you and your family.

Finally—and perhaps most important—spay and neuter surgery prevents the births of unwanted kittens that would otherwise be destined to die. It is simply the right thing to do.

Straight Talk About Declaw Surgery

This issue has started heated battles on the Internet and divides cat lovers all over the world. Cats claw. It is normal feline behavior. That didn't particularly matter when kitty was outside all the time. But when kitty became a house pet, suddenly his claw habits became personally important to the people in his life—and their furniture.

Let me be frank—I am adamantly opposed to declawing without pursuing other options first. Declawing should never be done as a matter of course, or offered as a "routine" part of kitten care. It's not.

Unlike spay and neuter, declaw is a cosmetic procedure that primarily benefits the human owner and has no health benefits to the cat. A caveat here, though: When it comes to a choice between the kitten losing his claws or losing his home and life, there's no contest. That's about the only time I'd reluctantly accept declawing as a viable option.

What's Involved

Declawing is the surgical removal of the toenail and last joint of the toe from which the claw grows. The surgery is performed under sterile conditions, and the cat is anesthetized. A surgical blade called a scalpel, or a specialized nail trimmer called a Resco, may be used to amputate this portion of each of the kitten's toes. A tiny stitch or tissue glue closes each wound. The operation is followed with firm bandaging of the paws for a day or two to control the bleeding.

Warning: Declawed kittens lose part of their defense arsenal and therefore aren't as able to protect themselves when they're outside. If they retain their rear claws, some kitties will still be able to climb trees. It's best to confine declawed cats indoors, for their safety.

Young kittens tend to recover more quickly from this procedure than older cats. For that reason, and also for economic considerations (only one anesthesia fee), the declaw is commonly performed at the same time as the spay or neuter surgery. In most instances, only the front claws are removed, those used for scratching and marking territory. The rear claws are left intact.

The most recent surgical techniques employ lasers rather than cutting blades. Lasers evaporate tissue rather than cutting it, and they seal nerve endings and blood vessels so there is less pain and bleeding. However, because laser procedures use heat—burning—to accomplish the amputation, healing takes longer.

Kittens will need special care and attention for several days following declaw surgery. The paws are tender for up to a week and a gentle, nonabrasive litter should be used temporarily to keep from aggravating the healing wounds. Shredded paper is often recommended. Most kitties are up and walking again within forty-eight to seventy-two hours after the surgery. Often, they will require pain medicine from the vet.

Another surgical procedure, called the flexor tendonectomy, leaves the kitten his claws but prevents him from extending them. The tendon that connects the second and third bones of the cat's toes and controls the extension of the claws is cut, and a tiny portion removed. After this procedure, the base of the nails tends to thicken and the claws may become more blunt. You'll still need to monitor and trim the cat's nails after this surgery.

Health and Emotional Impact

I'm not aware of any wide-ranging controlled studies of the emotional and physical impact on kittens that have undergone declaw surgery. Anecdotal testimony, however, asserts that some cats that lose their claws begin to rely instead on their teeth for defense. Cat show fanciers are so certain of the potential for emotional damage that they will not allow a declawed cat to be shown.

There are no health benefits to declawing your kitten. Some kitties experience a personality change after the surgery. It's hard to say if this is due to the loss of claws, the trauma of surgery, or the natural process of maturing.

Many kittens and cats show absolutely no negative effects to losing their nails. Do not let the presence—or absence—of claws interfere with your choice of a lovely shelter kitty. Some may have already had the procedure done.

Other Options

When your kitten still has his claws, I urge you to examine all options before resorting to declaw surgery. I see too many kittens declawed as a knee-jerk reaction to prevent a normal behavior even before the baby has caused any claw problems.

There are ways to deal with kittens in a humane manner that allows them to keep their claws and their natural propensity to scratch. Train your kitten from the beginning. Give him a "legal" target. It's not as easy as having the veterinarian remove the problem with a scalpel or laser, but it works. And in my book, it's the smart decision.

Kitten Purrs: Soft Paws vinyl nail covers come in a variety of stylish colors. These nail tips allow your kitten to keep his claws. The covers are glued over his own claws and offer a blunt tip that won't hurt your furniture even if he does make a mistake and claw it. Soft Paws are available from pet products stores or your veterinarian's office and from www.softpaws.com.

10

RECOGNIZING AND TREATING SICK KITTENS

Doing Your Part

You are the most important person in your kitten's life, the source of all her favorite food, attention, and play, and the guardian of her health. Of course, your veterinarian is a vital part of kitten care. The doctor you choose will provide important advice, preventive care, and expertise in diagnosing and treating problems as they arise. But it's up to you to recognize there's a problem in the first place. That means you must become intimately familiar with "normal" kitten behavior and appearance, so that a deviation from the norm sounds an alert.

In the best of all possible worlds, you'll only need to call on your veterinarian for routine preventive care three or four times during her first year of life and only once or twice a year thereafter. But you live with kitty all year long. You know her best; you are most familiar with all her special quirks. So you are in the best position to know when something isn't right.

People often tell me they enjoy a close, almost mystical bond with their special kittens, so much so that their "intuition" tells them when there's a problem. For instance, you may wake up in the morning and simply "know" your kitten feels bad, even before you see that she's had an accident outside the box. The closer your bond, the stronger this intuition may become. Holistic veterinarians encourage pet owners to "listen" to that little voice inside, the intuition that offers warnings. Our subconscious may recognize clues we otherwise might miss.

The Home Health Exam

Make a habit of giving your kitten a home health check on a routine basis. It's easy to do, and can double as a bonding experience. Your kitten will love all the attention.

A good time to give kitty a thorough once-over is in the evenings, or whenever she's winding down for the day. Place her on your lap, and begin at her head and face. Check her eyes, peek into both ears, and be sure her nose is clean. You'll want to make sure there is no abnormal discharge forming. If she'll let you without fussing too much, take a look inside her mouth, too, to make sure her gums are a healthy pink.

Finally, pet your kitten all over her body, starting at her head and running your fingers gently down both her sides, under her tummy, and around her flanks. She'll think it's a love-fest, when you're actually checking to be sure her skin is healthy and there are no scabs, bumps, or sores. You can "finger-comb" her at the same time, to check for telltale mats that tend to form in the creases of her legs or behind her ears. Don't forget to check under her tail to be sure there's no sign of diarrhea or worm debris.

This home health check will feel good to your kitten and help you become familiar with what's normal for her. Any change in the status quo should send up a red flag and prompt you to contact your veterinarian for an expert opinion and diagnosis. She'll be able to tell you what, if anything, needs to be done to address the change.

Tip: Don't forget to check the kitten's food intake and her litter box every single day. Input and output offer a great deal of information about health status. Hit-or-miss litter box behavior may be a behavior or training issue, but in many cases it's prompted by a health issue.

Home Medicating the Kitten

There will come times when you need to treat your kitten at home. Never fear, your veterinarian or the technician will be more than happy to demonstrate the best way to do this.

Kittens who are ill may be sent home from the vets with medicine for you to administer. Healthy kittens often need preventive treatments—like flea medicine—that should be given at home. Unfortunately, kitty won't "open wide" and take her medicine on command. Treating your kitten can be compared to giving medicine to a reluctant four-year-old child. But with children, you can explain what's happening and cajole them into putting up with the process. Kittens won't understand or care why you're trying to give them a pill. And the furred baby will use her claws and needle-sharp teeth to express her displeasure. She's also tiny, squirmy, and difficult to hold safely.

Safe Kitten Restraints

Kittens that are very sick are easiest to treat because they feel too ill to argue. But you'll need to protect yourself—and the baby—during some kinds of treatments by carefully restraining her. In these cases, it's best to have an extra pair of hands. The other person restrains baby while you treat the problem. Ask your veterinarian to demonstrate the techniques below.

Kittens have a great deal of loose skin at the shoulders and back of the neck. That's called the "scruff." Mom-cats carry their tiny kittens by the scruff. You shouldn't lift her by the scruff once she's older—her weight can make it hurt—but this loose skin makes a great handle to keep her still.

Gently grasp the scruff with your dominant hand—right one if you're right-handed, for example. When done correctly, baby won't be able to turn her head around to reach that hand with her teeth. For small kittens that may be all you need to gently hold her immobile on a tabletop while the second person administers the medicine.

Larger kittens may need their paws contained, too. Hang on to kitty's scruff with one hand and capture both rear paws with the other hand. Then gently lay her down on her side, on the tabletop. She can't reach you with her teeth or front paws, and the bunny-kicking rear feet are also contained.

An excellent kitten restraint that also works well for adult cats is the pillowcase. Simply put the cat inside, with her head (or other body part that needs attention) sticking out the opening. The pillowcase contains her pistoning feet, and often, the cat stops struggling once she realizes her efforts are ineffective.

Pilling

Kittens have tiny mouths, and it can be hard to get a pill down them. Unlike dogs, who tend to gulp tasty treats even with pills hidden inside, kittens and cats are harder to fool. You can try hiding a pill in your kitten's moist food, but nine times out of ten, she'll simply eat around the medicine. Ask your veterinarian if the pill can be crushed and mixed in a strong-flavored treat, like tuna juice or a dollop of canned food.

The key to successfully pilling your kitten is doing it quickly, and then offering a treat to salve any bruised feelings—or nasty taste. Here's what to do.

Place the palm of your hand on top of the kitten's head, fingers pointed toward her nose. Tip her head so her nose points to the ceiling—the mouth usually falls open a bit when you do this. Then gently press on her lips on each side of the mouth with your thumb and index or middle fingers. Pressing the kitten's lips against her teeth almost always prompts her to open wide.

Be ready with the pill in the other hand, and when she opens her mouth, push it into her mouth and over the hill of her tongue. You'll see a V indentation on the back of her tongue—aim for that.

Gently and quickly close her mouth as soon as the pill is in place. Stroke her throat until you see her swallow. Kitties almost always lick their noses after they've swallowed.

Have kitty's favorite treat in the world ready to offer her as soon as you've closed her mouth on the pill. Give it to her right away. In almost all cases, the kitten will be distracted enough to forget about the pill, and when she gobbles up the snack, the pill goes down the hatch, too.

Kitten Purrs: Kittens (and cats) are notoriously difficult to medicate, and the stress of "arguing" with them can make kitty even sicker. Compounding the medicine, though, makes a huge difference. Veterinarians can ask the compounding pharmacist to turn pet medicine into a flavor, dose, and form that your kitten will beg to take like a treat. That way, you don't have to divide pills into tiny doses, either. Ask your veterinarian about compounding prescriptions. The service is available over the Internet, as well. The site I use for Seren when she needs medication is www.peerlesshealth.com.

Liquid Medicine

Kittens more readily accept oral medicines that are liquid. They also tend to be much easier to give to the baby, because you don't need to lever her mouth open. All you need is a medicine syringe or eyedropper, and the medicine.

Medicine syringes are available from your veterinarian. Often, liquid medicine comes with its own applicator, but the syringe—minus the needle, of course—should be a part of every pet owner's home medicine chest. They are easy to use, allow you to measure the dose accurately, and are well accepted by kittens and adult cats alike.

Draw up the prescribed amount in the eyedropper or syringe. As with pilling, place the palm of one hand over your kitten's head to hold her still, and tip her head to the ceiling. Insert the end of the applicator into the corner of kitty's mouth, between her lips. Then squirt the medicine into her cheek. Withdraw the syringe, and hold her mouth closed until you see her swallow.

Ear Treatments

The key to ear treatments is hanging on to the kitten and not allowing her to shake until you're finished. Otherwise, you'll end up with the medicine sprayed all over you, rather than inside her ear where it belongs. It's a good idea to wear an old shirt when you must treat kitten ears. Despite your best efforts, she's likely to nail you with at least some of the medicine when she shakes her head after you're finished.

There is a trick to safely cleaning a pet's ears. Care must be taken not to damage the fragile eardrum, and using Q-tips can be dangerous for that reason. Your veterinarian will demonstrate how to use these cotton swabs, if that's necessary to the treatment.

Most times, though, medicated drops or ointments are prescribed. Dripping two or three drops of the medicine or ointment into the ear may be all that's required. Tip the baby's head so the appropriate ear faces the ceiling, and let gravity do your work. Once the medicine is applied, gently massage the base of the kitten's ear. That spreads the ointment or drops deeper into the canal where it can do the most good. Often, the kitten will appreciate this massage, because it helps scratch a deep-seated itch she can't reach.

When the veterinarian has diagnosed ear mites, you'll need to clean the ears thoroughly, once a week for at least three to four weeks. That gets rid of any hatching mites that were missed during the first treatments. Commercial over-the-counter products are available, or your vet may prescribe a mite treatment.

Hold the kitten's head steady, apply several drops of the liquid mite medicine into the ear, and massage the base of the ear. Hang on to the tip of the ear with a firm grasp to keep her from shaking her head too soon. Massaging the ear base helps flush mite debris out of the canal, so you can wipe it away with a cotton ball. It may take two or three sessions on each ear to get them clean.

Holistic veterinarians advise that any type of oil—including mineral oil, baby oil, and vegetable oil—will work to cure ear mites. Oil suffocates the bugs. Of course, you must first be sure of the diagnosis. Then you can safely use something like olive oil to soothe the sore ear and kill the mites. Remember to treat the ears for at least three weeks to get all the bugs.

Warning: Ear infections or mite infestations can make the ears so sore and itchy, the kitten may not allow you to touch her ears. Other times, she may damage herself with scratching until the ears bleed, or the ear flap swells like a tiny balloon. That's called an aural hematoma. In these instances, it's best to visit the veterinarian to ensure kitty gets the treatment she needs.

Eye Treatments

In most cases, you can gently tip the kitten's head toward the ceiling and drip the liquid medicine into each eye. Sometimes, when it's an ointment, you'll need to apply it very carefully, being careful not to poke her.

A kitten face is usually so small that you can hold her with one hand and gently open her eye with the same hand. Carefully pull down her lower eyelid, squeeze the prescribed amount of ointment into the cupped tissue, and then close her eye. The natural motion of blinking will spread the ointment where it needs to go.

It's important to restrain your kitten while you medicate her, to ensure she's not hurt accidentally when she wiggles. If you don't have an extra person around to help, you can often restrain the baby with the "knee trick." Get down on the floor and place your kitten between your knees as you kneel above her. She should face out. You control the exit, and she can't back up anywhere to get away. This trick also leaves your hands free to medicate her ears or eyes, or give a pill.

And remember, whenever not contraindicated by her health, always follow a treatment with a tasty treat, so the kitten will be less likely to argue about subsequent treatments.

Skin Treatments

Putting medicine on the skin is probably the easiest treatment of all. The problem, though, is that kittens want to lick off the medicine as soon as it's applied. After you apply the ointment, salve, or other medicine to the affected area, distract the kitten with a game. Play with a feather or fishing-pole toy for ten to fifteen minutes, to allow the medicine to be absorbed.

An Elizabethan collar, which fits around the baby's neck and extends several inches, like the stiff decorative collars popularized by the English queen of the same name, can prevent a kitten from licking off medication. This collar restraint keeps the cat from reaching her body with tongue or teeth, or from scratching her ears or face. Elizabethan collars are available from pet supply stores or the vet's office.

Elizabethan collars may not come in the right size for a tiny kitten, though. You can make a homemade "body suit" using a baby T-shirt that will protect skin sores from industrious licking. The kitten's head goes through the neck, her front feet fit through the armholes, and the excess is safety-pinned under her tail.

Ten Common Kitten Health Concerns

It's never a good idea to try to diagnose and treat a serious kitten health problem yourself. There's a reason why veterinarians go to school for eight to ten years to get a degree. Plus, they have access to all kinds of tests to confirm a suspected diagnosis.

It is important, though, that you become familiar with some of the most common health concerns your kitten might face. Most are easy to prevent. Many are treatable, particularly when caught early.

Diarrhea

Any time you share your life with a pet, you must get used to dealing with—ahem—bodily functions. Healthy stools are well formed, and tan to dark brown in color, depending on the kitten's diet.

In fact, when a kitten raids the garbage or has a sudden change in diet, there's often a change in the stool. Diarrhea is soft to liquid bowel movements, and may occur in a range of colors. Blood in the feces is always cause for a vet visit.

Diarrhea may be a sign of many different health problems, such as internal parasites or viral infection like panleukopenia (both discussed below). When your kitten has diarrhea, she can lose large volumes of water, which can make her sicker.

Kittens can quickly become dangerously dehydrated when they have a bout of diarrhea. You can check for dehydration with the

It's important to monitor the litter box for signs of diarrhea or worms. Be aware that kittens can get sick from some illnesses simply by sharing a contaminated box with an infected cat. Diarrhea can be a sign of many different kitten health problems.

(Photo credit: Amy D. Shojai)

"scruff" test. The loose skin at the back of kitty's neck should be very elastic. When gently lifted off her shoulders and released, the scruff should immediately spring back into place. A loss of elasticity where the skin remains tented, or very slowly returns to normal position, means kitty has some degree of dehydration. See the veterinarian immediately.

Diarrhea is always a concern in kittens, and should be addressed by a veterinarian as soon as possible. Kittens older than six months old, that otherwise act as if they feel fine, may benefit from Kaopectate until you can get to the veterinarian. The usual dose is ½ teaspoon every hour, for up to four hours.

External Parasites (Ear Mites, Fleas, Ticks)

Kittens are the perfect target for parasites. They're low to the ground, fluffy for easy hiding, and probably less than scrupulous when they groom themselves. Most times, skin parasites are more aggravating than dangerous, but with tiny kittens they can cause serious problems.

Ear mites are tiny, spiderlike critters related to spiders and ticks. They prefer to colonize the ear canal. Sometimes they spill onto the skin and cause a rash, too. But mostly, ear mites bite and suck lymph—the clear fluid found in the skin. They cause intense itching, and can lead to ear infections. You'll see your kitten paw and incessantly scratch her ears. Often you'll also see a dark brown, crumbly material inside the ears. Ear mites are very contagious and veterinarians recommend that all pets in the household (other cats, dogs, rabbits, ferrets) be treated if one is infected.

Fleas are specialized blood-sucking insects that have been around for millennia. They probably bugged prehistoric kittens, too. They can be more than mere itchy aggravations. A heavy flea load can cause severe anemia in a tiny kitten and, like tiny vampires, bleed her to death.

Warning: Anemia in kittens can be deadly. Your kitten will act weak and lethargic, and the inside of her ears and mouth and gums will be very pale. See a veterinarian immediately if you suspect your kitten suffers from anemia.

Fleas also prompt an allergic reaction in some pets. When that happens, it only takes a single bite to cause severe itching. Kittens become sensitized to the saliva of the flea. Flea-allergic cats often develop a skin rash called *miliary dermatitis*, which feels like tiny scabby bumps all over the skin.

You may not see your kitten scratching if she has fleas. You may not see any fleas—cats are very good at grooming the bugs away. Stand the kitten on a white paper towel, and brush or comb her fur to check for flea debris. Any black pepperlike material indicates fleas. That's the digested blood excreted by the fleas.

Ticks are also blood-sucking parasites. They attach themselves to your kitten by burying their heads beneath the skin. The bodies fill with blood and inflate like balloons.

Ticks leave sores on the skin, and in sufficient numbers, can cause anemia just like fleas. Dogs tend to have a worse problem because they don't groom as well as cats do. More serious than the .bite, though, are the diseases that ticks can spread to your kitten. Flea products like Frontline will also keep ticks off your pet.

Warning: Ticks can spread diseases to people, too, so never remove a tick with your bare hands. Using tweezers, grasp the critter right at the base of the head where it disappears into the skin. Exert a firm, gentle pressure to pull it away. A bit of kitten skin may come with the tick—that's fine. Dab the place with some Bactine or Neosporin, and watch the area to be sure there's no swelling. The skin will naturally spit out any stray bits of tick left behind.

(Photo credit: Amy D. Shojai)

Scratching can be a sign of fleas, ticks, allergies, or other skin disorders.

> **Tip:** Professional pet groomers recommend using petro-
> leum jelly to remove ticks. Place a dab of the jelly right on top
> of the parasite so it's completely covered. Then wait five min-
> utes. In order to breathe, the tick will have to back out and
> pull its head out of the skin. That's when you grab it with a tis-
> sue and flush it down the toilet.

Feline Immunodeficiency Virus (FIV)

FIV is the feline equivalent to human AIDS. Like human HIV, the
kitty version attacks the immune system, making afflicted animals
more susceptible to other illnesses. They get sick quicker and have a
more difficult time getting well. Chronic illnesses can include claw
or mouth sores, intermittent fevers, skin infections, and swollen
lymph nodes.

Thankfully, this disease is considered relatively difficult to catch.
The virus is thought to be spread primarily via bites from infected
cats. Biting literally "injects" the other cat with infected saliva. By
the way, you'll be relieved to know that researchers have been unable to find any evidence that people can get FIV from their cats. It's
kitty-specific, just as the human virus is people-specific.

The first signs of illness develop four to six weeks after infection,
but the transient fever, swollen lymph nodes, diarrhea, and other
vague signs may not be noticed. Most kitties recover from these initial signs and remain healthy for years, but can be carriers of the
virus, capable of infecting other cats. It's important to know if your
kitten is positive for FIV so that you can prevent her from spreading
the disease.

There is no cure for FIV, nor is there a preventive vaccine. However, with the right nutrition and medical support, infected cats live
otherwise normal, healthy lives, often for years following diagnosis.
Many live well past ten years old, and remain healthy. Typically the
disease is present for three to six years before the cat becomes sick
with true immunodeficiency. Discuss care options with your veterinarian so that you know what to expect and how best to protect
your kitten.

Blood tests are available. Usually, a first test determines if exposure has taken place, by looking for antibodies the kitten's body has produced against the disease. That doesn't mean your kitten is infected—only that she's been exposed. If the kitten tests positive for antibodies, then a second test is needed to confirm infection. Most veterinarians recommend that these tests be repeated when your kitten reaches six months of age, to be sure of the diagnosis, because kittens younger than six months of age do not always test accurately.

Warning: When your kitten tests positive for FIV, the responsible choice is to keep her inside to prevent exposure to other outside cats. You should also discuss safety issues for the other cats in your home to protect them from risk of the disease. Some households manage to segregate the FIV-positive cat in one area of the house, away from the other felines.

Feline Infectious Peritonitis (FIP)

This is a scary virus because it's very complicated and not completely understood. It's classified as a coronavirus. There are lots of these types of viruses, and some do little more than cause a bit of diarrhea in your kitten. But FIP is fatal, and there's no treatment available.

Unfortunately, there's not yet a convenient and accurate way to tell if a kitten has been exposed or infected with the deadly virus. Some specialized laboratories can do genetic tests that will diagnose the disease. Those available in most veterinarian offices will offer clues but no concrete answer.

For many years it was thought that FIP was primarily transmitted from cat to cat, probably through contact with litter boxes or nose-to-nose contact. The greatest risk continues to be for those felines living in shelters and catteries and multiple-cat homes. Today, though, evidence seems to indicate that many cats sick with FIP were first infected with the mild diarrhea-causing coronavirus, which then transmuted into the deadly FIP version. Researchers say the mutation could happen years after the initial infection with a coronavirus—prior to that time the cat remains healthy and normal. In most cases, if FIP is to develop, they believe it will happen within six months to a year after the initial infection.

Kittens can be exposed to the mild forms that may be in the environment. The coronavirus can live outside the body for many weeks. That means there is no good way to protect your kitten from the disease. The good news is that a coronavirus can be easily killed with household cleaners—four ounces of bleach in a gallon of water works well—so keeping things clean can help.

There is a preventive vaccine available for FIP. However, researchers I've spoken with at different veterinary teaching universities question the effectiveness and safety of the shot. If your kitten is an "only" cat, there's probably no good reason to get this vaccination.

Kittens from shelters or in multiple-cat homes are at highest risk, but even in these instances, veterinarians such as Dr. Dennis Macy at Colorado State University suggest it should be used in only very unusual situations. Ask your veterinarian about the best choices for your kitten's situation. Ongoing research continues to find answers to the puzzles of today, and hopefully, there will soon be a safe, effective option to protect our kittens from FIP.

> **Technical Stuff:** The signs of FIP tend to be very vague. There are two general forms of the disease. The "effusive" or "wet" form results in a progressive, painless swelling of the abdomen with fluid. The "dry" form may include signs as varied as anemia, fever, weight loss, and depression. Cats may suffer liver or kidney failure, or central nervous system problems such as paralysis or personality changes. Although blood tests can indicate exposure to a coronavirus, these won't say anything about the mutated FIP form. Instead, veterinarians must rely on analysis of the fluid in the body, or biopsy of a tissue sample.

Feline Leukemia Virus (FeLV)

This disease is considered one of the most devastating and common causes of death in pet cats. Infection with FeLV can prompt a wide range of infectious diseases that are caused either directly or indirectly by the virus, including cancer, anemia, reproductive disorders, and immune suppression. The immune suppression means the kitten gets sick very easily and has trouble recovering.

Technical Stuff: FeLV is a retrovirus that has the ability to insert its genetic code into healthy cells of the cat's body. That turns the cells into virus factories that pump out more of the deadly disease. FeLV programs the cat's body at the cellular level to self-destruct.

FeLV is extremely contagious and is spread directly from infected cats through contact with saliva or waste. Kittens can become infected from their mother's milk or even before they're born. In most instances, though, it takes repeated exposure over a long period of time for a cat to become infected.

About 40 percent of infected cats become sick and die. About 30 percent develop "latent" infections, which means they don't become sick, but they harbor the virus in their body. The remaining 30 percent of cats are able to fight off the disease and develop immunity to FeLV.

There are several tests for diagnosing FeLV. More than one may be needed, because the virus is present in the bloodstream only during certain stages of the disease. The tests won't identify latent infections, though. It is vital that you have your kitten tested for FeLV before you bring her into contact with your other cats. That's especially important if she's from a shelter, or a stray rescued from the street, because she won't have a known health history. You could be risking the lives of your resident cats. **Warning:** Cats that are infected with FIP or FIV are also often positive for FeLV. Veterinarians have a test that will look for FIV and FeLV at the same time.

There is no cure for FeLV. Some treatments may prolong the cat's life or help keep her more comfortable once she's sick. Once an infected cat becomes sick, half will die within six months and up to 80 percent will live only three years. When a kitten tests positive for the disease, you should remain extra vigilant to catch any health problem right away. Even the sniffles could turn deadly when her immune system is under attack.

Knowing the FeLV status of the other cats your kitten comes in contact with is the best way to protect her. A number of vaccinations are available to protect against the disease, but none is 100 percent effective. She'll need to test negative for FeLV before being vaccinated anyway.

Remember, up to 30 percent of cats that test positive for FeLV fight off the disease and become immune. Should your kitten test positive, talk with your veterinarian about protective steps for the other cats in your home. When the kitten otherwise appears healthy, it may be worthwhile to retest three or four months later.

If a cat in your care has died from FeLV, veterinarians recommend you wait at least thirty days before adopting a new pet. That gives the virus time to die, so it's not around to reinfect your new kitten.

Feline Panleukopenia Virus (FPV)

Also called feline distemper or feline infectious enteritis, FPV is a devastating, highly contagious disease that can kill a kitten within 12 hours. The baby becomes infected by swallowing the virus, often during self-grooming or oral contact with infected litter pans. The virus can survive for years in the environment, and most outdoor kittens are exposed during their first year of life.

Signs vary from cat to cat. Most commonly, a sudden high fever, refusal to eat, vomiting, and profuse diarrhea with a painful tummy will be seen. This is an emergency, and your kitten needs veterinary care immediately if she is to survive.

There is no specific treatment other than supportive therapy such as fluids that fight dehydration, blood transfusions, medicine to control vomiting and diarrhea, and nursing care that keeps her eating. Hospitalization followed by attentive home nursing care may be recommended. Kittens that survive for five to seven days will usually recover, but they can remain contagious for up to six weeks.

A highly effective preventive vaccination for FPV is available. It is part of the core vaccinations recommended for all kittens and cats, and will provide long-term immunity. Don't take a chance on your kitten catching FPV. This disease is potentially deadly, and now highly preventable. Be sure to get your kitten vaccinated against this disease.

Heartworms

Feline heartworm disease (FHD) is caused by a roundworm that lives in the heart and pulmonary arteries. Until relatively recently, experts didn't believe cats could get the disease, and in fact, heartworms are much more common in dogs than in cats.

The disease in cats is usually much more serious than it is in dogs, who often go for months or years without suffering related health problems. Dogs can ultimately develop signs of heart failure, but that's rare in FHD. Dogs can also be more easily and safely treated for the infection.

Cats may show no health problems at all and then suddenly drop dead. Other times, cats may show signs of difficulty breathing, coughing, wheezing, or chronic vomiting that has nothing to do with hairballs or other common causes.

Several blood tests can detect heartworms by looking for antibodies the cat's immune system produces, or the antigen that the worm produces. None of these tests will detect all cases, so often both types are run and may be repeated. X-rays or ultrasound tests may also be required.

Unfortunately, the treatment used in dogs to get rid of the worms can be as dangerous to cats as the worms themselves. That's because killing the adult worms can have catastrophic consequences for the cat if the pieces move in the bloodstream.

A much better option is to prevent the heartworms altogether. Heartgard for Cats is a monthly chewable tablet available only from your veterinarian; it also prevents the intestinal hookworm parasite. The treatment is recommend for all kittens and cats, six weeks of age and older. My cat Seren sits up and begs for her monthly treatment, so they must put something very tasty in the tablet.

So remember, FHD is easily prevented, but hard to treat and can be deadly to cats. It may not be a problem in your geographic region, but more than thirty-eight states have reported FHD. Risk is greatest where the mosquito thrives. Check with your veterinarian to see if prevention is a good option for your kitten.

Technical Stuff: Heartworms are transmitted by mosquito bites, and cats can only be infected when contagious dogs are nearby. Here's how it works. The mosquito bites an infected dog and swallows baby worms, called microfilariae. The immature worms mature inside the mosquito and are deposited on the skin of subsequent dog—or cat—victims. This immature heartworm enters the skin, and goes through several molts, or developmental stages, as it travels inside the body. Finally the parasite reaches the heart and pulmonary arteries, where it matures into an adult worm. When a dog is infected, the heart is large enough to accommodate enough worms to produce babies—the microfilariae that are shed into the bloodstream. That completes the life cycle. Kitty hearts and arteries, though, are so small that they typically support only one or two worms and microfilariae are almost never present in the cat's bloodstream. That's why it takes an infected dog to infect a cat. The American Heartworm Society says about 70 percent of cats are at risk in areas where there are heartworm-infected dogs. More information about this complicated issue is available on the Auburn University Web site at www.vetmed.auburn.edu/distance/cardio/home.html.

Intestinal Parasites (*Coccidia, Giardia, Roundworms, Tapeworms*)

Kittens also suffer from intestinal freeloaders. Worms and protozoa can set up colonies in the baby's digestive track and make her very sick. They tend to interfere with the body's ability to properly process food. Consequently, diarrhea is a common sign associated with these parasites.

Many kinds of intestinal parasites affect pets, but the most common complaints for kittens include coccidia and giardia (protozoa), and roundworms and tapeworms. There's no home treatment for these problems, but it's a good idea to learn to recognize the signs so you can get your kitten prompt veterinary care.

Coccidia and Giardia are primitive single-cell organisms. Coccidia colonizes and attacks the lining of the kitten's intestines. Infected kittens can develop a fatal diarrhea that's mixed with blood-tinged mucus. Giardia gets in the way of nutrient absorption, so the kitten suffers intermittent soft, smelly diarrhea, poor coat from malnutrition, and problems gaining or maintaining weight. Kittens contract these bugs by swallowing the infective stage of the parasite, which is often found in contaminated soil. Drinking from mud puddles may be all it takes to pick up giardia, and kittens can spread it among themselves, too. Eating infected mice can infect your kitten with coccidia. Diagnosis is made by examining a stool sample under the microscope. Drugs are available to get rid of these parasites. There is also a preventive vaccine for giardia.

Roundworms are found in almost all kittens. They get infected when nursing the mother cat's milk, by swallowing infective larvae in the environment or by eating an infected rodent. They are rarely dangerous, but in large enough numbers, roundworms can interfere with nutrition, cause intestinal damage, or block the intestines. Infected kittens typically have a swollen, potbellied appearance, a dull or lifeless coat, diarrhea, and sometimes mucus in the stool.

Kitten owners are often surprised and disgusted to find the spaghetti-like worms either thrown up or passed with the stool. Medicine to get rid of roundworms is a standard part of early kitten care at the veterinarian. It is safe enough to use in kittens as young as three to four weeks of age.

Tapeworms are an extremely common pest of cats. That's because the intermediate host for the immature worm is the flea. When kittens and cats groom themselves and swallow infected fleas, they contract tapeworms. Therefore, if your kitten has tapeworms, you must also treat her for fleas.

Tapeworms absorb nutrients from the kitten's food and rob her of what she needs to grow. Left untreated, massive infestations can interfere with digestion and elimination by blocking the intestinal tract. Tapeworms are made up of a chain of egg-filled segments that are sporadically passed with the bowel movement. The white segments can move independently like little inchworms. You'll see these telltale worms in the litter box, or stuck to the fur under the kitten's tail. They look like grains of rice when they dry out. Tapeworms are easily killed with medicine from the veterinarian. The best option, of course, is preventing fleas.

Ringworm

It's not a worm, it's a fungal infection of the hair, skin, and claws, and kittens are highly susceptible to infection. Ringworm lives in the soil or can be contracted from other cats that carry the infection. A normal immune system can usually keep ringworm at bay. But in very young kittens with immature immune systems, or those that are already sick, ringworm can flare up.

It spreads from hair to hair in ever-widening circles—hence the name "ring." It leaves behind bare or inflamed scaly patches of skin. Ringworm is the most common cause of hair loss in kittens. Special tests are used to diagnose ringworm. Treatment may involve a combination of oral medicine, topical treatments like baths and dips, or vaccinations that reduce the severity of the infection.

Warning: Ringworm is highly contagious to other pets, and to people. If your kitten is diagnosed with ringworm, consult with your veterinarian and your own doctor for advice on how to reduce the chances of contagion. Ringworm is particularly dangerous for very young children, and for immune-compromised individuals such as those undergoing radiation therapy, or with HIV. These individuals should have no direct contact with the infected kitten until she has been cured and tests negative. Diluted bleach solution (one part bleach to ten parts water) kills the fungus so use that to clean your hands after handling kitty, and thoroughly wash her bedding and grooming tools.

Tip: In an otherwise healthy pet, ringworm is a condition that will "self-heal" in about 60 days, even without treatment. Treatment will speed the recovery, though, and can help prevent reinfection. Ringworm fungus spores can live in the environment for over a year. Confine the affected kitten in one room that is easily cleaned with disinfectants like bleach solutions, to contain the household contamination.

Upper Respiratory Infections (URI)

Sometimes called "kitty colds," URI can make life miserable for adult cats and be potentially life-threatening to kittens. Rather than one virus, URI is caused by a complex of diseases. Most result from infection with feline herpesvirus 1, also called viral rhinotracheitis; from feline calicivirus; or from a combination of the two. A third agent, a primitive bacterium called chlamydia, or feline pneumonitis, can also be involved in some URI cases.

URI are extremely contagious, so close cat-to-cat contact in some shelters places these kittens at higher risk. Nose-to-nose kitty greetings, sneezing, and contact with contaminated bowls or litter boxes spread the disease. Chlamydia and rhino agents won't survive for long outside the cat's body, but calicivirus can survive for up to two weeks at room temperature in the environment.

Signs of URI can be any one or combination of a stuffy, gunky nose, sneezing, runny eyes, and eye or mouth sores. As a consequence of the stopped up nose or sore mouth, the cat typically refuses to eat—and that can cause the most danger to young kittens.

Like FPV, kitty colds are treated primarily with supportive care. Severe cases may require hospitalization. Your veterinarian may suggest that you provide necessary nursing care at home.

Simple nursing care of kittens sick with URI is the most important therapy. The baby must be tempted to eat if she is to recover, and almost always, an owner is best able to accomplish feeding the reluctant kitten. Nursing care includes keeping her eyes and nose clean of the crusty secretions. You can wet a cotton ball with warm water and gently soak and wipe them away.

Remember, kitten appetite is spurred by the smell of food, so if her nose is stuffy, she loses her appetite. Keep her nose clean to help her appetite return, and she'll recover more quickly.

(Photo credit: Amy D. Shojai)

Diseases like FeLV and upper respiratory infections can be transmitted via saliva. Grooming each other or nose-touch greetings can spread a variety of illnesses.

Tip: A humidifier can help the stuffed-up kitten breathe more easily. If you don't have a humidifier, try running hot water in the shower, and spend time in the steamy room with your kitten.

The illness rarely lasts longer than a week or so. However, kittens that get sick once can suffer recurrent episodes of URI, which typically flare up during times of stress, such as when boarding. Kittens with suppressed immune systems, as happens with FIV and FeLV, are more prone to URI. Highly effective vaccinations are available that will prevent kitten colds or reduce the severity of symptoms.

Vaccinations will keep kittens healthy and prevent many of these devastating diseases. These standard treatments protect not only the kitten, but also other cats in your home.

11

Ten Common
Emergencies and
What to Do

Accidents Happen

Kittens are accident-prone, fragile, and more likely than cats to become injured. The "Christopher Columbus" kitties, those with boundless energy and curiosity, are the most likely to get into trouble because of their desire to explore. Also, kittens learn by example and experience. They are innocents when it comes to many dangerous situations and simply don't know any better than to approach a strange animal, dart in front of a car, or fall into the hot tub.

Of course, preventing accidents is the best choice. But if the unthinkable happens, you can save your kitten's life by knowing emergency first aid. You should always follow up with professional veterinary treatment, as well. Here are some of the most common emergencies, and what you can do.

Animal Bites

Kitten teeth are like needles, and playing with the other furry babies can expose your youngster to bites. In nearly all cases, playful bites don't break the skin.

Worse bites come from adult cats, particularly those not willing to put up with the kitten's pestering antics. Adult cat teeth are also sharp and make puncture wounds that plant bacteria deep beneath

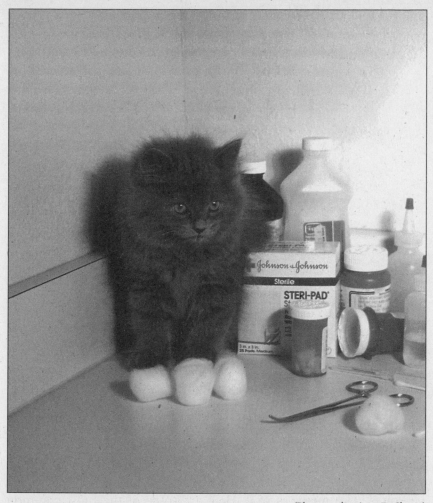

(*Photo credit: Amy D. Shojai*)

Keep first-aid supplies like cotton swabs, bandages, and antiseptics on hand. Squirt bottles work well to clean wounds. Hopefully, this blue baby won't ever need emergency attention.

the skin. Infection can result even when the bite looks minor. Without prompt treatment, a cat bite typically swells and gets hot when it becomes infected.

The most dangerous bites are from dogs. They may not look bad, because the entry wound can be small from the long fanglike canine teeth. But dogs tend to grab and then shake—tearing the muscle beneath the skin. Even worse, the kitten's internal organs can be bruised or punctured.

If your kitten is bitten, here's what to do:

1. Separate the animals by spraying water at them from the hose or tossing a blanket on top of them. That way you don't risk being bitten.

2. If the wound bleeds, put a soft, absorbent cloth like a towel or washcloth against the bite, and apply firm pressure.

3. When the kitten's abdomen gapes open from a bite, which can happen with dog-teeth tears, cover the area with a wet cloth, and hold in place by wrapping Saran wrap all the way around the body.

4. Severe bites may cause the baby to stop breathing. Administer artificial respiration described below, until you can get help.

5. Finally, bundle the kitten in a soft blanket or towel to keep her warm, and place her in an open box or carrier for the ride to the veterinarian's office.

Artificial Resuscitation

All kinds of kitten accidents may cause her to stop breathing. In these instances, you must immediately breathe for her and try to resuscitate your kitten, or she will die within three to five minutes. Rescue breathing can be performed on the way to the veterinary emergency room—kittens can and do survive life-threatening accidents when their people are able to provide rescue breathing. Here's what to do:

1. First, make sure the kitten has stopped breathing by feeling for warm air coming from her mouth and nose, and watching for the rise and fall of her chest. Pets that have stopped breathing will be unconscious and insensitive to your voice.

2. Cradle your kitten in your lap while another person drives the car to the emergency room. Straighten her neck by lifting the chin so her throat offers a straight shot into her lungs.

3. Mouth-to-mouth breathing won't work. Too much air escapes because you can't seal pet lips with your mouth. Use one hand to close your kitten's mouth.

4. Put your mouth completely over her nose and gently blow—imagine you're puffing breath to inflate a paper bag. Use your other hand to feel her lungs expand. Air will go directly through the nose and into her lungs when the mouth seals correctly. Don't blow too hard or you could hurt her—it doesn't take much breath to do the job.

5. Between breaths, let the air escape naturally out of her lungs before giving the next breath. Give ten to fifteen breaths a minute until she begins breathing on her own or you reach the veterinarian.

Tip: When other forms of resuscitation fail, try acupuncture. Needling the philtrum—the slit between the nose and the upper lip—releases natural adrenaline (epinephrine), a drug used by veterinarians to jump-start the stopped heart and breathing.

Insert a clean needle or pin deep into the slit at the halfway point between the nose and upper lip. Repeatedly move the needle in and out and rotate it while gently moving the head and neck of the kitten. Continue needling this point (technically called Governing Vessel 26 or GV26) in the car on the way to the emergency clinic. It may work immediately, or could take a while to see positive results. The veterinary literature reports that stillborn kittens given up for dead have been revived an hour after birth after using this technique for 20 to 35 minutes.

Car Accidents

When I worked in veterinary offices as a technician, we abbreviated "hit by car" to HBC. This kind of trauma can be deadly, and if the kitten is to survive, immediate veterinary emergency care is vital.

Being struck by a car can cause a wide range of damage, from broken bones and bleeding to internal injuries and an inability to breathe. Even if the kitten seems okay and walks away, problems can develop from shock or hidden damage within minutes to hours later.

Kittens are so tiny that it's nearly impossible to do anything for their broken legs—and a fractured leg is usually the least life-threatening of possible injuries. A spinal injury can be devastating, and it's hard to tell how extensive such an injury is without an exam. Here's what to do if your kitten loses a contest with a car:

1. When the kitten has stopped breathing, perform artificial resuscitation, as described in the previous section of this chapter.

2. Control bleeding by applying direct pressure, as described previously in "Animal Bites" on page 198.

3. It's important to transport the kitten to the emergency room as soon as possible—but you must move her very carefully to prevent more injuries. To do that, you should slide her—don't lift!—onto a solid, rigid surface. A rigid cookie sheet, bread-board, or even a coffee-table book will work. Place a towel across the kitten's body, and tape over the cloth behind her front legs and in front of the rear ones to hold her secure, so she won't move during transport.

If you have nothing else, use a towel or other length of material (perhaps a jacket?) spread on the ground beside the kitten, and slide her onto the fabric. Grasp the four corners, and use the material as a stretcher.

4. Have somebody call your veterinarian to warn her a HBC case will shortly arrive. Then drive to the emergency room.

Drowning

Kittens and cats instinctively know how to swim. But they run into trouble if they fall into water, can't get out, and become exhausted. Hot tubs, swimming pools, toilets or—for very small kittens—a water bowl can all cause drowning. You may find your pet floating in or near a body of water where she collapsed after dragging herself out.

Drowning causes suffocation—the kitten can't breathe—and

she'll quickly fall unconscious. You have a very short time in which to give first aid. When the water is very cold, you may have an extra few minutes to spare because the low temperature can slow body function and help prevent brain damage. Here's what to do if you suspect your kitten has drowned:

1. Grasp her by the hind legs and hang her upside down. Have a second person pat or thump her briskly on both sides of the chest for ten or fifteen seconds, and shake her a bit. That helps drain away water still in the mouth, windpipe, or lungs, and it may be enough to jump-start her breathing again. If it doesn't, begin rescue breathing, as described in the "Artificial Resuscitation" section of this chapter.

2. After two or three breaths, make sure her heart is beating by listening to her chest. If there's no heartbeat, start heart compressions (CPR or cardiopulmonary resuscitation). Cradle her chest in your right hand with your thumb over the left side behind her "elbow" (above the heart), and your fingers on the other side. Squeeze rhythmically to compress up to 50 percent. Alternate one or two chest compressions with ten to fifteen breaths a minute.

3. As soon as she starts breathing, dry her off and warm her up. Most pets drown in water colder than their body temperature. Wrap her in a dry towel and get her to the emergency room.

Falls

Kittens, like their adult counterparts, love to climb to high perches. And although they have a natural balance ability that allows them to land on their feet, kittens can still be hurt when they land. Falling from a relatively short distance, like from a toddler's arms, won't allow them time to get their feet under them. And falling from higher distances, like slipping off a shoulder, can break their fragile front legs. The worst falls, of course, are from higher distances, like the top of the stairs, from a balcony, or out an open window. Kittens injured from a fall may limp, hold up a leg, or refuse to move. If they crack their chin or head in the fall, a common occurrence, they may bleed from their mouth or ears, or act dizzy. Any of these symptoms need to be addressed by the veterinarian. Here are some first-aid treatments for falls before you go to the emergency room:

1. When the kitten has trouble moving or refuses to move, carefully slide her onto a rigid flat surface for transport in the car, as described above in "Car Accidents."

2. The blunt trauma can bruise or tear internal organs, even if there are no external signs of problems. That can cause life-threatening shock that can kill within fifteen or twenty minutes when the blood circulation starts to shut down. You can slow the progression of shock so you'll have more time to reach the clinic. Give your kitten a teaspoonful of Karo corn syrup or honey to lick—if she's unconscious, just rub a bit on her gums where it will be absorbed. Then wrap her in a blanket to keep her warm and get to the car.

Electrocution

Kittens love nothing so much as to hit and attack moving, swinging objects. Prime targets include lamp and computer cords, spiral telephone cords, and even the lights from holiday decorations. When the kitten's bite penetrates the electrical cord, she risks electrocution.

You'll know your kitten is in trouble if you find her unconscious near an electrical cord. Even if she remains alert, electrocution damages the internal organs. That causes the lungs to fill up with fluid and makes it hard to breathe. Often, the breathing and heartbeat stop. Here's what you should do:

1. Before anything else, shut off the power to that particular outlet. Often the electricity causes the pet to bite down even harder on the electrical cord and not let go. And you can get shocked if you touch a pet that's still in contact with the electricity. If you can't turn off the power, then try to knock the kitten

out of contact with the electrical source, using a nonconductive yardstick or the wooden handle of a broom.

2. Once it's safe to handle the baby, check her for breathing. If you hear gurgling sounds, turn her upside down by her hind legs (as in "Drowning") for ten to fifteen seconds to help clear the lungs.

3. If the kitten has stopped breathing, begin immediate artificial mouth-to-nose respiration, as described in "Artificial Resuscitation." Check for a heartbeat and begin CPR if necessary.

4. Wrap the baby in a warm towel and get to medical help as soon as possible.

Poisons

Kittens, like all babies, tend to put things in their mouths—even dangerous substances that can poison them. And cats and kittens are so sensitive, many otherwise "safe" substances for people or dogs are toxic to felines.

Swallowed Medicine

The most common kitten poisonings occur when human medicine is swallowed. That can happen accidentally when the baby plays with pills by batting them around and mouthing them. Other times, the wrong dose is given by mistake. All too often, human medicine like aspirin or Tylenol is given by the owner with the best of intentions, but both are very toxic to kittens.

- If you see your kitten swallow pills she shouldn't, or realize you've given the wrong dose, the best thing to do is to make her vomit. The easiest way to do this is with a squirt of 3 percent hydrogen peroxide (available at all drugstores) into the mouth. The bubbling action tastes nasty and prompts the kitten to empty her stomach. You can use an eyedropper and squirt about a teaspoonful into the kitten's mouth. If she doesn't vomit within five minutes, take her to the veterinarian where they have more effective methods for emptying the stomach.

- When you only suspect your kitten has eaten the wrong medicine, call your veterinarian before doing anything else. Describe the type of medicine, so she can best advise you. If the kitten vomits, take a sample along with the medicine to the doctor's office so they can analyze the poison and know what antidote to prescribe.

Fur Contamination

There are many toxic chemicals around the house. Many are found in household cleaners you store beneath the sink in your kitchen or bathroom. Kittens would never intentionally hurt themselves by drinking something that burns, but if they walk through a spill or a liquid splashes on them, they may swallow the poison when they lick themselves clean.

Most often, though, on-body poisons result when the wrong flea product—in the form of a shampoo, spray, or dip—is used on the kitten. Dog products, even if safe for puppies, are often toxic to small kittens. Here's what to do when kitty gets into something dangerous.

1. Wash the kitten under lukewarm running water for at least ten minutes. That not only flushes away the poison, but also dilutes the effects and prevents more from being absorbed by the skin. If the chemical burns, running water also stops the progression of skin damage and soothes the pain.

2. Wrap the kitten in a warm towel to prevent chills, and as she dries, call your veterinarian for advice. Depending on the toxin, the kitten may benefit from oxygen therapy or an antidote at the clinic.

Poisonous Plants

Kittens don't tend to indulge in recreational chewing quite as much as puppies and dogs do. But they can swallow poisons from plants when they claw the leaves and then lick off the toxin when grooming themselves. Depending on the plant, you should either offer the kitten water or milk to soothe the mouth or stomach irritation, or induce vomiting (as described previously). It's a good idea to contact your veterinarian or poison control center for specific instructions.

The American Veterinary Medical Association publishes information about pet poisons, including toxic plants, on their Web site at www.avma.org/pubhlth/poisgde.asp. You should also keep handy the telephone numbers of both your local and the ASPCA National Animal Poison Control Center. Consultations for NAPCC can be charged to a credit card by calling (800) 426-4435 or to a phone bill at (900) 680-0000, or you can visit their Web site at www.napcc.aspca.org.

COMMON PLANT POISONS CHART

POISON SOURCE	FIRST-AID
Azalea, daffodil, tulip, wisteria bulbs	Give lots of water or milk to wash stomach, dilute poison and coat stomach
Caladium, dieffenbachia, philodendron, Jerusalem cherry, potato (green parts and eyes), mother-in-law plant, nightshade	*Do not* induce vomiting, keep airway open, CPR if necessary, offer milk or water to wash out mouth
Crown of thorns, English ivy, chinaberry, foxglove, holly, larkspur, lily, lily of the valley, mistletoe, monkshood, morning glory, oleander, periwinkle	Induce vomiting

Heatstroke

Normal kitten body temperature ranges from about 100 to 102.5 degrees. Cats don't have an effective way to cool off when it's very hot. And when the outside temperature is the same as or warmer than their body temperature, they can overheat with devastating results. Usually, heatstroke occurs when the kitten has no access to shade, is trapped in a closed car in the sun, or has no cool water to drink. Kittens can also suffer heatstroke, as well as body trauma and head injuries, if they get shut in the hot clothes dryer.

A body temperature between 104 and 106 degrees, with bright red gums and tongue, sticky saliva, and panting indicate mild heatstroke. Body temperatures over 106 degrees are a symptom of severe heatstroke that can kill. The gums turn pale, the kitten acts weak or dizzy, and can develop a bloody nose and bloody vomiting or diarrhea. You must give immediate first aid to save the baby's life.

- For mild heatstroke, offer the kitten cool water to drink and put the baby in front of the air-conditioning or a fan. Usually, mild heatstroke victims recover pretty quickly when the outside temperature becomes lower than their body.
- Severe heatstroke requires an immediate cool (not cold!) water bath. Continue to monitor the kitten's body temperature until it falls to 106 degrees or below. Then get the kitten to the veterinarian for further treatment.

Hypothermia

Cold temperature can be as dangerous as hot weather. Adult cats that have full coats of fur are better able to protect themselves from cold, but very young kittens have trouble regulating their body temperature and keeping warm. As the body temperature falls, her breathing and heartbeat slow down, she shivers and acts sleepy. And with severe hypothermia, she can lose consciousness and die. Here's what to do to save your kitten's life.

- As long as the kitten is still shivering, her body will try to warm itself up. Simply wrap the baby up in a warm blanket and set her in front of the heat vent. You can offer her some warm chicken broth to help warm her up from the inside. If you're outside without access to warmth, put the kitten inside your clothes so your own body temperature warms her up.

- The shiver reflex stops when the body temperature drops too far. When this happens, you'll need veterinary help to warm up the baby. During the trip to the vet, keep her as warm as possible with a warm blanket and a hot water bottle wrapped in a towel cuddled to her tummy.

PART 4

KITTEN SOCIABILITY AND TRAINING

12

Making Sense of
Kitten Talk

Yes, kittens do have a language. When they are raised properly by Mom-cat, they learn all the intricacies of what I like to call "felinese." As they mature they can then communicate more clearly and understand other cats better. Proper feline communication helps them settle kitty disputes before they turn into wars.

Kittens talk to their special people, too. Misunderstandings often occur, however, because it takes a while for kittens to learn "human" language and for people to figure out felinese.

That's because people rely on verbal communication and mostly pay attention to the sounds their kitten makes. However, vocalizations are only one small part of the kitten vocabulary. The way things smell and the position of the body also speak volumes. In fact, people often "tell" their kittens something without meaning to, simply by the tone of their voice, the way they position their body, and even with certain odors they give off.

The human body is a chemical factory that produces all kinds of subtle scents that people rarely, if ever, notice. These odors send clear messages to our pets, because of their more sensitive noses. For example, when a person is startled or frightened, the body pumps out cortisol (a natural hormone) in greater amounts, which changes the way we smell. That's how dogs and cats often recognize an owner's emotional state, even when we "act" nonchalant.

You can learn to understand a good portion of felinese just by observing your kitten. Careful observation will help you understand your kitten better, anticipate his needs, and avoid misunderstand-ings.

This chapter covers some of the more universal aspects of kitten language. You must remember that every kitten develops his own individual communication quirks, similar to the way people from around the world talk with accents or in other languages, or use dif-ferent words to describe the same object. As you live with your kit-ten and pay attention to his voice and body language, you'll become more familiar with what kitty is trying to tell you.

Scent Communication

The sense of smell defines life for your kitten. An individual's scent is like a feline name tag that identifies her as friend or foe. Cats use scent information to determine sexual status, to communi-cate, to interact socially, and to identify territory. Scent is so impor-tant that it rules what the kitten eats. If he doesn't like the smell of his food, he won't eat it. To offer some perspective, people have 5 to 20 million scent-analyzing cells lining their nose. Your kitten has about 67 million. (The king of scenting pets, the Bloodhound, has 300 million.)

We don't have the sensory ability to truly understand the intrica-cies of the kitten's scent language. What we can do is recognize and understand the kitten behaviors that are prompted by scent. Mark-ing behavior is one of the most obvious.

Paws That Claw

Kittens have scent glands between their toes in the pads of their feet. When they scratch an object, they not only create visible marks, they also leave behind their personal scent. Just going through the motions of scratching has meaning. When cats want to signal dominance, they pointedly scratch objects in the presence of another cat (or dog) they want to impress.

Such paw-marking behavior doesn't rely on claws. Kittens that have been declawed will continue to go through the motions for the rest of their lives. The scented marks help establish territorial boundaries for kitty. He'll often claw or paw to leave his scent near doorways, his litter box, sleeping areas—any real estate that has particular importance to him. Basically, the scent posts a flag for other cats, letting them know this property is occupied and "owned" by another kitty.

Please remember that clawing is normal behavior for kittens and cats. It both feels good to them and serves as a communication tool. It is impossible to prevent your kitten from scratching. The best way to deal with kitten claws is to offer your new pet a "legal" claw target so he'll leave your valuables alone.

Bunting

The toes are only one place on the kitten's body that boasts scent glands. Kittens have these scent glands in the skin of the chin, lips, cheeks, forehead, and tail. The behavior of rubbing the head and body against people, other animals, and objects is called *bunting*.

Bunting spreads your kitten's signature odor upon whatever he rubs, and this "sharing of the scent" identifies family members and safe objects with familiar odor. Your kitten is paying you a huge compliment when he head-bumps you or rubs your ankles and twines his tail about your leg. He's marking you as part of his family, a favorite part of his territory or property. This specialized scent has a calming influence on the kitten.

Face rubbing is thought to be a subtle sign of deference, with the subordinate kitty approaching and bumping or rubbing against the more dominant pet or person. Nose touches and hip leans are considered by your kitten to be gestures of friendship. You may notice kitty cheek-rub as a greeting behavior, too, after you come home from work. He's not only sniffing your shoes or purse to "read" where you've been, but also bunts to freshen the "family scent" and so welcome you home.

Social grooming—that is, kittens grooming each other or even you—is also thought to figure into this mechanism of sharing familiar scent. You'll know your kitten considers you, the dog, or the other cats a true part of the family when he wants to clean you.

Urine Spray

Urine contains specialized scent particles called pheromones, which tells other cats the sexual status of the kitty that left the urine. Male and female cats crouch to urinate and release the urine over a flat surface—the litter box. When a cat wants to use the urine to mark territory, the posture is different. The spraying cat stands erect, backs up to the target, holds the tail straight up with just the tip quivering a bit, and releases the urine backwards against vertical surfaces like trees, stones, your wall, or your furniture.

Urine from an intact male cat has a particularly strong odor that can be hard to eliminate once it gets into carpet or upholstery. Territorial spraying is a sign of dominance and is used to mark territorial boundaries. It is normal behavior for sexually intact cats, especially males.

The pheromones in the urine announce to the other cats that King Tom rules this area, and the spraying helps suppress the sexual behavior of less dominant cats that venture into the territory. Intact females who spray tend to do so to announce their receptiveness to the feline Romeos in the area.

Most often, kittens won't start to spray until they are six to nine months old and reach sexual maturity. Neutering greatly reduces

---

Technical Stuff: Kittens have a second scent-detecting mechanism in addition to their nose. It's called the Jacobson's organ (or the vomeronasal organ) and is found above the roof of the mouth, between the palate and the nasal cavity. This organ is used primarily to detect pheromones, specialized scents generated by the animal body and used especially to communicate sexual information. Rather than sniffing scent particles up his nose, the kitten captures the scent on the tip of his tongue and transfers it to a duct behind his front teeth that communicates with the Jacobson's organ. Kittens make a distinctive sneering grimace called *flehmen* when they scent an odor with the Jacobson's organ.

the incidence of territorial spraying. However, altered cats of either sex may resort to spraying behavior when they feel insecure. Stress can prompt kitty to spread his own familiar, comforting scent around the room. In these instances, spraying acts as a kind of stress-buster for the bothered kitten.

Sounding Off—Vocalizations

Cats have long been regarded as mysterious, inscrutable creatures, but that's just because nobody bothered to figure out what they were saying. For the most part, the cat's vocal repertoire is tied to body language and serves as an expression of feline emotion. Kitty vocalizations are used alongside body language the way inflection is used in human speech to clarify the meaning of the words. Your kitten has the ability to make a wide range of sounds. He also can learn a large human vocabulary, especially when you use certain words with consistency.

It's important that you talk to your kitten. At first, he won't know what the words mean, but believe me, he'll understand the emotions in your voice. With time, he'll learn to associate certain words with specific actions. For instance, he'll learn that *food* means something yummy, and will run to his bowl when that word is mentioned.

Talking to your kitten does something else. Since kitten language is predominantly silent, talking helps tell your kitten he should pay attention to your voice. He'll learn that humans are vocal creatures, that communicating with us offers great rewards, such as a cuddle session or a treat. Those rewards will prompt him to make more effort to understand what you want, and try to communicate to you what he needs.

Me-wow

Once kitty recognizes how verbal people are, he may begin to vocalize more. In fact, kittens and cats almost never "meow" at each other. They have a huge range of other vocalizations they use amongst themselves. Meows seem to be reserved primarily for dealing with people.

Kittens often develop a repertoire of meows, each with a specific meaning, from soft and sweet, to long and drawn out yodels. Meows are a demand to the human for service: let me in, let me out, fill my bowl, pet me, play with me. As kitty becomes more passionate about his request, his demands become more strident and lower-pitched complaints.

Not all kittens are talkers. Some are quiet and barely heard, while others chatter all the time. Every kitten has his own distinctive voice. For instance, Siamese-heritage cats tend to be quite vocal, with penetrating meows, while the Chartreux is known to be a rather quiet breed that may chirp more than meow.

Experts have counted as many as sixteen distinct feline vocal patterns. They fall under four general categories: *murmur patterns* that include purrs and trills; *vowel patterns* describe the various meows (cats have command of several diphthongs, too); *articulated patterns* are sounds like chattering and chirps that express frustration; and *strained intensity patterns* are warning sounds like hisses and growls.

Trill of a Lifetime

The kitten trill is used to express happiness. Your kitten will likely use this type of vocalization as a greeting when you return home from work, perhaps mixed with meows.

Vocalizations like meows, trills, and purrs may be used to reduce the distance between the kitten and his target—you. They are solicitations for more contact and closer interaction.

Purr-sonal Satisfaction

The mother cat's purr serves as a vibration beacon that tells newborn kittens her location. Kittens begin to purr back an answer as early as two days of age. Purring can be nearly silent, or can rumble like a Mack truck, depending on the kitten.

Some behaviorists suspect purring may be a specifically kitten-

(Photo credit: Amy D. Shojai)

Meowing is aimed at humans as a demand to do something. Usually the meow becomes more strident and lower-pitched the more he complains.

like trait that adult cats retain, because they often indulge in kneading behavior at the same time. Kittens knead, or tread with the front paws, against Mom-cat's breasts to prompt her milk to flow as they nurse, and adult cats often retain this behavior.

People often consider purrs to be signs of contentment and expressions of affection, but cats and kittens rarely purr when they are alone. Purrs are aimed at other cats, or people, and are "the feline equivalent to a smile," says my colleague Gina Spadafori. I like that characterization a lot. After all, people smile for all kinds of reasons, and it doesn't necessarily mean we're happy.

Purrs rumble at all sorts of occasions, even when kitty is frightened or in pain. Some behaviorists suggest that the purr is a sign of submission that signals to the other cats and people that "I offer no threat" or "comfort me." That may be why the purr is used both in times of contentment to express joy and during times of stress to relieve tension.

It's interesting to note that only small cats have the ability to purr. "Big cats" like lions roar. Tigers have a kind of "silent" purr that is beyond the range of hearing and happens simultaneously with their roar. This low-frequency tiger sound has the power to briefly paralyze victims, so the big cat can have his way with them. Might the kitten's incessant purr have an ulterior motive, to hypnotize humans to do his will?

Cherish your purring kitten—nothing touches the emotions like cuddling a rumbling baby. The purr is a feline lullaby that soothes the singer as well as the listener's soul.

Technical Stuff: Experts still haven't nailed down the exact mechanism that creates the purr. Cats that lose their "meows" due to injury are often still able to purr, and there are several theories how the sound might be made. The most common explanation suggests that the false vocal cords, or vestibular folds, make the sound by rubbing together as air passes through as kitty breathes. Another theory points to the rapid contraction and relaxation of the muscles surrounding the voice box and diaphragm, which may produce turbulent airflow that makes the sound in the windpipe. The last explanation suggests that purring involves the turbulent flow of blood through a large vein in the cat's chest controlled by the muscle contractions of the diaphragm; the resulting vibrations are transmitted through the windpipe to the sinus cavities, which amplify the sound.

Chatterboxes

Cats produce chirping, chattering sounds out of excitement, frustration, and solicitation. These sounds, like meows, are demands but are rarely aimed at humans. Instead, they target the bird or the squirrel on the other side of the window that kitty can't reach. Your kitten may produce these types of sounds when he experiences situations beyond his control.

He sits in the window, watching, chittering, and chirping kitty curses at the strange critter crossing the yard. He demands that the creature *come* within reach, *hold* still to be captured, and *stop* teasing him.

My cat Seren's own special sounds of frustration are like a miniature lion coughing—*eh-eh-eh-eh*! Generally, she makes this ratcheting sound whenever she's thinking about doing something that she knows is illegal and will get her in trouble. She's frustrated because she knows she shouldn't give in to temptation, but she wants to sooooo badly. She gives herself away, tattles on herself. She'll also use this *eh-eh-eh-eh* as a solicitation when she knows a scrumptious treat is in the offing, as a way to try and speed up the delivery.

Warning: Kittens that are agitated and chattering about the presence of some critter they can't catch may decide to take their frustration out on a target they can reach—you. He won't mean to do it, but could lash out in reflex if you touch him when he's so wound up. You must pay attention to the context—why is he chattering? Second, read his other body language to figure out his state of mind. It's best to wait until your kitten has calmed down before trying to touch him, especially when his fur is fluffed and he's still hurling curses.

Growl Tiggers and Hissy Fits

Kittens can act like little spitfires. They hiss, spit, growl, and scream to show fear, aggression, warning, and imminent attack. While purrs, meows, and trills tend to be distance-reducing signals that invite you to come closer, a hiss, spit, growl, and scream are distance-increasing signals. Kitty means business and is telling you to stay away or suffer the consequences.

Kittens and cats spit when they are startled. You could call it a kind of feline gasp of fright. The hiss and growl usually indicate degrees of fear. Hissing means "stay away!" It is a warning. Some experts theorize the feline hiss evolved to sound like the universal warning made by snakes—humans and animals alike recognize the hiss's meaning.

Snarls—showing the teeth with or without sounds—and growls are used as defensive communication. The louder and more strident, the greater the emotion. Cats may be either frightened or aggressive when they use these signals. You must look to the body language to determine the cat's state of mind.

Our pet cats aren't able to roar like their big cat cousins. When terrified or enraged, especially during a fight with another cat, some cats do produce an extraordinary hair-curling scream.

Some types of feline verbal communication may be beyond our ability to hear. Cats can detect mouse squeaks at high frequencies far beyond human detection. Experts speculate that certain feline vocalizations may be so subtle, or so high in frequency, that only other cats hear them.

Cats evolved to have several types of communication and each has special advantages. Vocalization allows communication over long distances or when it's hard to see body signals—at night, for instance. But silent communication is safer, more intense, and can be sustained for longer periods. A hiss or growl can only last one breath at a time, but a silent stare, fluffed fur, or body posture can be held indefinitely. Body posture also allows communication between nearby individuals when a vocalization would alert dangerous predators. Finally, a scented note left on a prominent landmark—that is, urine spraying, clawing, or cheek scent—will last for hours to days, even without the cat's presence.

Kitten Body Language

Body language communicates both emotion and regulates social distance between individuals. How your kitten holds himself, his body position in relation to others, and the way he moves or holds his tail, ears, eyes, and fur either invite others to approach or warn them to keep away. By posturing in certain ways, your kitten signals that he's friendly or shy, aggressive or submissive, playful or fearful.

Don't rely on the position of any one part of the body to figure out what's going on inside his head. Kitten body language includes nose-to-tail signals. A wagging tail has different meanings depending on what the rest of the body is doing. Vocalizations, if any, must also be considered.

Eye of the Cat

Kittens use their eyes to communicate volumes. The position of kitty's eyelids and the dilation of the pupils indicate his mood. Droopy, sleepy-looking eyelids indicate trust in the kitten, and wide-open eyes are the sign of an alert pet.

A direct, unblinking stare is a sign of dominance, and is considered a challenge. When you stare with admiration at your kitten, be careful not to return eye contact for too long since it can incite some dominant kitties to attack.

On the other hand, a wide-eyed kitten that bumps your face with his cheek has given you a huge compliment. He's showing his trust by putting his open eyes in a vulnerable position.

Warning: Nearly any strong emotion—fear, pleasure, excitement, anger—can cause the cat's pupils to suddenly contract to slits. When the pupils dilate to saucer proportions, your kitten is scared to death.

Tip: Try sending your kitten a "blink-kiss." When he's acting sleepy and his eyelids are relaxed and at half-mast, make brief eye contact and then slowly blink at him from across the room. Kittens will often return this blink-kiss in answer. It's kitty language for acknowledging affection.

What Kitty Sees

Kitten eyes are designed very similarly to human eyes, but with the night hunter in mind. Proportionally, the cat has the largest eyes of any carnivore. If people had a similar face-to-eye ratio, our eyes would be eight inches across.

Cats require only one sixth the illumination level to see, compared to people. In other words, they see much better in dim lighting than we ever could, and that makes them virtuoso hunters after the sun goes down. They also benefit from a specialized layer of reflective cells, called the tapetum lucidum, located behind the retina in the eye. These cells reflect back light that enters the eye, and basically gives the cat's eyes a second chance to use the light. When the light escapes, you see the night glow that shines from the eyes.

The specialized construction of the cat's eyes allows the dark center portion, called the pupil, to open very wide to make the best use of light. In bright illumination, though, it's able to contract down into a fine slit, which also helps kitty focus.

Technical Stuff: Kitten near vision isn't nearly so sharp as in humans, but kittens have much greater binocular (depth) and peripheral (side) vision. Cats have 130 degrees of binocular vision and 155 degrees of peripheral vision, compared to human's 120 degrees of binocular and 90 degrees of peripheral vision. Cats are experts at detecting motion, especially out of the corners of their eyes.

Cat eyes have the "equipment" to see colors. Specialized cells called cones, located on the back of the eye in the retina, allow him to see differences between certain reds, greens, blues, and yellows. Other cells (rods) allow kitty to see shades of black, white, and gray. Cats don't seem to care one way or another about colors, though. Patterns, like the stripes of a neighbor cat, appear to be more important to the cat than color.

(Photo credit: Ralston Purina)

This fearful kitten shouts his distress with ear-talk. Sideways ears like little airplane wings are a sure sign of dismay and concern.

Early Ear Warnings

Ear position is a barometer of your kitten's emotions. Erect, forward-facing ears indicate interest. His ears remain erect but turn to the sides to show degrees of aggression. The more of the backs of the ears he shows, the greater is his agitation and threat to attack.

Fearfulness is measured by the degree to which the ears flatten to the kitten's head. The ears turn to the sides as he feels uneasy or threatened, and flatten tight to the head as fear or anger grows.

How Kitty Hears

The outside portion of the ear, called the pinna, is controlled by nine-teen separate muscles. That allows your kitten to swivel his ear 180 degress to catch all the interesting sounds in the world around him. The pinna acts as a kind of funnel to direct sounds down into the hearing portion of the ear.

Kittens are able to detect sounds beyond the range of human hearing. Kittens hear better than adult cats, and young adult cats hear better than older cats. A cat in his prime can hear the high-frequency squeaks of mice that are fifty to sixty kilohertz (people only hear five to twenty). With the aid of those swiveling ears, he can pin-point sounds that are only three inches apart up to three feet away.

Hearing is important if the kitten is to understand verbal communi-cation from other animals and from you. Some kittens are deaf, espe-cially white kitties with blue eyes, which may be born with an abnormality that results in gradual loss of hearing.

Deaf kittens can become wonderful pets and lead full lives. Some simple care considerations are necessary, though. Because the deaf kitten can't hear danger signals, he should be kept exclusively indoors, unless on a leash. His senses of sight and smell will become more important to him. You can help him keep track of you by always wearing a familiar perfume. He may not hear, but he can feel vibra-tion, so experiment with sounds. For instance, he might feel the vibra-tion of the floor when you stomp your foot or of the piano when you strike a chord on the lowest keys. You could turn that signal into a way to call him to supper.

Tail Talk

You can tell a great deal about your kitten by watching his tail "semaphore." Kittens greet Mom-cat (and you!) with happy erect tails held straight over their backs with just the end tipped over. It looks sort of like a finger waving hello.

Kittens show their frustration or irritation by flicking just the end of the tail. If these polite requests to stop whatever you're doing are ignored, the tail movement escalates to wags, lashing, or even tail thumps against the ground.

Warning: A wagging tail on a cat indicates agitation and basically means, "Go away, you bother me." The more vigorous the lashing, the more emphatic the warning. Ignore the cat's wagging tail at your peril—he's liable to smack you. When kitty is ready to attack, he keeps his tail low and close to the body.

A contented and relaxed kitten holds his tail curved down and up in a gentle U. The higher he holds his tail, the more interested he is. Bristled fur on the tail means either aggression, fear, or defensiveness, depending on how the tail is held. A straight tail with fluffed fur is aggressive; a bristled tail held in an inverted U (like the typical Halloween cat) shows fear.

Coat and Whisker Cues

A relaxed kitten's whiskers extend straight out from his muzzle. Interest causes whiskers to sweep forward, but when this is accompanied by erect ears turned sideways, kitty is signaling aggression and possible attack. A frightened cat's whiskers mirror his ears, and will slick back against his cheeks in the same way he flattens his ears.

Muscles in the skin adjacent to the hair roots will contract in an involuntary reaction to fear. This causes piloerection, which prompts the cat's fur to stand on end and turns the tail into a bottle brush.

Pet Postures

Mom always told me, posture counts. Holding your head up, shoulders back, and "pretending" to be confident even when you feel shivery inside gives an impression of confidence. Consequently, people treat you differently, as though you truly are in charge. That reinforces your mood, and your posture improves even more.

Cats use the same type of body language to communicate with other animals. An erect posture signals dominance because it demonstrates confidence. Confident kittens face the world head-on.

Less confident kittens and those who are shy turn sideways and present their profile to the other animal. A fearful kitten arches his back, and an involuntary reaction makes his fur stand on end. The classical sign of the self-inflated Halloween cat may look aggressive,

(Illustration: Wendy Christensen)

Here, the kitten shows all signs of aggression—but is it real? Sometimes kittens "pretend" to be upset and fluff their fur and act out in an exaggerated fashion as a type of play.

but actually he is scared to death. Cats may try to bluff their way out of such situations, with fluffed fur making them look bigger so they'll scare away their adversary.

If that doesn't work, kitty shows submission by trying to look smaller than he really is. In effect, he's saying, "I'm no threat, see how little I am?" as he crouches on the ground with ears slicked against his head, and tail and four feet tucked tightly beneath him.

Don't be fooled by the kitten rolling onto his back. In dogs, this is a sign of submission. In cats, it puts all four clawed paws at the ready and is a defensive position. Again, you must look for other body signals to interpret true meaning. Kittens that roll on their backs and present their tummies may also be soliciting play. Watch the ears and the tail talk to determine if your kitten is fearful or aggressive when she rolls (ears slicked back, tail lashing, hissing or growling) or is playful (ears forward and meowing or trilling).

One obvious signal that solicits play and attention is the lordosis position—what I call the "elevator butt" pose. Kitty lowers his front end to the ground and sticks his tail up in the air as high as possible. This is very similar to the "play bow" that dogs use to invite a game. Seren does this to invite a friendly scratch at the base of her tail. Lordosis position is also the invitation that intact female cats use to signal they are ready for romance.

Kittens often use exaggerated signals, almost caricatures of aggressive or fearful communication, to invite play. For instance, the kitten may stand on his toes, turn sideways and fluff his fur like a Halloween kitty, then prance and tippy-toe sideways, just to get you to chase him. You must always take into account the context of your kitten's behavior to understand what he's trying to tell you.

(Illustration: Wendy Christensen)

In this case, kitty wants to play. Note the forward-facing ears and whiskers.

Tip: Kittens communicate affection and trust by sharing close proximity with others. Declarations of love and devotion include sleeping or eating together, mutual grooming, and playing together. Sleeping in your presence, especially with his back to you, is the ultimate sign of trust.

13

GAMES KITTENS PLAY

The Health and Play Connection

Play is a normal function of kitten life. Babies begin playing as early as two to three weeks of age, and cat play continues for the rest of her life. It's fun for the kitten and entertaining for people. It's healthy both physically and emotionally.

Historically, kitten play has been considered an instinctual method to "practice" for adult life issues, such as hunting. Adult pet cats that played were thought to act out these behaviors as a substitute for frustrated hunting activities. That seems simplistic, though, and falls short of the whole answer when you consider that many adult animals in the wild continue to play.

Play does, in fact, help the kittens hone various skills by practicing use of tooth and claw, chase and pounce. More than that, play teaches them how to react to the world around them. The kitten learns that patting a leaf makes it move, that biting her brother prompts a squeal and retaliation, and that she can bunny-kick a toy into submission. Play activity teaches kittens limits on what they can do, and how their actions and reactions affect the world around them.

Play also serves as a natural body-building exercise. A kitten's brain is almost fully mature at five weeks, but physical and motor development takes longer. Practice sharpens dexterity, builds physical prowess and skill, and keeps muscles toned and the mind engaged. Play is a great stress-buster for kittens and adults alike. It builds trust and reinforces social ties among individuals, and encourages loving relationships. Play can boost confidence in shy kittens and reduce obnoxious aggression in bullies. Most important of all, play is fun.

(Photo credit: Amy D. Shojai)

Kittens use their paws to reach out and "test" an object in play behavior to see how it feels and moves. They can learn to keep claws sheathed when playing with siblings—and humans.

When Is Kitty an Adult?

Kitten breeds tend to develop at different rates, with some—like Siamese-heritage—maturing earlier than others. Your kitten may look quite mature by the time she's six to nine months old. In fact, your pet won't "officially" be an adult until her one-year birthday. Even when she looks grown up on the outside, she's still maturing on the inside.

Sexual maturity and the ability to reproduce often arrive before full physical maturity. Certain breeds of cats may not develop their full hair coat or true eye color until they are two years old or older.

One sign of maturity is a decline in kitten play. Some cats continue to enjoy games all their lives, but most don't indulge in play nearly so often once they become adults. You can expect kitten play to peak at about three months of age, and then begin to decline. The kitten's behavior and attitude at age nine to twelve months is a good predictor of how she will play as an adult.

Adults typically fall into two broad categories: lap-sitters and ankle-rubbers. The lap-sitters tend to like snuggling and are more sedate, quiet cats. Ankle-rubbers are energetic, playful kitties.

A one-year-old kitten is equivalent in age to a human adolescent—about fifteen years. The second year brings kitty to her late teens or early twenties, depending on the cat. Each year thereafter is roughly equivalent to four years of a human's age. Today, it's not unusual for a well-cared-for kitten to live well into her late teens or even early twenties.

Social maturity develops even more slowly than physical maturity. Cats reach social maturity between two to four years of age. Prior to that time, the young cat may get along well with other felines in the house. At the two- to four-year mark, sometimes the youngster decides to test her social standing and move up in the world, and some behavior problems and squabbles may arise.

Kitten Games

Kittens are incredibly inventive when it comes to play. The intensity of kitten play escalates from four weeks on, peaks between nine and fourteen weeks of age, and then slowly declines as the kitten matures. The first play your kitten indulges in is self-play, when she lies on her back and plays with and bites her own feet and tail.

> **Technical Stuff:** Play behavior can be categorized as loco-motory, social, and object play. Locomotory play includes run-ning, jumping, rolling, and climbing; it can be done solo or can involve two or more kittens. Social play is interactive and includes wrestling and biting, pouncing, play-fighting, and tag. Object play means the kitten targets an interesting object, like a grasshopper or feather.

There are different styles of play, which can vary depending on the breed. For example, the Somali and Rex breeds are athletes who enjoy chase and climbing games, Siamese-heritage cats love to fetch, and Persians play more quiet, sedate games. Your kitten will have her own play foibles and will invent her own games along the way.

For instance, Seren and I have a couple of favorite games, in-cluding a combination of hide-and-seek and tag. I search for her, calling "Where's Seren?" as I go. When I get near her hiding place, she streaks out from beneath the bed (or other hidey-hole), bops me on the leg with both paws, and races away to hide again. She also uses this "hit-and-run" technique to invite me to play or pay atten-tion to her.

Warning: Kittens love to chase and capture objects that can be bitten. Toys are fine, but fingers and hands should be off-limits. Sure, those wiggling fingers are tempting to the baby. When she's tiny, she may not be strong enough to hurt you. Kittens grow, though, and their teeth and claws become very sharp. It's not fair to punish her if she plays too rough and draws blood, when you've en-couraged the habit. A cute habit in a kitten can become dangerous as she matures to adulthood, especially if she targets a child.

Wrestle and Box

Play-fighting is great fun for kittens. It burns up a great deal of energy, and also teaches the babies how to safely inhibit their bite and claws. During play, kittens take turns being the "underdog" kit-ten. They'll grapple each other, roll around on the floor, and bunny-kick each other for all they're worth. They rear up on their hind legs and use their paws to box each other, or to capture each other's tails. When the kitten play-bites the back of another kitten's neck, she's practicing the killing bite that adult cats use to dispatch prey.

Your kitten may turn into a fountain of kitty youth for your adult cat, too. Adults often enjoy playing with kittens, and an old-fogey resident cat may show new interest in play when Junior shows up. Just be sure to introduce them correctly, so that the play-fighting remains play, and doesn't turn into a war.

Social play won't be as common among adult cats. Unless they know each other very well, the play can easily escalate into a real fight. Cats who know each other are able to communicate their intention to play, and know it's only "pretend" and not real aggression.

Tag and Chase

A favorite kitten game is anything that involves racing around. Kittens will even "pretend" that something big and scary is chasing them, and dash around the room or up the cat tree. When they play tag and chase with each other, kittens often take turns being "it." As soon as the pursuer catches up with the target-kitten, they may wrestle a bit before switching roles.

Kittens and many adult cats indulge in what owners often call "the five o'clock crazies" or "zooming." Cats evolved to hunt in bursts of activity. When they are home alone all day, pent-up energy often becomes more than they can control. By the time you return home after an absence of several hours, it won't take much to trigger a burst of extravagant play. Often the kitten "zooms" around, racing up and down stairs and running laps around the house.

Mouse Pounce

Object play is often carried into adulthood. Kittens enjoy pawing, stalking, biting, and "capturing" objects. Bugs like crickets and butterflies are fair game, but kittens even treat rolling pencils and stuffed toys as though they are alive. Kittens may even play with "objects" that are invisible to us.

> **Kitten Purrs:** A wide range of fun, interactive toys are available from Ethical Products that allow your kitten the excitement of chasing "big game" without the risk. Toys include a battery-powered "mouse" that scampers around the room. Another favorite that tickles the cat's fancy is the ChipRunner, a battery-powered chipmunk enclosed inside a plastic ball that rolls around the room. These and other creative toys are available at pet supply outlets.

The pounce requires leaping skills, so kittens often practice jumping until they look like furry balls bouncing around the room. They prepare for pouncing by hiding in some hidey-hole, and then leaping out on the unsuspecting victim.

Stalking precedes the pounce. The kitten crouches low to the ground and creeps forward one paw-step at a time. When she's ready to make her move and pounce, she may signal the action by treading back and forth on her hind legs—almost as if she's revving her engines. She springs forward, and her front paws land smack-dab on top of the target, be it a feather or mouse, or your ankles.

Fish Scoop

Kittens use their paws not only to pat-test objects, but also like little hands to scoop up objects during play. This technique must have been developed eons ago when cats discovered tasty fish, and figured out a way to get them out of that obnoxious wet stuff.

Kittens (and adult cats) seem fascinated by holes. They love to peer into these hiding places and stick their paws inside to feel around, and perhaps scoop out a prize.

You can tempt your kitten into a game by intriguing her with objects that "disappear" before her eyes. Drop a wad of paper or foil into an empty tissue box, and watch her try to fish it out. My cat Seren often carries one of her sparkly fuzzy toys and drops it inside a shoe, and then has great fun fishing it out.

Another favorite game Seren still enjoys is the "disappearing ribbon." Hide one end of the ribbon, yarn, or even a long feather beneath a pillow or other object, then slowly draw the toy out of sight. As it disappears, your kitten is likely to pounce on the end, and fish underneath the pillow to try to capture the elusive prey.

Kitten Ballet

Kittens learn to invite others to play with exaggerated body language. For instance, they may roll about on the floor, presenting their tummy (and four paws full of claws!) to invite a wrestling match. They'll also rise up high on their tippy-toes and shuffle sideways to dance around other kittens.

That, of course, is a defensive posture used by adult cats. When kitty "pretends" to be fearful or fearsome, she overacts. Kittens that get very excited may self-inflate their fur, like the scared Halloween cat. You'll know the difference between play and real life by paying attention to the situation and the kitten's vocalizations. When hisses and growls erupt, playtime is over. Other kittens and cats recognize these signals as mock-aggression and react accordingly, joining in the game.

Besides the sideways sidle, kitten ballet includes graceful (and not-so-graceful) vertical leaps. The kitten may jump straight up in the air, spin and pirouette, chase her tail, and finish with an acrobatic dash up the drapes.

Ties That Bind—Play as a Bonding and Training Tool

Kittens look on humans as surrogate parents. To your kitten, you are the Mom-cat figure because all the food, attention, and fun stuff comes directly from you. It's up to you to provide guidance, promote good behaviors, and improve or correct negative habits before they become problems. Playing with your kitten can be a powerful bonding and training tool.

Make a point to play with your kitten for at least twenty minutes,

(Photo credit: Ralston Purina Company)

Kittens play all kinds of games, even vaulting over each other.

twice a day. Longer and more frequent play periods are even better. This helps exercise her body so she wears out and is less likely to find trouble. It also engages her kitty brain—create puzzles for her to solve to keep her interested. For instance, show her a treat, hide it beneath a scarf, and then encourage her to find it.

Playing such games increases the bond your kitten feels with you. When kitty is shy, it can build her confidence and help her become a more even-tempered pet. A stuffed toy she can bite and bunny-kick, or a ribbon toy she can chase and capture—what a brave kitten!—offer positive results. These games are self-rewarding. She wins and has fun at the same time. When dealing with a very shy kitten, like a feral baby that fears getting close to people, you can still interact from a distance with a fishing pole style toy. She'll learn that proximity to people can be pleasant and rewarding.

Rambunctious kittens and those who have developed poor bite and claw habits can learn through play to temper these behaviors. Such play also gives them a "legal" outlet to go crazy and be wild kitties. Play is a particularly effective training tool that can be used as a reward for good behavior, or as a lure to prompt kitty to do the right thing. Remember, the best way to alter an unacceptable behavior is to offer your kitten a better alternative. Taking away the poor target—your fingers, for example—leaves a void that kitty will fill with something else that's potentially just as objectionable—like your ankles. Kittens love to bite and claw, so give her a toy that allows her to indulge in this normal kitten behavior.

Kitten Purrs: PetsMart and Hasbro, Inc., have collaborated to create the Paws 'n More toy line for the developmental needs of puppies and kittens. More than twenty pet toys and accessories help young pets learn through play, promote health with physical activity, and help socialize the youngster. Highlights in the kitten line include the Nip 'n Tug Kitty Koosh, a version with a toy mouse, bells, and even a handy pocket that can be filled with catnip. The Catch-A-Fish Mobile For Cats keeps kittens active with spinning fabric fish. The complete Hasbro Paws 'n More line of pet care products and toys is available at PetsMart stores nationwide, and on-line at www.petsmart.com.

Five Unique Kitty Abilities

Kittens display a wide range of extraordinary physical prowess during their play. It can be exhausting just to watch them. We marvel at their flexibility, speed, and sense of balance. Here's how they do what they do.

PRETZEL KITTEN

Cats and kittens have incredibly elastic bodies, because their spines are held together with muscles instead of ligaments, as in people. Your kitten also has five more vertebrae in her back than you do. The combination of muscles and extra bones allows kitty to bend her body up to 180 degrees.

TREE-HUGGERS

The kitten's shoulder blades are on her side, not on her back like ours. She also has a unique shoulder joint attached to the chest by muscles, not by the collarbone. That's why kitty can turn her forelegs in nearly any direction. That not only gives her a longer stride when running, but also offers the ability to grab around trees and climb them. Her claws allow her to hang on and scramble upward. Kittens that climb too high may cry for you to rescue them because they don't want to back down the tree. Claws curve in the wrong direction to make face-first descents easy.

FAST TRACK

Adult cats can run up to thirty-one miles per hour. Kitty's tail acts like a counterbalance and helps her make quick turns at high speeds. Cats can run up trees as fast as they race along the ground. Teach your kitten to come when called—now—because when she grows up, there will be no catching her.

LEAPIN' KITTEN

Cats are able to jump five times their height from a standing position. They come down in stages, though, by "walking" or jumping halfway down the tree or refrigerator, and then pushing off to leap to the floor.

UNCANNY BALANCE

The kitten's balance is maintained by an organ deep inside her ears called the vestibular apparatus. Her flexibility, vision, and motion control combine with this sense of balance to allow the cat to fall on her feet. She uses a series of spine, shoulder, and flank contractions to twist in midair and land kitty-correct.

Technical Stuff: Inside the cat's ears are three small fluid-filled structures called the utricle, saccule, and semicircular canals. They are lined with microscopic hairs, and the utricle and saccule contain chalklike substances that float in the liquid. Each time the kitten moves her head, the fluid and the chalk move against the sensitive hairs, and tell the brain about the body position and speed of movement.

Warning: Falls from a short distance—such as from the arms of a child—may not allow enough time for the righting mechanism to work. Kittens often sustain dangerous injuries from falls when they aren't able to land correctly, or when the distance is so great that they can't avoid being hurt.

14

KITTENS *ARE* TRAINABLE!

The subject of kitten and cat training is one of my favorites, because I love to see amazement bloom on skeptical faces. The old saw that "cats are aloof, independent, and untrainable" is a myth. It's not only simplistic, it's insulting, as well. It paints the entire feline species with the same inaccurate brush, making them one "type" rather than the myriad fascinating individuals we know them to be.

I often travel around the country to give kitten and cat training demonstrations at adoption events. Typically, a kitten or adult cat from a shelter serves as the demo-kitty, and boy do these felines wow the crowd! Kittens and cats that have never before seen a leash strut their stuff for television cameras, they sit up and wave at the audience, and they give owners with "problem cats" renewed hope that with simple training methods, a damaged bond can be healed.

C.A.T. (Cat Attitude Training)

Over the years, I've developed a kitten and cat training program called C.A.T., which stands for *Cat Attitude Training*. Although I've described aspects of this program in my regular pet-care column and demonstrated some techniques to the public as the national spokesperson on the Purina Cat Chow Way of Life Tour, the description of the entire C.A.T. program that follows represents its first appearance in print, in its entirety. In my experience, the C.A.T. program usually

shows results after only a limited time spent with the cat. That's because the demo-kitties I select are chosen for their curiosity and aptitude for learning. Used correctly, though, C.A.T. can improve the
behavior of any kitten or cat. Just imagine what you can achieve with
your kitten during a lifetime together.

People tend to think of cat training in the same terms as obedi-
ence-training a dog to "heel" and "sit" or do tricks. Certainly, your
kitten can be trained to perform these activities, and I'll address that
later in this chapter. More important, however, training your kitten
teaches him what you expect in terms of behavior. It prepares him
for life with people, prevents normal behaviors from turning into
problems, and rewards both you and your kitten with a stress-free,
loving relationship.

Think of kitten training as life insurance for him, and love insurance for you. Training your kitten to do the right thing preserves
your bond, and keeps him from losing his home and life.

Kitten Preschool—How Kitty Learns

All cats can be trained, but frankly, the younger they are, the
faster they learn. Kittenhood is the ideal time to begin your baby's
education.

Kittens learn from the moment they're born. Mom teaches them
by example how to wash themselves and use the litter box. They
may learn to fear children, for instance, if Mom-cat reacts unfavor-
ably to them.

Learning can be categorized in a couple of different ways. *Classical conditioning* forms an association between an outside event, like
running the water in the sink, and a reaction, such as a bath. Depending on the reaction, the kitten associates the event with a pleasant or unpleasant experience and behaves accordingly. *Operant
conditioning* deals with relationships among stimuli, responses, and
consequences. The kitten learns that what he does is critical to what
happens next. For instance, he receives a treat for a "good" behavior,
like scratching the cat tree.

Kittens behave in certain ways because the action is self-rewarding. It feels good to scratch or go to the bathroom as soon as the

(Photo credit: Amy D. Shojai)

Kittens can't read your mind, and won't know that a tabletop is off limits unless you tell them. They love high places, so these kittens are just doing what comes naturally.

urge strikes. Trial and error lessons are the most powerful because they self-train the kitten when the action (patting the cricket) rewards the behavior (the cricket jumps—what fun!).

In the same way, kittens learn that biting Mom-cat's tail prompts a scary *Sssssttt!* and an end to the game. That's no fun at all. When they play nice, though, they are rewarded with Mom's fun interaction and a cuddle or grooming session.

The key to successful kitten training is to figure out what motivates your kitten to do what he does, and use that to elicit the response you want. In effect, kitten training fools the kitten into believing it was all his idea. You'll need a good understanding of kitten language, social structure, and behavior to create effective kitten motivations. Kittens are insatiable when it comes to learning. In most instances, they need to be instructed only once or twice to understand what you want.

Warning: Kittens use some of these same training techniques on you. For instance, when your kitten wants to be fed, he creates a stimulus (meowing incessantly) to motivate you to feed him. When you give in and feed him, he stops meowing—that rewards you and reinforces the training. Of course, when you give in and offer kitty food, you've also rewarded him for meowing.

Socialization and Bonding Benefits

I've talked a lot about bonding in this book. It bears repeating here, because proper training can enhance that bond, while inappropriate training techniques cause the opposite effect.

Socialization affects your kitten on the most basic level. It refers to the sensitive period in your kitten's development when he learns from positive and negative events. The prime socialization period for kittens falls between two to seven weeks of age; however, socialization continues through twelve to sixteen weeks.

Early experiences during this "window" teach him to tell the difference between safe and positive events, and scary and dangerous ones. Kittens that are well socialized to other pets, people, and places—that is, exposed to positive interactions with them—learn that people, pets, and new places are nothing to fear. Socialized kittens become more confident, well-adjusted babies who grow into well-adjusted adults. At its most basic level, that's what C.A.T. training is all about.

Conversely, kittens that experience negative, scary interactions—or no contact at all—with humans and other animals have a more difficult time adjusting to them. For instance, if Mom-cat fears dogs and teaches her babies by example, or a kitten is frightened by a dog during this period, the baby will be reluctant to accept dogs when he grows up. Feral kittens that never interact with humans during this important period become terrified of people.

Just as children learn the three "R's" when they go to school, your kitten's socialization relies on the three T's: Touching, Talking, and Timing.

Tip: Feral kittens that fear close contact may still benefit from "touch" therapy using a surrogate hand—like a pencil or the end of a long wooden spoon. This keeps your hands safe, but introduces pleasant touch to the frightened baby by gently stroking him from a distance. Build up his tolerance a little bit at a time before introducing him to your hands.

Touching the baby in a positive manner reminds him of Mom-cat's grooming. It feels good, and teaches him that your hands are extensions of you. Touching and petting your kitten should be a rewarding experience for him.

Talking to your kitten helps him learn that your words are important to his happiness. The more he pays attention to what you say, the quicker he'll learn to understand and anticipate what you want.

Timing has to do with promptly interrupting unacceptable behaviors, and immediately rewarding good behaviors. More about that later in this chapter under "Kitty Delights" (rewards that work), and in chapter 15 under "Effective Kitten Corrections."

Kitten training is simply an extension of the socialization process. The earlier kittens experience positive interactions with training, the more readily they will respond and embrace these concepts. Training should always be positive, so that kittens look forward to it and embrace the notion because it rewards them for doing so.

Kittens can be trained at any age, and even adult cats benefit from training. They learn more readily, though, the younger they are. Don't wait to begin training your kitten. Start as soon as you bring him home, and the positive benefits will last a lifetime.

The Kitten-People Partnership

Those of us who love kittens were not surprised when the medical community finally ackowledged what we've known all along—kittens are good for our health. Several specific studies measured the health of pet owners compared to people who don't have pets.

They concluded, among other things, that people suffering from heart disease survive longer if they have a pet; and simply stroking your kitten can reduce stress, lower blood pressure, and help prevent stress-related illness. Older people who have cats are emotionally and physically healthier because the pet keeps them more "connected" to life. They make the extra effort to provide food and litter for their furry companion, when they might otherwise neglect a trip to the grocery store. That means these folks don't need to see the doctor as often, and when they do, they don't need as much medicine and they recover more quickly.

Also cats and kittens are now involved in animal service fields. In animal-assisted therapy some extraordinary kittens have learned to act as ears for their hearing impaired human partners, or to warn seizure- and migraine-prone partners of impending attacks. In most instances, these skills cannot be trained; they are possible only because of the close and loving bond developed between the person and the individual cat. Since the 1980s, pets' participation in a wide variety of animal-assisted therapies have made pets frequent visitors to hospitals and nursing homes.

Rules for Humans

When training kittens, consistency must rule, or else! Don't allow your kitten on the countertop one day and chastise him for it the next. First of all, it's not fair to him to change the rules in the middle of the game. Also, inconsistency sabotages any training progress you've made. Kittens learn very quickly, and a single lapse in enforcing the rules will tell your kitten that "sometimes" he can get away with disobeying. He'll take that to heart, believe me.

Therefore, before you start a training program, it is vital to get your whole family together and decide on the rules of the house. Kittens are just like children. If they know that "Mom" will let them get away with something but "Dad" is strict, they'll simply modify their behavior accordingly.

Here's an example from my experience with my cat Seren. We have wooden blinds on our windows rather than drapes, and as a kitten, Seren quickly learned to sit on the tabletop and stick her head through the slats to peer out. She caused a great rattling noise that sounded as if the blinds were crashing to the ground. Each time she rattled the blinds, my husband leaped up to chase her away—and voila! A new kitten game was born. Today, she still paw-rattles the blinds when she wants his attention. She doesn't do it when I'm home alone—she knows it won't work with me.

Patience Is Key

Don't expect to wave a magic wand and produce a trained kitten. Kittens love the status quo, and any change to their routine must be made in a gradual manner if they are to accept it. So training demands patience.

After all, you are dealing with a baby. Babies make mistakes. Mistakes are part of the learning process—kittens learn through trial and error. Frankly, so do people. So have patience with your new kitten, and patience with yourself. Give yourself permission to experiment and figure out what works best in your situation.

Remember, there is a communication gap between you and your kitten. Both of you are learning each other's language. Misunderstandings are inevitable, but you can reduce these setbacks by paying attention to how your kitten reacts to you. Every kitten is different. What works for one kitten may be the wrong approach for another.

Tip: A time-out works wonders for soothing upset feelings. I'm talking about your feelings as well as your kitten's. Training requires a calm temper. Anger won't get you anywhere, and losing control of yourself can actually backfire. To be effective, training must be positive and fun for the kitten. Scaring him by getting aggravated or angry may even cause some backsliding. So when you feel tempers flare, give yourselves a break. Give the baby a time-out in his own room. Meanwhile, you might take a walk, or count to ten.

Effective "Kitten Talk"

What you say is not nearly so important as how you say it. Certainly, one of the most important words your kitten should learn is *no*. More important, however, is learning his name—and you certainly don't want him to hear *no* so often that he confuses the two.

I encourage you to talk to your kitten on a routine basis. Use your normal tone of voice, and intersperse the kitten's name in your conversation. The key here is for him to associate his name with only positive, good things. "*Cleo*, what a *smart, lovely* kitten you are! *Cleo*, you make me so *proud* when you claw your cat tree, what a smart *Cleo*!"

Conversely, when you need to interrupt bad behavior or communicate your displeasure, avoid using his name. Choose words he can't mistake for anything else. Short, percussive words work best. You can even use made-up words and assign meanings to them, perhaps creating a "No!" word that gets the kitten's attention more readily. Just be consistent, so he's not confused.

One of the most effective word-interruptions for young kittens is a short, percussive *Ssssstt!* that sounds like Mom-cat hissing to discipline a kitten. Don't overuse the hiss, or it will lose effectiveness. Reserve it for truly serious corrections, such as biting.

It doesn't matter that he won't understand all the words. Believe me, he will understand the pleased tone of your voice, and the affection. Conversely, he'll recognize annoyance and disappointment. He'll also pay close attention to the expression on your face and to your body position, so be aware of what you're telling him. Mixed signals—saying *no* or hissing while smiling or laughing at his antics—dilutes your message and confuses him.

Kittens communicate with both vocalizations and body language. Whether you mean to or not, your facial expressions and body positions tell kitty all sorts of things. For the most effective kitten talk, especially when communicating something you want kitty to do, talk in the language he understands. Stand tall and face toward him to communicate confidence. Kittens react more readily to higher-pitched voices, but forget about Minnie Mouse impressions. When kitty doesn't pay attention, make your request more emphatic by lowering the pitch of your voice, the same way kitty does with his meow-demands.

Warning: Angry shouting won't teach your kitten anything except to be afraid of you and avoid you. In cat society, felines routinely bluff each other by making lots of noise and growling and hissing at each other—he'll think you're playing that game. His answer will likely be to run and hide, the cat version of crying uncle. Yelling won't teach him what he's done wrong, only that you sometimes go nuts and make lots of noise.

Timing Is Everything

Kittens learn using the three T's. We've already covered touching and talking. Timing is equally important, for several reasons. First, kittens have the attention span of a four-year-old child. They are oh-so-bright, and absorb information very quickly, but they are also easily distracted.

Create a routine that your kitten can anticipate and look forward to. Routine is comforting to kittens and cats. Even if the exercise is new, kitty will feel most comfortable when trained in the same place and at the same time each day.

Keep training sessions brief, no more than five to ten minutes for kittens younger than twelve weeks old, and up to fifteen minutes for older kittens. Several short sessions throughout the day are much more effective than one marathon session.

Tip: Finish each training session on a positive note. You want the kitten to have fun, not be stressed or worn out from failure. A great technique is to begin and end each training session with a favorite game, particularly if what you're teaching is new or challenging to the baby.

Timing is even more important when correcting misbehavior. That's because kittens have a memory for infractions that lasts about sixty seconds. If kitty has an accident outside the litter box, he'll only remember what he's done for a brief time. Corrections that take place too long after the infraction *do not work*. Kitty won't be able to associate your upset with the mess he made unless he is literally caught in the act. If you come home and find claw marks on your new sofa, there is no way to effectively tell the cat he made a mistake.

It is vital that any correction be timed to coincide with the inappropriate behavior. A simultaneous correction is best. Catch him in the act, or within sixty seconds of the infraction, so he associates the "wrong" behavior with the correction. That's the only way he'll learn that the misdeed results in an unpleasant consequence, and so know to avoid it.

Warning: Effective correction interrupts the behavior or takes place immediately after (within sixty seconds) the behavior. By contrast, punishment is a way to get back at the kitten, to avenge the behavior. Please, get rid of the punish idea altogether! Granted, it may help vent your anger in the short term, but it causes long-term damage to any relationship with the kitten. Revenge has no place in kitten training, or in training any pet, for that matter. Kittens associate punishment with your presence—and learn to fear you. For more about effective and humane kitty corrections, turn to chapter 15.

Effective Training Tools

In the world of dog training, negative or coercive training techniques work to a degree because the dog is usually such a generous, forgiving soul. He'll wag his tail and cower, but then lick the hand that slapped or shoved him into position, and come back for a belly rub. Of course, professional dog trainers know that positive training is much more effective.

Cats, on the other paw, are not as forgiving as dogs. Corporal punishment never works. It simply makes your kitten fear your hands or other objects, and avoid interaction with you.

Dogs can often be physically moved into the position you want—for instance, pushed and pulled into a "sit" or a "down" posture. Cats resist being "managed" in this way and are better lured into position, so that it seems to be their idea. They learn much quicker this way, too, because the body action comes from their brain, not from you tugging them this way and that. Bribes are legal in kitten training. Find out what kind of lure tempts your kitten and reserve that for his training sessions.

A range of training tools is available. The best provide a positive benefit to the kitten by either triggering the desired behavior or rewarding the performance. The most effective training tool for your kitten, though, depends on his individual preference. A one-size-fits-all approach doesn't work. In general, you need to fit the tool to the individual kitten's personality. Find out what floats your cat's boat, and use that.

Kitten Purrs: Clicker training, popularized by Karen Pryor, is an innovative technique long used in dolphin training and now commonly employed to train dogs. It is equally effective in cats. A clicker is used to tell the cat *that* (click!) is the desired behavior, followed by a treat to reward him. Because the sound of the clicker is so different from the voice or other training cues, pets seem to more easily focus and understand what is expected. To learn more about clicker training, visit Karen's site at www.clickertraining.com.

Kitty Delights—Rewards and Lures That Work

Kittens appreciate praise. Be sure to fill your voice with emotion that says how pleased you are. "What a *smart* kitty you are!" Verbal praise works best when partnered with a more tangible reward, like petting. Use petting and scratches in all your kitten's favorite places as a reward, too. Pay attention to his "sweet spots" such as his cheeks and the base of his tail.

Toys and games are a favorite, and really get the purr a-rumbling when used in training. Again, which toy or game should be used depends on the kitten. Perhaps he loves Da Bird fishing pole style toy, or a sparkly fuzzy ball toy he can carry around. Once you've figured out his favorite, reserve it for use only as a reward. Make him earn it before the games begin.

One of most effective training tools for kittens is a feather. Pheasant feathers are my favorite. They are so long and flexible, they can be used to "snake" across the ground in temptation, or work from a distance to tease the kitten into the behavior you desire. Feathers also work well as lures to tempt kitty into the position you want (get those paws onto the scratching post) and can be part of games used as rewards for good behavior.

Food bribes are legal, and bar none, treats are the most universally effective training tool for cats and kittens. The treat should be something completely different from his usual diet and reserved only for those training sessions or for rewarding particularly good behavior. If he usually eats dry food, for example, then "treat" him with canned food. Commercial treats are designed not to upset the nutritional balance of his diet, an important consideration with kittens. You don't need much—just a taste is all it takes.

Anything your kitten really likes to eat can be a potential bribe to use for training. For instance, my cat Seren adores cream cheese so much that just a tiny smear on the end of my index finger does the trick. Strong-smelling treats work best, though. Tiny amounts are enough to prompt the right behavior, and won't unbalance his diet. If you use commercial treats, break them into pieces so one treat provides two or more rewards. Professional trainers of animal actors use tiny tidbits of smoked turkey luncheon meat to tempt their kitties to perform.

> **Kitten Purrs:** Kitty Kaviar is a favorite at our house. The pungent treat is made from dried bonito (a type of fish) and can be sprinkled over food, or hand-fed as a training bribe. The natural protein product is available at www.kittykaviar.com or from www.vir-chew-all.com.

Litter Box Training

Almost all kittens will already know what a litter box is for, and how to use it, by the time you adopt them. They learn by following Mom-cat and watching her. You'll need to do Mom's job when your baby is very young. Set up the box, place the baby on the litter, and scratch the litter with your fingers. It's a good idea to leave one fresh "deposit" in the box to offer a scent signal about what's expected. When he is productive, praise him extravagantly, and offer a favorite game or treat as reward. Covering waste is a sign of deference, and most kittens do this with little prompting.

Allow the baby to climb out of the litter box by himself and make his way from the area. That will help him remember how to find his way back to the box when nature calls again.

What to Expect, Productionwise

Kittens need to use the bathroom at predictable times. Generally, these are when they wake up from a nap, finish eating, and after a play period. To speed up the training process, place your kitten in the box right after he wakes up, finishes eating, or stops playing. Even if he doesn't always "go" on cue, this serves to remind him where the box is. You want to make sure every opportunity counts.

This is particularly important when the box is in a distant part of the house, but your kitten is playing upstairs in your office. When placing your kitten's litter box, think of convenience. Not for you—for your kitten. Even when your baby knows what he's supposed to do, and can find the box, very young kittens simply won't have the physical capacity to "hold" it for long periods of time. Make sure there's a litter box within a convenient distance for your kitten to reach in time. Give your pet every opportunity to be good and avoid mistakes.

Keep in mind your kitten's likes and dislikes so that you make his litter box the *best* option he has, and he won't seek out alternatives. Kittens (like adult cats) don't want to have a bathroom near where they sleep or eat, and often like privacy. Choose a low-traffic area of the house for his bathroom.

Scratching the Surface—Claw Training Basics

Kittens—and adult cats—claw. It is a natural behavior, and one you will never eliminate, so don't even try. Instead, train your kitten to use a "legal" target so he can indulge his claw needs without risking damage to your furniture. Remember, kittens can't read minds, and he won't know that he shouldn't claw your antique desk. It's up to you to explain in terms he can understand.

Claws are an extension of the end of each kitten toe, where two small bones rest nearly on top of each other. They are held together by tendons that create a hinge mechanism. Relaxed claws are sheathed inside a fold of skin at the end of each toe, so that the paw looks soft and smooth. Kitty straightens the hinged bones by flexing the tendon, to push the claw down and forward. That not only extends his claws, it also spreads the paw pad to nearly twice its former width.

After choosing the right style of post, the most important training consideration is where to put it. Because clawing is a marking behavior, kitty wants the whole world to see his scratch marks. Hiding the scratching post in a back room defeats the whole purpose of marking.

Think of all the reasons why your kitten claws and use them to find the perfect location for the post. Kittens often claw more than one place in the house, too, so don't limit him to a single post—offer him several in all his favorite locations: near his bed, where he eats, and in the living room where the family gathers. He wants you to see, and admire, his scratch graffiti.

Why Cats Claw

Scratching is one type of feline marking behavior. It is vitally important to the cat's health, for both physical and emotional reasons.

First of all, scratching feels good to your kitten. When he reaches outward, sinks claws into a surface, and then draws them back toward himself, he flexes and exercises his shoulder muscles. Think of clawing as kitty calisthenics that help keep his muscles toned. For that reason, cats often seem to enjoy a scratch after they wake up from a nap.

Clawing also strips away the old outer claw coverings, and reveals the sharp new nail beneath. This keeps the kitten's toes and claws healthy. Trimming his nails reduces the potential for damage.

Finally, the visible claw marks communicate to the world that the target (and real estate surrounding it) is owned by kitty. Scent glands in the paws leave similar messages. Clawing typically targets "important" places, such as near a favorite sleeping place, the food bowl, or a favored pathway like the hall into your bedroom.

The key to scratch-training your kitten is to offer him an irresistible target in the perfect location, so he doesn't feel the need to seek other options. Introduce him to the scratching post by kneeling down and pretending you're a cat—scratch the post yourself in front of him. Don't forget to tell him how good it feels, and what fun you're having. That's often enough to get baby to test the object himself—and get hooked. You can also tease him with a feather or ribbon dangled against the scratching surface, so that when he grabs for the toy, he feels how great the scratching post is.

> **Tip:** You can use catnip to tempt your kitten to use the proper scratch object. Rub the dried herb onto the claw surface, or use a commercial catnip spray product. Two out of three kittens will begin to react to catnip after they're six months old—but one third of cats don't inherit the "catnip gene" and will never react.

"Liberation" Training

Learning to accept the crate and walk on a leash liberates your kitten by offering him safe options for leaving his home. Every kitten will need to venture beyond your house at some point in his life. He'll need to visit the veterinarian for necessary vaccinations. He may need special coat care and to spend time at a professional groomer. If you have a kitten you plan to show, he'll need to travel even more often.

Many cats learn to fear their carrier because the only time they see it is when they're forced inside and end up at the vets'. They associate the sight of the crate with scary needles or rude thermometers. You want to do the opposite, and train your kitten to associate the carrier and rides in the car with fun, positive experiences.

Remember, kittens and cats are creatures of habit, and any change to their routine can be upsetting to them. Liberation training requires patience on your part, so that kitty is gradually introduced to the idea. The last thing you want to do is have him become frightened of the situation.

Kitten Purrs: One of the best ways to speed the acceptance of new, strange items like the halter or crate is to use Feliway. This spray is an analogue of the cheek pheromones—scent chemicals—that cats naturally produce and spread by cheek-rubbing. Cheek scent has a calming influence and basically tells kitty, "Everything's cool, don't worry!" Spritz a bit on the inside of the crate and onto the halter and leash so that they aren't so scary and the kitten more readily accepts them. You can find Feliway at most pet supply stores or at www.peerlesshealth.com.

Crate Training

The key to training kitty to accept the carrier is creating familiarity. You do that by introducing him to this new situation in a series of nonthreatening, gradual steps.

Begin by making the carrier (crate) a part of the furniture. In other words, set it on the floor in the corner of kitty's room, and let him explore at his leisure. Don't make a big deal out of it. Simply allow the kitten to approach, cheek-rub the outside so it smells like him, and explore the inside on his own.

After several days, once he's accepted the carrier as a normal part of his environment, enhance the attraction. Take the door off or leave the zipper open so it's easy for him to come and go. Then toss inside a favorite toy or treat that he already likes. Ping-Pong balls are great fun inside hard crates. This helps him associate the crate with fun things. Put a fuzzy blanket inside. For some kittens, the crate can double as a bed.

The next step is to put the door back on, and wait until kitty goes inside on his own. Shut the door, praising him all the while, and talking calmly to him. Be matter of fact—treat this as normal and no reason for kitty to get his tail in a twist. After five minutes, open the door and give him a treat or toy reserved only for his best performance. Praise the dickens out of him! He should know that staying calmly inside the crate earns him good things. Repeat several times over the next few days, each time letting the kitten out after five minutes.

By the end of the week, you can begin increasing the time he spends in the crate. Pick up the carrier while he's in it and carry him around; then let him out. Take him in the carrier out to the car, sit there and talk to him, and then bring him back into the house and release him—don't forget to offer the treat. Soon, you should be able to take him for car rides in his carrier without him throwing a fit. He'll learn that most times, the carrier means good things for him—and the vet visit isn't the only association it has.

Warning: Kittens and cats should always ride in a carrier when traveling in your car. Otherwise you run the risk of a frisky baby distracting the driver. Even a well-behaved pet can become a furry projectile should you be in an accident. If that happens, you want the kitten safely protected by the carrier, and not scared and running loose inside—or outside—the crashed car.

Halter and Leash Training

Like crate training, you need patience to get your kitten to accept the halter and leash. Use similar steps to help him learn there's nothing to fear and much to gain.

(Photo credit: Ralston Purina Company)

Here I am with Puma, a six-month-old shelter baby adopted immediately following this C.A.T. demonstration during the Purina Cat Chow Way of Life Tour event. Puma learned to walk on a halter and leash within ten minutes.

As before, make the halter and leash a part of the furniture. Leave them on the floor for your kitten to find. During a petting or grooming session, try using the halter to pet kitty so that his own scent becomes impregnated in the fabric. Making the halter and leash smell like him goes a long way toward making them less frightening.

Use the leash as a toy and tempt your kitten to play chase with it. Drag it along the floor like a ribbon toy, and praise kitty when he catches it. That helps associate the leash with fun times.

After two or three days, when the leash has become part of kitty's normal environment, settle down on the floor with him for a petting session. In the middle of petting, put the halter on him, first rubbing him with it and making the equipment part of the petting.

Once it's on, engage him in his favorite game—a feather toy works well, or use the end of the leash. The idea is to distract him from the odd feeling of the halter on his body. This works especially well with younger kittens. Encourage him to chase the feather, to get up and move around. He'll quickly learn that the halter doesn't interfere with his movements. After five minutes, take it off.

As with the crate training, short five-minute sessions repeated several times a day over the first three days work wonders. You can then gradually increase the amount of time that he wears the halter. Be sure to give him a scrumptious treat each time you take off the halter, so he recognizes there is a lovely end in sight when he puts up with the bother.

Once your kitten wears the halter without protest, clip on the leash, pick up the end, and simply follow him around. Don't try to influence his movements at first. Unlike leash-trained dogs that are supposed to "heel" and follow the owner, leash-trained cats direct the action.

Warning: Do not pull and tug on the leash if he tries to fight it—simply pick him up and calm him down. Unless the halter fits perfectly (which can be hard to do with tiny kittens), pulling backwards against the leash can allow kittens to slip out of the halter and escape. That's a lesson you *don't* want him to learn!

After several days of short sessions in which you follow him around, begin to gently guide his movements. One or two pull-release tugs are enough. Don't drag him—that invites him to fight the leash, and can turn the positive experience into a negative one.

A good way to train kitty to follow your tug-guidance is to lure him with a feather toy in the direction you want him to go.

Eventually, when both you and kitty feel secure on the leash, you can explore the porch or back yard together. Leash training opens up the world to your feline friend and allows him a safe and controlled outdoor experience.

Tricks for Treats

Yes, your kitten *can* be trained to do tricks. Most cat training deals with real-life issues, such as proper clawing and litter box behavior, but some kittens certainly have an aptitude for performing. The key to trick-training kittens and cats, though, is building on their own natural behaviors. Basically, you find an action your kitten does anyway, and you teach him to do it on command by rewarding the behavior with a toy or tasty treat. Meat baby food can work wonders for tempting kitty to perform. Just be sure there is no onion added—that could be a problem for some kitties.

Here are four examples of kitty tricks. Pay attention to the fun behaviors that your kitten does naturally, and use these techniques to train him to perform them on command. For instance, maybe you can promote his jumping ability and train him to leap through the circle of your arms, or even to "speak" on command if he's a talker.

Come

All kittens and cats can be trained to come when called. They often train themselves to do this simply by paying attention to what happens—for instance, prior to dinner time. When they learn to associate the sound of kibble hitting the bowl or the whirrr of the can opener with food, they'll come running for this "trigger." Use that natural impulse to train kitty to come when called. Use the command "Come!" each time you fill his bowl. Do this faithfully, for two weeks. Next, load your pockets with his favorite treats, and give the "Come!" command at another time, from a different place in the house. When he arrives, give him the treat. Do this without fail for another two weeks. Then for weeks five and six, continue to practice the "Come!" command at mealtimes, and at different times and places—but only give him a treat every third or fourth time. This teaches kitty that he'll *almost always* get a treat when he comes—he never knows *when* for sure, so he'll be more likely to respond every time on the chance he'll get the reward.

Warning: Never call your kitten to you in order to correct or chastise him. That only teaches him *Not* to come when called—he'll quickly learn to expect punishment. If you must perform some unpleasantness upon his kitten-person (such as a nail trim or bath), rather than call him to you, you should go and collect him. Otherwise you risk undoing your training.

Sit

All cats and kittens sit. Consequently, you can associate a command—trigger word—along with a treat or reward to the action so they'll learn to sit on command. Use kitty's favorite treat or toy—pheasant feathers work especially well. Wait until kitty is standing in front of you, hold the feather or treat directly over his head, and move it slowly backwards. In order to follow the lure with his eyes, his furry tail must touch down. When it does, time your "Sit!" command to coincide with the action, and give him the treat or access to the feather. Some cats, like my Seren, will learn to run to you and sit down just to see if they can get their own personal "treat machine" to pay up!

Beg

From the sitting position, use the lure to tempt the baby to sit up. Many cats do this naturally, and they are the best prospects for this trick. Reward any attempt at first, even if he can't keep his balance. With practice he'll improve.

Wave

All kittens and cats reach out with their paws to tap or touch a tempting object. You can use this natural behavior to teach the command "wave." Simply link the behavior to the command, and reward kitty when he performs. Do this consistently, so that he recognizes the benefit.

15

UNDERSTANDING KITTEN MISTAKES

"Bad" Versus "Normal" Behavior—
Do the P.E.T. Test

Kittens don't make mistakes on purpose. They are not vindictive. Cats do not set out to "get back" at their owners out of pique. Bad behavior is the number one reason kittens lose their homes and their lives.

It's vital to understand bad kitten behavior if you are to preserve your loving bond. To help you do this, you can use the P.E.T. test to figure out what's causing the problem. P.E.T. stands for Physical health, Emotional issues, and Traits of personality and instinct.

Physical Health

Sick kittens tell you they feel crummy with "bad" behavior. For instance, an upset tummy prompts a deposit outside the litter box or a sore spot that's touched produces a reflexive hiss and bite. Any sudden change in behavior is a wake-up call that kitty needs your help. Before anything else, have her health checked by the veterinarian.

Emotional Issues

Emotional issues caused by stress also affect behavior. For instance, a change in routine (such as your new work schedule) might increase her scratching, because marking your chair makes her feel more secure. Perhaps you've begun dating a new boyfriend, and the stress prompts kitty to wet on your pillow—not out of anger, but to make it "smell" safer (like her!) and to announce you are her property. The death of another pet, your son going away to college, even a re-arrangement of the furniture may prove so stressful to some cats that they become depressed and hide under the bed for days at a time. So-cial hierarchy issues between pets also cause stress-related bad behav-iors. He may spray urine outside the box due to a stray cat trespassing on his turf or an upstart kitten invading his house; or he may become aggressive toward another animal that threatens his so-cial standing.

Traits of Personality and Instinct

These traits include a kitten's individual personality, as well as in-herent behaviors that are hot-wired into every feline brain. Kittens naturally scratch, climb, and cry—you can't stop these instinctive behaviors. Personalities also vary, from wired in-your-face energetic kittens to your friend's adult sixteen-year-old Persian who sleeps eighteen hours a day. People who have never shared their life with a kitten may have inaccurate notions about what to expect. Also, our memories of beloved childhood pets filter out the negatives and paint rosy portraits of Saint Fluffy, who could do no wrong. New kit-tens tend to suffer in the comparison. You need to develop realistic expectations about your kitten's instinctive, natural behaviors. Once you understand why they behave in certain ways, you can train kit-tens to use "legal" alternatives by employing positive rewards.

Your new baby is not a saint. She's not a stuffed toy, either. It is un-realistic to expect her to be perfect, especially when you both have very different ideas about what you want—and need—out of the rela-tionship. Above all, your new pet needs your love, support, and per-mission to be a normal kitten, with all the intrinsic feline frustrations that may bring. After all, kitty accepts you with all your imperfections (even when you insult her mouse gifts!). Owners learn to accept and even to cherish the unique feline foibles of their kitten friends.

Rules of the House—Setting Limits and Enforcing Them

It's hard enough for you and your kitten to understand each other without further muddying the water with inconsistencies. Figure out ahead of time what rules matter to you. Make sure that everybody in your household understands the set limits, so that kitty isn't confused with mixed signals. It's not fair to her, or to you, for your family to be wishy-washy when enforcing the rules of the house. Your kitten won't understand why "sometimes" she can climb the drapes and get a laugh (from your son), and the same behavior another time prompts anger (from you).

When devising your rules, build in some wiggle room, particularly in areas where the kitten's innate personality or instinctive behaviors are likely to clash. For instance, your Somali kitten is an active breed that loves heights, so forbidding her access to all high furniture perches will drive you both crazy. Be realistic. Provide her with legal opportunities—perhaps the back of the La-Z-Boy or top of the TV—so she'll more readily honor your specific kitten-free zones and leave alone the mantel with its fine china display.

Almost all misbehaviors arise from misunderstandings about what constitutes a realistic expectation. Kittens claw. Kittens play. Kittens cry, and bite, and poop. These are normal behaviors you cannot—you *should* not—attempt to stop. Understand why they do the things they do, so you can offer them alternative outlets. That keeps them happy and healthy, and keeps your love alive.

If you're both lucky, you will have ten or more years together. Kitty may even live into her twenties. Strong relationships are built on mutual trust and, to a degree, on compromise. Believe me, your kitten will never stop trying to "train" you to conform to her own kitty ideal. She won't give up on you, even when that perfect vision never comes true. Nor should you consider giving up on her.

Work it out. To be fair, set realistic rules of the house. Decide what's important to you, while keeping in mind what's important to your kitten. Then consistently enforce the rules. Don't change them midstream. And be sensitive to your kitten, should she make a mistake. Be a "pet detective" to figure out why she lapsed, so you can correct the problem without risk of making it worse.

Effective Kitten Corrections

I hate the word *punishment* which smacks of retribution, and much prefer to talk about corrections. The best way to deal with kitten misdeeds is to interrupt the behavior with a humane correction.

A correction works to interrupt the behavior by startling the kitten so she stops what she's doing. It doesn't take much to break her concentration. Once that's done, you have a few seconds to engage her attention and direct it in a more positive, acceptable behavior. After she's changed the behavior, always reward her. For instance, *interrupt* the kitten from scratching the sofa, *redirect* her claws onto the "legal" cat tree, and *reward* her for scratching the right target. Not every correction works for all kittens, so you must define the "ideal" kitten correction for your pet.

P.U.R.R. Program

The most successful plan for fixing problem behaviors includes four key elements. If you miss one, you're likely to fail. These are easy to remember, if you just think of the acronym *P.U.R.R.* It stands for Prompt interruption, Understand the issue, Replace the target, and Retrain.

- Prompt interruption means you must stop the behavior right when it's happening—not after the fact.
- Understand the problem. Educate yourself about what motivates kitten behavior so that you have realistic expectations, and know how to meet kitten needs.
- Replace the target with a more appropriate, legal option. You cannot stop normal kitten behavior, but you can modify the behavior and give kitty an irresistible alternative.
- Retrain your kitten. Do that by immediately praising her cessation of the "bad" behavior and bribing or rewarding her to do the "right" thing.

Using Good Sense

Every kitten and cat is different. (Where have you heard *that* before?) What works to correct one kitten may not faze another, so you'll need to experiment a bit to find the perfect kitty correction.

Scent corrections either repel or attract the kitten. For instance, Vicks VapoRub has a strong menthol odor that keeps the kitten from chewing dangerous items like electrical cords. Catnip attracts kitty's interest so she'll use a "legal" claw target.

Noise corrections are used to startle the kitten enough to stop an objectionable behavior midstream. These must be sudden, out of the ordinary, and used sparingly or kitty will lose her "startle" reflex. Hissing like the mom-cat is one effective example.

Tactile corrections come out of nowhere to physically startle the kitten. One very effective example is the squirt gun. Cats dislike getting wet, and a "zap" with a stream of water from across the room seems a mysterious force to them. Other tactile corrections include booby-trapping forbidden objects with material that's unpleasant to the kitten. For instance, cats seem to hate the sensation of walking on aluminum foil, so foil spread on forbidden countertops may keep them off. It's also self-correcting— you don't have to be there for kitty to encounter the foil.

Corrections like sounds serve only to interrupt a behavior, not to stop it permanently. Others such as double-sided sticky tape offer unpleasant consequences, which both interrupt the behavior and reduces repeated offenses. Corrections stop the behavior at *that moment*, or repel the kitten from *that target*. She'll simply move to the other end of the sofa to claw unless you also offer a better alternative.

Common Complaints

Kittens are nothing if not inventive. I once was asked how to stop a kitten from swiping makeup sponges, soaking them in the dog's water bowl, and then bombing the dog with the wet missiles from the tops of doors.

Stop the kitten? My goodness, that baby deserves applause!

The most common kitty complaints, though, are more serious. I'll walk you through them, and show you how to evaluate the problem with P.E.T., and how to correct it with P.U.R.R. With patience, you can turn "bad" behaviors into positives and keep your bond intact.

Biting

Use the P.E.T. test to determine if the biting stems from a physical, emotional, or innate kitty trait. A health problem may prompt your kitten to bite, either in reflex from pain or out of stress from fear or for defense. However, most kittens bite in response to normal exuberance when they play, so biting shouldn't be unexpected. Socialization helps temper the biting, and you'll need to teach kitty some limits if the mom-cat fell down on the job.

How do you do that? Remember P.U.R.R. Prompt interruption means right as she chomps your ankle or nails your hand. For biting, there are two corrections that work extremely well. In most cases, the *ssssst!* that imitates the mom-cat stops young kittens cold. Make the sound very percussive.

Another effective bite-stopper is a scream. This works well on older kittens and adult cats. Do not yell—a yell won't work, but a short, sharp, and very loud *scream* does. Think about it: That's what kitty's brothers and sisters would do, and it tells your baby in no uncertain terms what you think of the behavior. She probably hasn't a clue that biting hurts you. Screaming will not only startle and interrupt the behavior, it will also teach her an important lesson. Scream therapy is also quite good for your own stress relief. Be sure to warn your family members before you indulge in the scream interruption technique.

After the hiss or scream interruption, figure out why she bit you. Did you pick her up when she warned you away with ear and tail language because she's scared? Does she have a sore place you accidentally hurt? Or is it just normal kitten play?

Remember, if you've let her play with your hands like toys, she won't know any better and may bite you without meaning to. Avoid using your fingers or hands as toys. Replace these with a "legal" biting outlet like a stuffed animal she can chew and claw to her heart's content.

To retrain your kitten to inhibit her bite, use the scream or hiss to stop the behavior, and when it's due to normal play, simply stop the game. She'll learn that any time she bites, the fun stops. The only way for playtime to continue is if she learns to inhibit her bite and claws.

Kittens that are fearful, or are excessively aggressive, benefit a great deal from "play therapy" that offers them a legal target. Use a stuffed toy, or a fishing pole style interactive game, and let her expend her energy. Encourage the kitten to bite and chase the toy (rather than your hands or ankles).

Tip: Often we encourage kittens to bite without meaning to do so. Jerking back your hands or dancing around to keep kitty off your feet makes these objects move in even more enticing patterns. That prompts her to continue the game. Instead, grit your teeth and hold still. If she's latched on to your hand, instead of pulling away, push into her mouth. That will prompt her to open wide and release your hand. Do this in conjunction with your hiss or scream interruption.

Even minor cat bites that break the skin can be dangerous to people. They need immediate medical attention and often an antibiotic injection from your doctor to prevent the development of a serious infection from the wound.

Some kittens benefit from a time-out. Again, it must happen immediately after the bite incident so kitty will associate the consequence with her actions. When she bites you, deliver the interruption; then pick her up and put her in her room alone. That's no fun—nobody to play with! She'll soon learn that biting stops the play and attention, and will think twice about munching down on you.

Keep in mind that kittens have a short attention span. A time-out will be effective only when begun within sixty seconds of the bite. Five minutes is plenty of time to be alone, though. After that, she won't remember why she's there, only that she's alone. Let her out, and offer her the "legal" bite toy. If she nails you again, repeat the time-out.

Abscesses

An abscess is a serious health concern often caused by cat bites. Kitten and cat teeth are so sharp, a bite plants bacteria deep beneath the skin. When the surface skin heals over, these organisms are trapped inside, and swell into a painful pocket of infection. Kittens that play roughly and bite eventually "train" each other to inhibit their teeth and claws. But when they break the skin on each other, they can develop painful abscesses that, in turn, can prompt them to lash out at you in pain.

You'll see a swelling in the skin, often around the neck and head area, but sometimes on a paw or near the tail. The location depends on whether kitty was attacking or running away when she got nailed. The infection makes the sore spot feel hot, and it can burst and drain a noxious, smelly substance. Kittens and cats with abscesses typically run a fever.

Normal kitten temperature is 100 to 102 degrees. You can check your kitten for fever with a regular rectal thermometer. Grease the end of the thermometer with petroleum jelly or vegetable oil, grasp the kitten's tail to hold her still, and then gently insert into the rectum. Wait three minutes, withdraw, and read.

Abscesses are more often an adult cat problem, especially with intact felines. Cats that fight each other over territory or girlfriends often develop abscesses. Spaying and neutering greatly reduce the incidence of abscesses, which always need to be addressed by a veterinarian.

Clawing

Kittens that claw you, either in play or to mark you as their "territory," can be taught to stop, using the same techniques described to correct biting. Most clawing complaints have to do with kitty using your furniture for her nail recreation.

Take a look at the P.E.T. test, and you'll see that clawing is not a health problem. It's a normal behavior. Emotional stress can increase the incidence of claw behavior, so keeping your kitten happy goes a long way toward handling the problem. Kittens simply must learn to redirect their claws onto a "legal" target that you provide.

Prompt interruption stops the clawing behavior. There are many types of corrections that work.

SQUIRT GUN

This sends an unexpected stream of water to zap her tail and startle her out of the behavior. In the best scenario, kitty hasn't a clue where the water came from.

Warning: Always aim for the tail region, never the face. A squirt into her ears or eyes is not only painful, but could also do damage. You want to startle and stop the scratching, not injure her or make her hide the scratching behavior from you. Be aware that spraying water won't work for all cats. Seren likes being squirted and considers "squirt gun tag" a great game.

PENNY CAN

Fill an empty soda can with pennies or marbles, and shake it to make a terrible noise to interrupt the behavior. Similarly, you could clap your hands or slap a magazine against a tabletop.

TOY TOSS

A bean bag, stuffed toy, or "shaker" can tossed near the vicinity of the scratch action can stop her, or even lure her to investigate the object. Never aim to hit your kitten—it doesn't need to touch her to do the job.

There are also a couple of effective "preemptive" corrections you can use, when you know (or anticipate) where your kitten might claw.

STICKY PAWS

You can booby-trap the surface to make it unpleasant. Sticky Paws, a double-sided tape product, repels the kitten after only one experience. It self-trains the baby that if she claws, the tape sticks to her fur and pulls and feels nasty. Self-training interruptions are the most effective because you don't have to be there for them to work.

FELIWAY

This spray pheromone product uses your kitten's sense of smell, and has been shown to help deter her from clawing treated objects.

You absolutely must replace the scratch target with a more appropriate one. Not only the type of claw object, but also the placement determines if your kitten will accept and use the post. Kittens have different clawing styles (vertical or horizontal) and preferred surfaces to scratch. Choose a vertical or horizontal commercial claw object covered with carpet, sisal, or wood, to suit your kitten's tastes.

Retraining Kitten Claws, Step by Step

Now that you understand *why* your kitten claws, and what she *needs* out of a claw object, you're ready to begin the retraining process. Don't expect to fix the problem overnight. It will take patience, and there will likely be some relapses, but with diligence, you can both be satisfied.

1. Make "bad" choices unattractive. Booby-trap the sofa or other prime claw targets with Sticky Paws, Feliway, or other techniques. Be creative. Cover the upholstery with surfaces kittens dislike, such as aluminum foil. Spray citrus deodorizers on your furniture—most cats dislike this scent. Spread a tiny bit of Vicks VapoRub on wooden surfaces, or smear it on a washcloth that's draped over the fabric. The idea is to make the furniture so unattractive that kitty decides to avoid it.

2. Correct the behavior. Each time kitty claws the wrong object, she should receive an immediate interruption or correction. That teaches her there's an unpleasant consequence to her actions. The squirt gun or shaker may work well.

3. Review kitty's preferences and choose a commercial scratching post she can't resist. Place it directly in front of the illegal target she's used in the past. Spike the post with catnip, lure her on board with a feather toy, and praise and reward with treats when she uses it. Kittens and cats use scratching to mark all their territory—one scratching post won't be enough. You'll need a legal target in all the places kitty feels are important, such as near her bed, food, and favorite lookout places.

4. Kittens love the status quo. Any change can cause stress that prompts even more scratching. Wait until kitty has sworn scratch-allegiance to the "legal" target before moving the post, and even then, do so very gradually. The post must remain in the general vicinity or you risk the cat relapsing and going back to the furniture. But you can move the post to a more convenient location—to the side of the sofa instead of right in front of it, for instance. Aim for moving it about five inches a day, until you reach the preferred location.

Litter-ary Problems

Health issues can be a major cause of elimination problems. Intestinal parasites that cause upset tummies or diarrhea may prompt accidents outside the box when kitty can't get there in time.

Any sort of stress—often caused by a change in the kitten's routine—may also prompt accidents. Litter box aversion can develop when the kitten associates her bathroom with a bad experience. Perhaps the dog surprised her in the middle of her toilet, or maybe she had a painful bowel movement due to a hairball. She avoids the box because she remembers that scary dog or painful experience. Or maybe it just smells bad, from strong perfume or stale deposits.

Some cats or kittens may develop problems with asthma, which can be aggravated by dusty or perfumed litter. Affected cats show signs of gasping, wheezing, or loss of consciousness. An asthma attack from a reaction to litter can also prompt litter box aversion. If

---

Tip: If you have a kitty that's spraying constantly in just one or two places, you may be able to break him of that habit using aluminum foil. Cover the wall and down to the floor with the foil. When his spray hits, the sound not only startles him, but the splash back of urine onto him is distasteful. The foil also protects the surface or carpet for easy cleaning.

Kitten Purrs: The spray product Feliway is an analogue of the feline cheek pheromone, a natural scent produced by the cat that tells her, "Be calm, chill, everything's cool." It not only helps with scratch training mentioned earlier, but also applies to urine-spraying problems. A spritz of Feliway on the cat's favored urine-target dampens the urge to come back and repeat the offense. Regular use of Feliway reduces spraying behavior due to stress in a large majority of cases.

your kitten is asthmatic, choose your litter very carefully to avoid dust or aromas that may trigger an attack.

Older kittens and adult cats often express themselves by spraying urine. Intact kitties do this to announce they own a particular territory, and to tell other cats about their sexual status. Neutering and spaying will drastically reduce and in some cases totally eliminate spraying behavior.

However, any cat experiencing stress may spray urine to spread comforting "self-scent" around to make her feel more in control. Spraying urine often develops from stressful social situations between cats, or from changes in routine or environment. In these instances, if you can identify the "trigger" that prompted the stress, and eliminate it, the wetting usually goes away.

Lower Urinary Tract Disorders (LUTD)

One of the most common health causes of hit-or-miss bathroom behaviors is LUTD, sometimes in the past referred to as feline urologic disorder (FUS). LUTD is associated with a range of health conditions that may prompt inflammation or infection in the bladder and urinary tract, formation of mineral crystals in the urine, and sometimes blockage.

Veterinarians aren't sure exactly what causes LUTD to develop in some cats and not in others. Certain cases may be produced by bacterial infections, others by the acid-and-base balance of the urine that promotes different types of crystals, and still more by stress. Diet, medication, and stress reduction may be used alone or in combination to deal with the problem.

The signs of LUTD include any one or combination of (1) crying during urination, (2) excessive licking of the genitals, (3) straining at the end of urination, (4) bloody urine, (5) strong ammonia odor from the urine, (6) a break in house training, or dribbling urine in unusual locations, (7) frequent but nonproductive visits to the litter box, (8) listlessness, loss of appetitie, excessive thirst.

LUTD is typically an adult-cat problem, but older kittens may also develop these signs. Straining and crying may indicate a blockage of the urinary tract, which is a life-threatening emergency. *See your veterinarian immediately!*

With kittens, most hit-or-miss litter box behaviors are due to misunderstandings. Kittens must learn what's expected, that their toilet is in the box and not under the piano bench, for instance. Even more important, you must understand kitty's motivation. Sure, every baby has to "go," but what is it that attracts her and keeps her faithful to a particular toilet? Figure out what it is about the litter box that has made her misbehave. Here's a checklist to help you figure out the problem.

1. Location. Like real estate, the most important consideration for your kitten's toilet is location, location, location. Kittens and cats prefer privacy to do their business, so the litter box must be in a low-traffic area. Second, kittens are fastidious creatures, and don't want to sleep or eat next to their bathroom. Finally, young kittens may not have the physical capacity to "hold" themselves and need more than one box located within convenient reach.

2. Content. Not only the location, but also what goes inside the box matters to your kitten. Be sure that the litter you choose has no scent. Kittens have an exquisitely sensitive nose, and a perfume that smells good to you might repel your baby.

3. Cleanliness. Because of their fastidious nature, kittens want their bathroom clean, and may find an alternative location

(Photo credit: Amy D. Shojai)

Kittens may misunderstand what you want. This smoke-color beauty seems to think the litter makes a great bed.

(like under your bed) if you don't keep the box clean. Daily scooping is a must.

Warning: It's important to completely dump the box and clean it once a month, minimum, but avoid using strong cleaners. Hot water may be sufficient. Kittens may be turned off by the smell of disinfectant. Also, the slight but familiar "aroma" of their own deposits helps remind them what's expected, and makes them feel more comfortable.

4. Number. The one-plus-one rule should apply—that means one box per kitten or cat, plus one. Many kitties prefer to use one box for solids and the other for urine, or they don't like to go "after" another cat.

5. Size and Style. This won't matter for small kittens, but as she grows, a big kitten may "hang out" of the box and drop deposits outside. The bigger the box, and more room inside to maneuver, the better.

6. Status Quo. Once you've found a location, box filler, and cleaning routine that works for kitty, for heaven's sake, stick to it. Changing the brand of litter or switching box location or routine may prompt problems.

To retrain your kitten to use the litter box, it's only fair to give her every opportunity to do good. Time her bathroom visits—after vigorous play, a snack, or a nap offer ideal opportunities. If you see her "posing" and prepared to leave an unwelcome gift, scoop her up and place her in the box instead.

Warning: Avoid using "interruptions" with tiny kittens, or you may train her to hide when she eliminates. Once she's older and understands the concept of the box, an interruption like the squirt gun works fine to "remind" her to mind her P's and—other stuff. Move her to the litter box once the squirt breaks her concentration, and encourage her to finish her business there. Praise the dickens out of her, and give her a treat, when she's productive in the right spot.

Remember, unless you catch her in the act, kitty won't have a clue why you're upset when you find a pile or wet spot on the carpet. When it's not possible for you to supervise kitty's activity, the humane choice is to isolate her in kitten central—in her room where she has access to a litter box.

Invest in an "odor neutralizer" product available at pet supply stores, and use it to clean any accidents on your carpet or furniture. These products contain enzymes that "digest" the smell and get rid of it. A product called Tuff Oxi gets rave reviews from cat lovers, and is available from info@tuffcleaningproducts.com. Cleaners that simply wash or perfume the place will leave behind a telltale scent that may draw kitty back to the scene of the crime, to repeat her indiscretion. Avoid cleaners that contain ammonia. Feline urine contains an ammonia-like odor, so these types of products may actually prompt the kitten to repeat her accident on the spot.

Warning: Brand-new carpet can smell like cat urine, and this scent can tempt cats to use the carpet as a toilet. The material commonly used in carpet backing (and some plastic-backed bath mats) is home to microorganisms that produce various by-products that can smell like cat urine. If your kitties are using the bath mat, throw the mat away—there's no saving it. There's not much to do about brand-new carpet—except complain to the manufacturer and get it replaced. Hopefully the biologists will figure out a solution to de-stink new carpet sometime in the near future.

Tip: Cat urine, feces, and (I'm told) even human dandruff will glow under a true ultraviolet light, or Wood's lamp (your veterinarian will have one of these). That can help you find the "scene of the crime" to get it thoroughly clean. The surrounding lights need to be very low or completely off, and the ultraviolet light held pretty close to the urine source. An ultraviolet light doesn't come cheap, though, and unfortunately the inexpensive "black lights" often available at gift stores are not particularly effective.

For hard-case kittens, you can break them of "going" on your favorite Persian rug by moving their feeding bowls to the spot. She won't want to mess where she eats. Leave the empty bowl behind as a reminder. After a week, take the bowl away for a day, and then bring it back. Continue this every-other-day routine for a week, and then gradually leave the bowl in its original spot. In the meantime, take steps to ensure her litter box is the better alternative.

Loudmouth Kittens

Crying is one of the most common complaints of kitten owners. Be aware that just like human infants, crying is natural behavior for baby cats. I hear it again and again. "She cries all the time, what does she want?" Or they'll complain, "She wakes me at four A.M. every day and won't stop crying until I feed her. How can I make her stop?"

In answer to the first question, she wants your attention. She may not even know what she wants. It may be her way of saying, "I'm bored. Entertain me!" The more you try to give her what she wants, the more she cries the next time—heck, you've trained her to pester.

Kittens also cry, squeal, scream, or otherwise make sudden sharp sounds of distress if they're hurt or frightened. As you get to know each other, you'll learn to "hear" the difference between a distress call and a more mundane kitten complaint, such as she wants you to wake up and play with her.

Different personalities and breeds of kittens will be more vocal than others. If you are concerned about a loudmouth kitten, you might want to choose a less mouthy breed. Siamese-heritage kittens tend to talk a lot.

In the same way, kittens that wake you at the crack of dawn do so because (1) they're bored and want attention or (2) they're hungry. You will reward kitty if you respond in any fashion to these cries, especially if her meowing gets you out of bed to feed her. She has trained you to be a food dispenser.

There's absolutely nothing wrong with responding to your kitten's pitiful whines, as long as you don't mind being at her beck and call. In my house, Seren talks a great deal, especially in the early morning and late evening. After all, Seren is Siamese—and these are prime times for cat activity.

If you want to sleep later than 4:00 A.M., you'll need to practice some tough kitten-love. In other words, ignore the whiny baby. Give her attention *only* when she's quiet, and on your terms. Do not acknowledge her mews by moving, squirting her with the squirt gun, or saying a word. Especially don't allow her to badger you into filling her bowl with food. Anything you do will be interpreted as a reply to her pleas, and she'll redouble her efforts.

Of course, it can be difficult to ignore a whiny kitten pat-pat-patting your nose or burrowing into your armpit. Kittens can be very determined. If that's the case, rather than sharing your bedroom with the kitten, she should spend the night in her own room. You will get a good night's sleep, and she'll be forced to wait until a decent hour when you greet her with breakfast on your terms.

Second-Story Kittens

Kittens and cats love heights. Only her present stature keeps your kitten on the ground level, and believe me, she'll grow out of that. Individual kittens and cats may relish higher ground. For instance, the active Cornish Rex can not only leap great heights, but also loves to climb. The tops of refrigerators, high bookshelves, even the tops of doors may not be beyond this kitty's paws.

A yen for heights is instinctive behavior. A high perch offers a secure resting place from which to play lookout. A desire for lofty perches is also associated with feline social structure. Basically, the kitty that can claim the highest perch is also "top cat." Vertical space is incredibly important to the cat.

Of course, some second-story "property" in your home may be dangerous to the kitten, such as the stovetop. Few owners want their kittens playing among delicate collectibles, conducting "gravity experiments" by knocking breakables off the mantel one by one.

However, it's unreasonable to expect a kitten or cat to stay on the floor. Sure, she may follow your lead and "obey" when you—the Big Cat—are present to enforce the rules. But she'll certainly take advantage of your absence, to time-share the dining room table.

Decide what you can live with, and designate which second-story property is okay, and which should be a kitten-free zone. Be prepared to interrupt the kitten from treading an illegal surface. You can do this by watching for her to leap and spritzing her tail with the squirt gun or shaking the penny can just before she takes off. Kitties often prepare to leap by crouching down before the target, and "revving" their back legs by treading.

Depending on the target surface, you can also booby-trap it to make the resting spot unattractive and uncomfortable. For instance, my cat Seren learned she could reach the mantel by jumping first onto the TV cabinet, and from there onto the TV, and then the mantel. A single strip of Sticky Paws on the cabinet, on either side of the TV, stopped her cold—and protects my china.

Other countertop deterrents include aluminum foil, which cats hate to walk across. Plastic carpet runners placed nub side up on the surface make a singularly unattractive resting spot that kittens avoid. Pet products stores also carry snapper-type booby-traps (often in the dog section, called Snappy Trainer) designed to be set out on the countertop. When touched by the unsuspecting kitten, they pop like mousetraps (but without the danger of trapping the kitten), and startle her off the surface. They are also available at www.pet-expo.com where you can get a three-pack for about seven dollars.

> **Tip:** Cats love to sleep on cars because the engine is warm, and it's a great lookout. The plastic carpet runners, nub side up, also work to keep kittens (and cats) off your car. Of course, it's safer to keep the kitten indoors away from any vehicles—maybe you can explain that to your neighbors if they have trespassing, car-loving cats.

None of these corrections will work unless you replace the target with something better. Provide your kitten with a perch that is more comfortable, has a better view, and is higher than any of your off-limits furniture, and kitty will have no complaints. Many of these cat trees include scratching surfaces, so you can replace two targets at once.

Be sure to choose a cat tree or perch that has room for all your cats. Because elevation helps dictate what cat is in charge, it's important to offer options to the multicat home.

The Cat Tree Cure

A well designed cat tree or two, or several perches throughout the house, can cure a multitude of stress-related behavior problems in the multicat home. "Only" kittens and cats rarely develop stress-related behaviors as often as kittens and cats who must struggle with hierarchy issues. Because cats need to own property, the less space there is to share, the more behavior problems can develop. The rule of thumb is to have no more cats than you have bedrooms—that is, make sure you have a separate room available for every cat.

When that isn't possible, you can diminish stress by capitalizing on vertical space. Build up. Create multilevels in your home. Leave half a shelf empty, so kitty has a place of her own to perch. Provide multilevel cat furniture like trees and perches or hiding places. Enrich the environment so that even your one-bedroom apartment has vertical space that satisfies your several cats. That will cut down or eliminate inappropriate bathroom and scratching behavior prompted by stress.

PART 5

FELINE FASCINATIONS— TOP TEN LISTS

16

TEN FAVORITE CAT LEGENDS

In the Beginning—Creation Fables

No creature has been so beloved—and so reviled—throughout history as the cat. Likely these strong reactions have to do with their mysterious nature, marvelous physical prowess, uncanny sensory ability, and loving natures. These feline traits and abilities left our ancestors in awe of the cat.

People of the past sought answers to their questions about the cat and often devised delightful, eloquent myths to explain the inexplicable. Some of the most entertaining ones focus on how the cat came into being.

Noah and the Kitten

A story from Hebrew folklore declares that cats weren't around before the Great Flood. Noah had quite a time rounding up all the critters and loading them onto the Ark. Not only did he have to convince pairs of reluctant animals to become part of a floating zoo, he also had to ensure their safety from one another. After all, the lions were not only a danger to the gazelle, hare, and other prey creatures, but also to their human caretakers. What would become of them, thought Noah, if the lions became hungry for a midnight snack and gobbled up their housemates?

So Noah took his concerns to heaven and begged for an answer to this terrible quandary. God answered Noah's prayers, and all the creatures on the Ark rejoiced as the two lions fell into a deep, deep slumber. Seeing this, the other animals felt safe and gladly climbed aboard the Ark in answer to Noah's request. In fact, a pair of rats heard about the big to-do, and sneaked on the boat without an invitation.

The rains fell, the thunder boomed, the wind lashed for days and nights on end, leaving the people and animals frightened and sick. Once the sun returned to the sky, and seasickness subsided, their appetites returned, and Noah took stock of provisions. He discovered that the stowaway rats (immune to seasickness, it seemed) had found the grain, had been particularly fruitful, and had multiplied beyond anyone's wildest expectations.

Noah again sought heaven's help, for he knew the voracious rats represented as big a danger as had the lion's appetite. Once more, God answered his prayers. And lo and behold, the lion, in the midst of his slumbers, produced a gigantic sneeze.

And out of the sneeze sprang a pretty little kitten with a lion-size appetite for rodents—and a love for people as big as the Creator's heart.

Saint Peter and the Cat

Medieval legend offers another version of the cat creation story, which reflects the attitude toward felines during this age, when for the most part kitty was reviled as an evil being.

The story goes that the Devil was beside himself with jealousy when he saw that God had created men and women. What wondrous creatures they were! But, being nothing if not a true egotist, the Devil knew he could outdo the Creator.

And so, in an effort to mimic God and create humans, the Devil used his own special brand of creation. But far from creating an exalted being, he produced a sad-looking, pitiful creature that had no skin.

It was the first cat.

Rather than feeling proud of his creation, the Devil turned his back on the cat in disgust. But Saint Peter saw the pathetic kitty and heard her crying with despair and shame. He took pity on her, and gave the cat her only priceless possession, a glorious fur coat. That is why, to this day, the cat takes such vain care of her wondrous coat and washes herself, to honor Saint Peter and his kindness.

The Contest of Sun and Moon

An ancient fable explains that Sun and Moon challenged each other to a contest to see who could create the finest animal of all. Sun rolled up his fiery sleeves, concentration furrowed his glorious brow, and out of nothingness he brought forth a lion. The lion strode about the room, proud and powerful, and roared his approval. Impressed, the other gods congratulated Sun and complimented him on such a fine creation.

Moon was filled with jealousy. She gathered up shimmering moonbeams that trailed from her fingertips and fashioned a delicate yet muscular and sprightly cat. The playful cat scampered about, and even her loving eyes reflected the waxing and waning of her Mother-Moon.

But the other gods mocked the cat. "You've given us an imitation lion!" they cried, and called Moon a copycat. Sun created a mouse as a sign of his contempt.

Desperate to create something original, Moon tried again—and this time, from the shadow that colored the other side of her brightness, she fashioned a cunning monkey. But the monkey's silly antics only made matters worse, and the other gods laughed and laughed until Moon's face turned red with humiliation.

Furious over the mockery, Moon caused eternal strife to spring between the creatures that had been created. And to this day, the lion despises the monkey, and the cat wages war on the mouse.

Cats and the Weather

Our ancestors have been charmed, awed, and even frightened by the incredible predictive ability displayed by cats. Today we know that the feline senses are able to detect the most subtle changes in the world around them. Consequently, cats learn what these changes mean to them, and react accordingly.

For instance, the atmosphere charged with static electricity that heralds a thunderstorm likely feels pretty uncomfortable to the cat when her fur builds up a charge. Her whiskers and fur, each individual hair planted beneath the skin near sensitive nerve endings, alert her to wind changes and even subtle shifts in barometric pressure. Scent sense—the mere smell of moisture on the breeze—easily alerts the cat to impending rain. To the cat, these clues are more meaningful and accurate than the nightly television weather report.

Of course, ancient people saw only the cat's reaction and believed she employed magic to predict—or even incite—weather changes. Cats got credit (and blame) for a host of natural events, especially storms at sea. In fact, the light breeze that ripples the water during a calm as prelude to a squall is still called a cat's-paw. In many countries, bathing a cat was thought to prompt rain.

In Scotland, cats were evicted from houses during thunderstorms because they were thought to be living lightning rods. One legend says lightning was designed by angels to rid cats of the evil that infests them during storms. Both Scottish and Japanese folklore credit tortoiseshell cats with the ability to predict storms. Kitty scratching a table leg "raises wind" in Scotland, while a Japanese cat who washes behind her ears foretells rain. Playing with string stirs a tempest, and a playing cat was thought to actually cause a gale.

Nine Lives Legends

Throughout history, cats have been associated with the religious beliefs of various cultures. The legend that cats enjoy nine lives springs from this association and the reverence and awe ancient peoples had for the power of numbers.

The number nine—a trinity of trinities—has always been considered lucky and mystical. Multiply nine by any other number and the sum of the digits in the resulting answer is always divisible by nine—now that's powerful magic!

For instance, in ancient Egypt, cats were considered the physical incarnation of the goddess Bast or Pasht (also called Sekmet). Pasht was the female aspect of the god-trinity of that time. The Egyptian pantheon had three companies of nine gods each, and because of their protecting love for the cat, this may have given rise to the thought that she had nine lives. A Viking goddess of love and beauty, called Freya, rode in a glorious chariot drawn by loving cats and reigned over the "nine worlds," and according to Norse legend, it took nine nights' ride to reach the sacred river.

The cat's nine lives are even associated with early Christianity. According to a fascinating book, *The Cat in the Mysteries of Religion and Magic*, by M. Oldfield Howey (Castle Books, 1956), the ninth hour was the hour of Christ's death. Described as the Sun of Righteousness, and loosely associated with Osiris and Horus (Horus was "the god of light" and the beloved son of Osiris), Christ was represented by the sacred cat to emphasize he was the newborn, rising sun, the light of the world. The cat's ability to be "reborn" in each of nine lives had strong correlation to a holy trinity, rising from the dead and being reborn.

But likely the cat's incredible physical prowess cemented the cat's reputation for living beyond one lifespan. People noticed how cats seemed impervious to disasters that typically injured or killed other creatures—like falling from a great height yet landing safely on their feet.

Marks of Favor

Many charming stories try to explain various physical attributes of the cat, especially colors and markings. For instance, tricolored cats—often called calico—are considered by many cultures to be lucky, probably again due to the mysticism attached to the number three. Others stories have to do with physical differences—cats with extra toes, referred to scientifically as polydactyl cats, are said to be lucky. Other cats are marked forevermore by some spiritual or cataclysmic encounter.

Tail Tales

With few exceptions, cats have expressive, lithe tails. Those few exceptions, though, beg an explanation. For instance, the tailless Manx cat originated on the Isle of Man and is said to have lost her tail when Noah shut the door too soon and cut it off. Another version explains that Manx cats became tailless due to an altercation with Samson, who often swam in the Irish Sea. He tangled with a swimming cat one day, and was nearly drowned and only saved himself by chopping off her tail. Ever since, the Manx has been tailless.

There's even a story to explain why Siamese cats have kinked tails—well, they used to, anyway, until reputable breeders set out to eliminate the trait. Anyway, the story goes that one lovely Siamese kitty was entrusted with a jeweled ring, which she slipped over the end of her tail for safekeeping, ending up with a permanent kink. Yet another explanation says that many many years ago, a Siamese cat tied a knot in her tail to help her remember something . . . but she forgot it anyway.

"Temple Mark"

Many cultures around the world have considered cats to be beloved of the gods of the day, and they held a special place in the hearts of their prophets and seers. A story told of Mohammed notes that his favorite feline, Muezza, fell asleep on his sleeve while he prayed. Rather than wake her, the prophet had such regard for her comfort that he cut off the sleeve rather than disturb her nap.

Siamese cats are one of the oldest established breeds, and as such, enjoy a number of lovely legends. Oftentimes it was believed that spirits of the dead were enshrined inside the living bodies of sacred cats, like the Siamese. There are also references made to a holy "Temple Mark," said to distinguish the True Temple Cats of Siam. Two distinct markings on the backs of these cats are said to be the shadowy handprint of a holy being who once picked up the cat and forever left the mark on all Temple Cat descendants.

Sacred Cat of Burma

A legend describes how the Burman cat came by her distinctive looks. Mun-Ha, a venerable kittah (priest), lived in the Temple of Lao-Tsun. The priest spent his days contemplating the golden goddess with sapphire eyes, Tsun-Kyankse, the deity who held sway over the transmutation of souls about to be reborn into new living creatures. Mun-Ha had an oracle that dictated his decisions—his golden-eyed white cat Sinh, whom all the other kittahs revered. Sinh was one of one hundred white temple cats kept by the kittahs.

A night came when enemies from Thailand swarmed near the sacred temple, and brokenhearted, Mun-Ha died in the presence of his goddess with his divine cat nearby. Suddenly, the miracle of immediate transmutation took place, as Sinh bounded onto his dead master and faced the goddess-figure.

The hair along Sinh's back turned golden, and his yellow eyes became sapphire-blue like the eyes of the goddess. His four feet and ears turned earth-brown, but where they contacted the priest's venerable head, they whitened to the claws, to the toe-tips, purified by the touch of the holy man.

The transformed Sinh gazed at the other priests with a silent order, and the kittahs obeyed and successfully defended the temple from the invaders. Thereafter, Sihn refused all food and maintained his vigil of the goddess—and seven days later, without lowering an eyelash, he died and bore away into the goddess's care the soul of Mun-Ha, which was too perfect for the earth.

The priests assembled before the goddess Tsun-Kyankse to choose a successor. And wonder of wonders, there came a slow procession of the one hundred white cats of the temple. Their feet were gloved in white; their snowy hair reflected shots of gold; and the topazes of their eyes shone sapphire-blue.

All fell prostrate with fear before the cats, for the priests knew they bore the souls of their holy ancestors. The cats solemnly surrounded Legoa, the most youthful of the priests, and so revealed heaven's will that he be Mun-Ha's successor.

And from that day forward, all true Burman cats are marked by the presence of the goddess with blue eyes, golden fur, earth-brown feet with white toes, and are known as the Sacred Cats of Burma.

The Kimono Cat

The book *The Cat in the Mysteries of Religion and Magic* by M. Oldfield Howey features two pictures of a "sacred" cat from Japan, photographed by Dr. Lilian Veley in 1910. The stocky white cat is marked with black splotches of color, and has a "short, black, very broad, triangular tail" and looks very much like the modern Japanese Bobtail.

It is the marking found on the cat's back—a solid-colored silhouette-like shape of a woman in a kimono—that makes the cat sacred. Such cats were thought to hold the soul of an ancestor, and they were sent to temples to be honored and cared for in luxury for the rest of their natural life.

Why Tabby Wears an M

One of the most touching legends tells the story of a simple Tabby cat, and her gift on the very first Christmas day to a special mother and child.

There was no snow that night in Bethlehem. Instead, the small cat watched a star-spangled sky from her perch in the window of a stable. She liked the stable, for it was a warm, safe place to raise her furry babies, and the innkeeper sometimes left scraps out for her to nibble. Tabby wasn't particularly distinctive, and most humans didn't look at her twice. After all, her short gray-black fur was quite common. But Tabby's striped coat hid a heart bigger than cats twice her size.

This night, though, Tabby was out of sorts, for she'd not been able to hunt and catch dinner. Travelers had poured into town for days, so noisy they disturbed decent cat-folks' rest. Why, they'd even invaded Tabby's quiet stable, a place she had before shared only with other furry creatures. Tabby hadn't minded the human couple—they were calmer than most. She'd left that morning for her usual rounds, but when she returned, the stable was packed with people.

From her perch on the window, Tabby watched the last of the strangers leave. She slipped from the window and padded silently inside—and froze!

"Meewwww, meewww, meewww," cried a tiny voice.

A kitten? Tabby's ears turn this way and that to find the sound of the kitten's voice. It came from the manger, the very place Tabby often made her own bed. A woman knelt beside the manger, intent on the small mewling creature within. Tabby was drawn by the kittenish sound, though she knew her own furry babies were grown to cathood. She tiptoed forward very slowly and passed by a woolly burro, a warm cow, and all the other animals.

The woman looked up and saw the striped cat. "Oh, little cat," she murmured, "my baby cannot sleep, and nothing calms him this night." She sighed and turned back to the manger. "How grateful would I be to anyone able to bring him sweet dreams."

And, as Tabby watched, each stable animal stepped forward in turn and tried to soothe the woman's baby. But the kittenish sounds continued and finally Tabby could contain herself no longer.

Quickly, she washed herself—paws, face, behind the ears, to the very tip of her tail (so as not to offend the child's mother)—and then shyly stepped forward. She leaped gracefully to the manger and stared into the face of the most beautiful baby (human or kitten!)

(Photo credit: Ralston Purina Company)

The blessing from the Madonna legend clearly marks this tabby kitten's brow with an M.

she'd ever seen. He cooed and smiled, waving his tiny hands at Tabby, and she very carefully drew in her claws and settled beside him. Forgotten was her empty tummy; she could only hear her heart calling out to this sweet human-kitten.

And Tabby began to purr.

The wondrous cat-song filled the stable with overwhelming emotion. The animals listened with awe, and the child's mother smiled as her baby quietly went to sleep.

The child's mother placed her hand gently on the purring Tabby's forehead. "Blessings upon you, Tabby cat, for this sweet gift given to me and my child," she said. And where she'd touched Tabby's brow, there appeared an M—the sign of the Madonna's benediction.

From that day forward, all proper tabby cats are honored with an M on their brow for the great service they performed that first Christmas night. And Christmas nights often find Tabby cats staring into the night, purring as they recall a very special child their ancestor once sang to sleep.

17

Ten Fun Feline Facts
Explained

Catnip Indulgence

You see the greenish-gray herb called catnip advertised everywhere. It comes dried and packaged in tubs in the cat products section of the supermarket, or stuffed inside toy mice for your cat's enjoyment. There are even sprays with catnip scent available. And, of course, catnip fresh from the garden really gets cats interested. But not all cats love catnip. Kittens rarely respond before they're six months old, and only two out of three cats will inherit the "catnip gene" that makes them wild for it.

Like other mints, catnip has a strong, pungent odor. Susceptible cats sniff this scent, and it produces a reaction in the brain that prompts a loss of inhibition. Catnip-intoxicated cats may meow with pleasure, roll around, and act like furry drunken fools for five to fifteen minutes until the effect wears off.

Catnip is a great training tool. For instance it can be used as a reward or as a lure to get kitty to scratch the right object. Cats do not become "addicted." The herb is a great recreational indulgence, but the effect can weaken and wear off more quickly if catnip is used too often.

Technical Stuff: Catnip (*Nepeta cataria*) grows wild all over Europe, temperate Asia, and North America. It was introduced in America by early European settlers who brewed the herb into medicinal tea to settle upset stomachs. The plant grows two to three feet high in a mounded bushy shape, with heart-shaped, toothed leaves covered with a fine down. Crushing the leaves by biting or rolling on the plant releases a volatile oil into the air that acts like a feline hallucinogen when it reacts with nerves in the cat's nose and "scent center" in the brain.

Kitten Purrs: Cosmic Catnip, prepackaged dried catnip, gets rave reviews from cats and is available at most pet supply stores. The company says it's been specially prepared to preserve potency. It's also available in a spray bottle application that's great for gaining cat allegiance to a new scratch object.

Catnaps

Napping is one of the cat's favorite pastimes. There are various stages or levels of sleep, and the first level is a light sleep—called a catnap. These last up to fifteen to twenty minutes and are characterized by slow-wave pulses of activity in the brain. Kitty lies with his head up and paws tucked beneath him, or even sitting upright—ready to spring into action. During a catnap, kitty senses stay tuned to sounds and scents so that even with his eyes closed, he remains alert to the world around him. That's why he can come fully awake from a catnap at the sound or smell of a tasty treat being prepared.

Sleep Champs

Newborn kittens spend nearly twenty hours a day asleep, but even adult cats will sleep up to sixteen hours every day. Cats sleep so much, they spend two-thirds of their life asleep. That means a six-year-old cat will have only spent about two years of his life awake. Elderly cats sleep more than robust adults, and all cats tend to sleep more during cold or rainy weather.

Even while sleeping, your cat is not completely dead to the world the whole time. Cats don't spend hours at a time asleep, the way people do, but indulge in short periods of sleep alternated with activity. The kitty brain remains tuned to scents and sounds during 70 percent of sleep.

After the light sleep (catnap) phase, feline sleep progresses to deep sleep for about six or seven minutes. The deep sleep phase is also called *rapid sleep* because of the quick movement of the brain waves. Adult cats alternate between light and deep sleep, but during the first month of life, kittens fall directly into deep sleep and stay there.

Technical Stuff: Experts theorize that cats and other animals that have few natural enemies in the wild are able to sleep for longer periods of time, and that need for sleep increases in direct proportion to the amount of energy required for hunting. Cats tend to burn huge reserves of energy in bursts of activity during play and hunting.

Dream Cats

Yes, cats (and kittens) do dream. We can only guess at what visions they see as their paws wiggle, whiskers twitch, and tails lash with excitement. Perhaps he's capturing illusory mice or teaching the neighbor's dog a lesson in manners. It's likely they relive in their dreams the events of normal cat life.

Cat dreams occur during the deep, rapid sleep phase—that means kittens dream more than adult cats. Animals with the most highly developed brains tend to have the longest dreaming phase during sleep. People typically dream for up to two hours each night (whether we remember or not). Adult cats spend up to three hours each day indulging in kitty dreams.

This little guy is ready for a nap. Kittens often like catnapper beds designed just for them, but they can (and do!) sleep anywhere.

(Photo credit: Amy D. Shojai)

Eye to Eye

Cat eyes have fascinated us since the beginning of time, and are, indeed, one of the cat's most striking features. They are said to be the window to the feline soul. In fact, in nineteenth-century China people gauged time by the dilation of the cats' eyes. The Chinese believed the pupil grew narrower until twelve noon when it became a fine slit, and then began to widen again. On sunny days this truly works; since the brightest time of day likely falls during the noon hour, the pupil would compensate and narrow to a fine line during this period.

Eyes come in three basic shapes, determined by the position of the upper and lower eyelids and position of the eyes. Round eyes are typical of the Persian, while many cats, including most kitty-next-door types, have oval eyes. Oriental-type cats like Siamese seem to have almond-shaped eyes because they are slightly slanted and set to the side of the head.

Kitten Eye Color

All kittens are born with blue eyes, and in most cases the final eye color develops between three and seven months of age. One exception, however, is the Korat breed, which boasts luminous green eyes. It may take up to four years for the eyes of the Korat to develop their true adult color.

Cat eyes come in nearly all the jewel colors of the rainbow—from yellow-gold-amber-copper, to all shades of green and blue. The color of the eye varies by breed and is determined by genetics. Not only the amount and position of the pigment in the iris—the colored portion of the eye—but also the way light reflects off the eyes helps determine eye color. Some cats are termed "odd-eyed," which means each eye is a different color.

Glow-in-the-Dark Kitten Eyes

Shine a light toward any cat or kitten's eyes in low light, and they'll reflect back an eerie glow. Ancient peoples believed that the bright night-shine that spills from the cat's eyes at night was due to the light they drank during the day. This eye shine comes from the mirrorlike layer of cells, called the tapetum lucidum, at the back of the retina of the eyeball that serves to amplify existing light. That allows cats to see better in low light than humans or many other animals. The domestic cat's eyes use nearly 50 percent more available light than ours do, and require only one sixth the illumination. That's why your kitten is so active in the evening and night hours, when all you want to do is sleep.

Color Purr-ception

In the past, experts declared that cats saw only in shades of black and white. Today we know that cats and kittens do, indeed, have the "equipment" to see color. Millions of light-receptor cells on the retina at the back of the eye gather information about patterns of light. Cells called rods allow the cat to see shades of white, black, and gray. Cells called cones detect colors. Cats have many more rods than people do, which helps them see in low-light situations.

Tests have shown that cats do have the ability to see differences between certain reds, greens, blues, and yellows. People see combinations of red, blue, and yellow—but cat color sense is based on a two-color (dichromatic) system of blue and green. In very bright light, green and blue look brighter than red or yellow to the cat, because they have very few red-sensitive cones. That makes sense, of course, because cats evolved to see prey in the green-and-blue color schemes of grassy landscapes, where prehistoric cats lived and hunted.

Bottom line, color probably doesn't mean much to cats and kittens. They can see it, but they don't care much about it. Pattern seems to spark more interest in cats than colors do.

Hunting "Gifts"

Cats have been domesticated for centuries, but the wild child remains inside. Many cats become expert hunters adept at capturing critters, be they a feather toy on the end of a string, a moth at the window, or even a mouse or other prey creature. Cats often present these prizes to their owners with well-deserved pride. Such "gifts" may be displayed on the back step, in the food bowl, or (oh joy!) on your pillow.

Why does kitty bring his human family these less-than-savory gifts? Well, of course, the cat thinks he's offering you the highest compliment when he presents the result of his prowess for your inspection. Some behaviorists believe these cats look on humans as poorly equipped hunters who are unable to bring home the bacon without feline help. Others theorize the cat simply brings his trophy to his nest—the house—with plans to enjoy and eat it later.

Certainly, kitty seems to preen with pride when complimented on his exceptional skill. So praise your fearless hunter. And when he's not looking, dispose of the kill appropriately and replace it with a more wholesome treat.

Kneading Behavior

Kneading behavior harks back to the cat's babyhood. When a cat is born, she will press her paws rhythmically one after another in a treading action against her mother's breasts, which helps stimulate the milk to be released. Behaviorists believe that this action—called *kneading*—is a sign of feline contentment and reminds the cat of those feelings of safety, happiness, and comfort the cat felt as a newborn being cared for by her mother. What an honor—your cat is calling you Mom.

Mitten-Pawed Kittens

Kittens and cats normally have four toes on each hind foot, and five toes on each front paw. A mutation causes some cats to be born with extra toes—called polydactylism. The extras make the kitten look like he's wearing mittens when they double (or more) the size of his "thumb" claw on the front or rear feet.

In the past mitten-pawed kittens and cats were thought to bring good luck. A polydactyl cat may have one extra toe on one foot, or several extras on all four feet. Usually the mutation is harmless but it can result in smaller-than-normal toes with claws that may not retract, and so more care may be needed for appropriate kitty pedicures.

Water Phobias

Many cats seem to abhor water. They cower when the rain pours down and detest (shudder!) a bath. Yet at the same time, these same cats may enjoy dabbling paws in a stream of water from the tap or playing in their water bowl. So what's the deal?

Cats prefer routine above all else. Rain or a dunking in the bathtub is the unexpected at its worst. Water filling the sink for a bath may sound scary, too. Cats remember unpleasant experiences, so getting water in his eyes or ears just once may be enough to cement a phobia for life.

Cat fur sheds moisture, so even a cat caught in the rain has the ability to keep his skin warm and dry. But a dunking soaks the fur clear to the skin, strips away that insulating cushion of body-warmed air caught at skin level, and feels unexpected and distasteful to the cat. Wet fur clings to the skin, adds uncomfortable weight to heavily furred felines, and interferes with fur function. After all, dry fur can be fluffed to send a bragging message to other cats, or to allow a cool breeze to reach the skin.

Water preferences vary among individual cats. When the encounters are on the cat's terms, many kitties enjoy watery adventures. In fact, one gorgeous breed called the Turkish Van (or the Turkish Swimming Cat) loves water so much they may join you in the bathtub!

APPENDIX A

Ten Favorite Kitten Web Sites

I've come to the Internet rather late in my professional life, and I am by no means a "Net head." Nevertheless, I have found Internet resources invaluable for their educational impact—and for the fun they offer. Today, a computer and modem allows anybody to plug into the World Wide Web to visit a nearly limitless supply of kitten-related destinations.

I use on-line resources such as professional Web sites to help research my books; electronic bulletin boards to ask and answer questions; and subscriptions to e-mail lists or news groups that feature electronic communities of people with similar interests. E-mail has become one of my most important business and recreational tools. It keeps me connected to family, friends, and colleagues, and even allows me to conduct interviews with experts around the world.

My list of favorite sites includes far more than ten. But the ones I've featured here offer a good jumping-off place from which to begin your explorations. Most have multiple links that take you to other sites, in a never-ending chain of kitten delights. You should also try the search function on your browser. Search engines like www.altavista.com or www.dogpile.com are on-line directories of every subject imaginable. Simply type in your subject (for example, *kittens*), and hundreds to thousands—maybe even millions—of kitten-oriented destinations are listed.

Kitten Care Plus!

KittenCare.com (www.kittencare.com) offers a great cross section of kitten-specific information as well as general cat care content. I particularly like the list of links, which includes valuable animal hospital and feline veterinary locators and shelter directories. Just punch in the state where you live, and area clinics and veterinarians are listed for your consideration. This site also offers information resources for folks who deal with kitten rescue as well as general kitten care highlights, uplifting success stories, favorite cat books, and on-line "cat communities" where you can interact with other folks who love kittens as much as you do.

Of course, when care issues and questions arise, the first place to look for answers is your veterinarian. The veterinarian who personally knows your kitten and can examine him is in the best position to answer specific questions, but many on-line veterinary sites offer general information. Vet Care Forum (http://go.compuserve.com/animals) is one of the best, with a staff of volunteer veterinarians available to answer nearly any animal behavior, training, and medical care question in the message boards. There are also many files available on a wide range of topics. Simply click the mouse on the "VetCare" message board, post your question, and check back for a response. You'll receive input from many experienced kitten and cat people who are able to offer suggestions to help solve any problems, or explain something that has you puzzled.

Complementary & Alternative Veterinary Medicine (www.altvetmed.com) is one of my all-time favorite veterinary resources. Many people these days are interested in offering a wider range of care options, and this site offers links to informational sites on holistic veterinary medicine—acupuncture, chiropractic, herbal medicine, homeopathy, nutritional therapy, and other therapies. There are also a number of good articles on "natural" topics, and directories that can help you find a veterinarian who practices the complementary therapies that particularly interest you.

My all-time favorite cat site is Cats Forum (http://go.compuserve.com/cats), billed as "the on-line home of the most experienced and friendliest cat people you will ever meet." I think that's true, and I hope you'll visit and see for yourself. Cats Forum features more than a dozen topic-specific message boards for questions, answers, and on-line discussions on everything from cat care and behavior; rescue, stray, and feral issues; to cat show topics and breeder information. You'll find sympathetic support in the "Grieving for Pets" section. There are many articles and informational threads to access in the on-line library where you can share your own stories, and even cute kitten pictures. There are even sections where your kittens can "talk" to other cats and animals from around the world in a "Critter Chat" forum. Participants interact by typing messages in the "voices" of their pets, using phonetic spellings to create "critter-speak." No human identities are allowed. The result is a freewheeling, imaginative world that's lots of fun for the people who take the time to indulge. I'm convinced Seren loves it!

Pedigrees and Show Cats

The folks who show and raise pedigree kittens take great pains to remain up to date on everything there is to know about their particular cat breed. Type the name of any feline purebred into an Internet search engine and you're sure to find dozens and dozens of Web sites with lovely pictures and information.

One of the best places to start is the Internet Cat Club (www.netcat.org). The members of the club combine their love of pedigreed cats with computer savvy, and the site offers a venue for networking with other cat lovers who have similar interests. Along with many articles on showing and health related issues, Internet Cat Club also provides links to Cat Fanciers Association clubs, purebred rescue contacts, and breed-specific mailing lists.

Another great site for breed-specific and show cat information is the Cat Fanciers site (www.fanciers.com). Pages and pages of links cover everything from general cat and care information, breed descriptions and cat books, to breed clubs, cat registries, and show schedules. There are also many fun links to unique, fun, fascinating, funny, and delicious cat-related sites. You'll want to create a link to this site because there's no way to explore everything at one visit.

This Himalayan baby likes to snuggle and sleep in warm blankets fresh from the dryer. On-line chat and bulletin boards offer places to share stories about your kitten's favorite napping places, unique personality, and other advice.

(Photo credit: Amy D. Shojai)

Kitten Rescue

Oh, there are so many wonderful rescue sites available! National animal welfare associations as well as many regional or privately funded groups host countless educational Web sites. They provide information on adopting homeless kittens and cats, rescue operations, and uplifting success stories. One of the best, the San Francisco Society for the Prevention of Cruelty to Animals, serves as a benchmark that many other animal welfare organizations try to emulate. You can learn all about their programs at www.sfspca.org.

Alley Cat Allies (www.alleycat.org) provides educational information on the care and management of feral cat colonies. The site provides a state-by-state index of feral cat support organizations that can help provide caring people with solutions to the issues concerning wild cats living in their community.

Feral cats are different from stray kitties. Strays are pet cats and kittens that have at some point lived with people and have become lost or abandoned. Many times they welcome a return to life with people, and are happy to be pets again. But feral cats are born and raised in the wild without contact with humans; they have a difficult time living with people and may never become "tame."

Alley Cat Allies, and other feral cat help-groups, offer ways for people to provide necessary care with Trap, Neuter, and Return programs (TNR), while allowing feral cats to continue to live happily and healthfully on their own terms. Their program helps colonies stay healthy, reduces scavenging and illness, and eliminates reproduction. TNR offers an alternative to the wholesale extermination of wild cats that some communities feel forced to implement.

Kitten Fun

I've saved some of the best for last. You'll surely find more favorites as you explore the Information Kitten-Highway, but I came across these and just had to share them.

When you have a new kitten, health and behavior concerns are vital. But you can't call the kitten "hey, you!" forever, and the sooner he learns his name, the better. Check out Kittynames.com (www.kittynames.com) for a fun resource that offers hundreds of choices, top picks, and even the true "meaning" of a particular name.

What stage in maturity has your kitten reached? If you know kitty's birthday, you can figure out what to expect at El Sham's Kitten Calendar (www.dataweb.net/~sham). This is a fun and educational way to figure out what to anticipate from your kitten, from birth through about twelve weeks of age. There's also a "pregnancy calendar" that tracks the mom-cat's development, at the same site.

Everybody loves kitten pictures. You'll find thousands on the

Internet. But heck, there are many sites that welcome your contribution, too. Don't be shy about posting pictures of your own precious baby. And if you want to go all out, maybe you'll want to hire an artist to capture the beauty of your kitten in an original work of art. Again, there are many available. One of my favorites features watercolor cat artist Drew Strouble (www.catmandrew.com). There are many works immediately available, and Drew also works on commission to paint a portrait of your special feline. Wendy Christensen, the illustrator for *Complete Kitten Care*, also specializes in feline art. Visit her portfolio page at www.catwriters.org/articles/w-christensen.html.

APPENDIX B

Resources

Cat Associations

A cat association is a national organization that registers cats, keeps records of their ancestry in pedigrees, publishes breed standards, sponsors cat shows, and determines who will judge them. Catteries are individual establishments that strive to produce the "ideal" cat of a given breed. These cats are then shown in contests sanctioned by the cat association in which that cat is registered. The goal is to determine which cat is closest to the breed standard of perfection.

Catteries often hold membership in local cat clubs, which in turn hold membership in one or more cat associations. There are a number of cat associations. Breed standards may vary from association to association; not every cat association recognizes the same cat breeds.

American Association of Cat Enthusiasts (AACE)
P.O. Box 213
Pine Brook, NJ 07058
Phone: (973) 335-6717
E-mail: info@aaceinc.org
Internet: www.aaceinc.org

American Cat Association (ACA)
8101 Katherine Avenue
Panorama City, CA 91402
Phone: (818) 782-6080

American Cat Fanciers Association (ACFA)
P.O. Box 203
Point Lookout, MO 65726
Phone: (417) 334-5430
E-mail: mcats@bellsouth.net
Internet: www.acfacat.com

Australian Cat Federation (ACF)
P.O. Box 3305
Port Adelaide SA 5015
Australia
Phone: 08-8449-5880
E-mail: ccaafc01@sentex.net
Internet: www.acf.asn.au/

Canadian Cat Association/Association Feline Canadienne
    (CCA/AFC)
289 Rutherford Road, South, Unit 18
Brampton, ON L6W 3R9
Canada
Phone: (905) 459-1481
E-mail: office@cca-afc.com
Internet: www.cca-afc.com

Cat Fanciers' Association (CFA)
1805 Atlantic Avenue.
P.O. Box 1005
Manasquan, NJ 08736-0805
Phone: (732) 528-9797
E-mail: cfa@cfainc.org
Internet: www.cfainc.org

Cat Fanciers' Federation (CFF)
P.O. Box 661
Gratis, OH 45330
Phone: (937) 787-9009
Internet: www.cffinc.org

Federation International Feline (FIFe)
FIFe General Secretary
Penelope Bydlinski
Little Dene, Lenham Heath
Maidstone, Kent ME17 2BS
England
Phone: +44 (0) 1622 850913
E-mail: penbyd@compuserve.com
Internet: www.fifeweb.org

Governing Council of the Cat Fancy
4-6, Penel Orlieu
Bridgewater, Somerset TA6 3PG
England
Phone: +44 (0) 1278 427575
E-mail: gccf_cats@compuserve.com
Internet: ourworld.compuserve.com/homepages/gccf_cats

Happy Household Pet Cat Club (HHP)
Internet: www.HHPCC.org

The International Cat Association (TICA)
P.O. Box 2684
Harlingen, TX 78551
Phone: (956) 428-8046
E-mail: ticaeo@xanadu2.net
Internet: www.tica.org

Traditional Cat Association (TCA)
18509 NE 279th Street
Battle Ground, WA 98604-9717
E-mail: info@traditionalcats.com
Internet: www.siamesecats.org

World Cat Federation (WCF)
Geisbergstr. 2
D-45139-Essen

Germany
Phone: +49 201-555724
E-mail: wcf@wcf-online.de
Internet: www.wcf-online.de

Animal Welfare and Information Sources

Alley Cat Allies (feral cats)
1801 Belmont Road, NW, Suite 201
Washington, DC 20009
Phone: (202) 667-3630
E-mail: info@alleycat.org
Internet: www.alleycat.org

American Humane Association
63 Inverness Drive East
Englewood, CO 80112-5117
Phone: (800) 227-4645
E-mail: info@americanhumane.org
Internet: www.americanhumane.org

American Boarding Kennels Association
1702 East Pikes Peak Avenue
Colorado Springs, CO 80909
Phone: (719) 667-1600
E-mail: info@abka.com
Internet: www.abka.com

American Society for the Prevention of Cruelty to Animals
   (ASPCA)
424 East Ninety-second Street
New York, NY 10128
Phone: (212) 876-7700
E-mail: website@aspca.org
Internet: www.aspca.org

Animal Protection Institute of America
P.O. Box 22505

Sacramento, CA 95822
Phone: (916) 731-5521

Delta Society
289 Perimeter Road East
Renton, WA 98055-1329
(human/animal interaction)
Phone: (425) 226-7357
E-mail: info@deltasociety.org
Internet: www.deltasociety.org

Feral Cat Coalition
9528 Miramar Road
PMB 160
San Diego, CA 92126
E-mail: rsavage@feralcat.com
Internet: www.feralcat.com

Massachusetts Society for the Prevention of Cruelty to Animals
    (MSPCA)
350 South Huntington Avenue
Boston, MA 02130
Phone: (617) 522-7400
Internet: www.mspca.org

National Association of Professional Pet Sitters
6 State Road, Suite 113
Mechanicsburg, PA 17050
Phone: (717) 691-5565
E-mail: nappsmail@aol.com
Internet: www.petsitters.org

Pet Sitters International
201 East King Street
King, NC 27021-9163
Phone: (336) 983-9222
E-mail: info@petsit.com
Internet: www.petsit.com

SPAY/USA
c/o The Pet Savers Foundation
2261 Broadbridge Avenue
Stratford, CT 06614
Phone: (203) 377-1116
E-mail: alwaysspay@aol.com
Internet: www.spayusa.org

Magazines and Newsletters

Catnip
P.O. Box 420235
Palm Coast, FL 32142-0235
Phone: (800) 829-0926

Cat Fancy Magazine
Subscription Service Department
P.O. Box 52864
Boulder, CO 80322-2864
Phone: (800) 365-4421
E-mail: fancy@neodata.com

Catwatch
Cornell University College of Veterinary Medicine
Ithaca, NY 14853
Phone: (607) 257-5355

I Love Cats Magazine
c/o Editor Lisa Allmendinger
16 Meadow Hill Lane
Armonk, NY 10504
Phone: (908) 222-0990

PetLife Magazine
3451 Boston Avenue
Fort Worth, TX 76116
Phone: (800) 856-8060

Whole Cat Journal
P.O. Box 420234
Palm Coast, FL 32142
Phone: (800) 829-1926

Recommended Books

Adoption Information

Competability: A Practical Guide to Building a Peaceable Kingdom Between Cats and Dogs, by Amy D. Shojai. Information about the differences between cats and dogs, and how to help them live together

The Guide to Handraising Kittens, by Susan Easterly

Hand-raising the Orphaned Kitten, by M. L. Papurt

Shelter Cats, by Karen Commings. Learn more about the types of shelters and what you can expect—and even about volunteering

The Stray Cat Handbook, by Tamara Kreuz

Breeds, Breeding, and Showing

Barron's Encyclopedia of Cat Breeds: A Complete Guide to the Domestic Cats of North America, by J. Anne Helgren

The Complete Book of Cat Breeding, by Dan Rice

It's Show-Time!, by Phil Maggitti and J. Anne Helgren

Health Care

The First-Aid Companion for Dogs and Cats, by Amy D. Shojai. Covers over 150 everyday accidents and emergencies

New Choices in Natural Healing for Dogs and Cats, by Amy D. Shojai. An overview of many holistic therapies

The Purina Encyclopedia of Cat Care, by Amy D. Shojai. An A-to-Z reference on health, care, breeds, and behavior—particularly for adult cats

Miscellaneous Cat Fun

The Cat's House, by Bob Walker. Offers ideas about ways to enrich your cat's indoor environment

300 Incredible Things for Pet Lovers on the Internet, by Bob Vella

My Cat's Tale: A Journal of My Cat's Life and Times, by Lorie Glantz with Amy Shojai. A "baby book" for your new kitten.

Care Organizations

American Animal Hospital Association
P.O. Box 150899
Denver, CO 80215-0899
Phone: (303) 986-2800
Internet: www.aahanet.org

ASPCA National Animal Poison Control Center
Consultations for NAPCC can be charged to a credit card by calling (888) 426-4435 or to a phone bill at (900) 680-0000, or you can visit their Web site at www.napcc.aspca.org.

American Association of Feline Practitioners
200 4th Avenue North, Suite 900
Nashville, TN 37219
Phone: (615) 259-7788
E-mail: aafp@walkermgt.com
Internet: www.aafponline.org

Animal Behavior Society
Susan Foster
Department of Biology
Clark University

950 Main Street
Worcester, MA 01610-1477

American College of Veterinary Behaviorists
Department of Small Animal Medicine and Surgery
College of Veterinary Medicine
Texas A & M University
College Station, TX 77843-4474
Phone: (409) 845-2351

American Holistic Veterinary Association
2218 Old Emmorton Road
Bel Air, MD 21015
Phone: (410) 569-0795
E-mail: ahvma@compuserve.com
Internet: www.altvetmed.com

American Veterinary Chiropractic Association
623 Main Street
Hillsdale, IL 61257
Phone: (309) 658-2920
E-mail: amvetchiro@aol.com

American Veterinary Medical Association
1931 N. Meacham Road, Suite 100
Schaumburg, IL 60173-0805
Phone: (847) 925-8070
Internet: www.avma.org

The International Veterinary Acupuncture Society
Edward Boldt Jr., DVM, Exec. Director
P.O. Box 271395
Ft. Collins, CO 80527-1395
Phone: (970) 266-0666
E-mail: ivasoffice@aol.com
Internet: www.ivas.org

Pet Supply Sources

Angelical Cat Company (furniture)
2500 North University Drive, Suite 13
Sunrise, FL 33322
Phone: (954) 747-3629
E-mail: generalinfo@angelicalcat.com
Internet: www.angelicalcat.com

Arcata Pet
600 F Street
Arcata, CA 95521
Phone: (800) 822-9085
E-mail: sales@arcatapet.com
Internet: www.arcatapet-online.com

Cat Fence-In
P.O. Box 795, Dept. E
Sparks, NV 89432
Phone: (888) 738-9099
Internet: www.catfencein.com

Care-A-Lot
1617 Diamond Spring Road
Virginia Beach, VA 23455
Phone: (800) 343-7680
E-mail: CustomerService@carealotpets.com
Internet: www.carealot.org

Drinkwell Pet Fountain
Phone: (800) 805-7532
Internet: www.vetventures.com

Doctors Foster & Smith
2253 Air Park Road
P.O. Box 100
Rhinelander, WI 54501
Phone: (800) 381-7179
Internet: www.drsfostersmith.com

Fat Cat, Inc.
340 Avenue D, Suite 40
Williston, VT 05495
E-mail: comments@fatcatinc.com
Internet: www.kittyhoots.com

Feliway
Internet: www.peerlesshealth.com

Feline Evolution CatSeat (toilet training)
Evolve-Products
117 N. Crawford
Norman, OK 73069
Attn: Feline Evolution Product Order
Phone: (877) 902-4222
E-mail: feedback@felineevolution.com
Internet: www.catseat.com

Feline Furniture (Hidy-Tidy)
P.O. Box 4128
Bisbee, AZ 85603
Phone: (520) 432-7766
E-mail: sales@hidytidy.com
Internet: www.hidytidy.com

LitterMaid
Phone: (800) 548-6243
E-mail: consumer.affairs@applicamail.com
Internet: www.littermaid.com

Noah's Pet Supplies
5376 Highland Road
Baton Rouge, LA 70808
Phone: (888) NOAHS PET
E-mail: noah@noahspets.com
Internet: www.noahspets.com

PeerlessHealth.com
P.O. Box 225
Denison, TX 75021
Phone: (903) 463-2418
E-mail: shojai@peerlesshealth.com
Internet: www.peerlesshealth.com

Petco
Phone: (877) 738-6742
Internet: www.petco.com

PETsMART.com
35 Hugus Alley, Suite 210
Pasadena, CA 91103
Phone: (888) 839-9638
Internet: www.petsmart.com

Pet-Expo.com
Phone: (888) 738-3976
E-mail: info@futurepets.com
Internet: www.pet-expo.com

Purr-Fect Privy
P.O. Box 462
Lakehurst, NJ 08733
Phone: (800) 434-1919
E-mail: info@pfprivy.com
Internet: www.pfprivy.com

R.C. Steele
Phone: (888) 839-9420
E-mail: cs@rcsteele.com
Internet: www.rcsteele.com

Rover Vinyl-Tech Industries
Kali-Ko Kathouses
20 Kiji Dava
Sundog Industrial Park

Prescott, AZ
Phone: (800) 658-5925
E-mail: rover@roverpet.com
Internet: www.roverpet.com

SnuggleKittie
Phone: (800) 463-4107
E-mail: info@snuggleme.com
Internet: www.snuggleme.com

Soft Paws
Phone: (800) 989-2542
Internet: www.softpaws.com

Sticky Paws
Phone: (817) 926-3023
E-mail: kittichik@aol.com
Internet: www.stickypaws.com

That Pet Place
237 Centerville Road
Lancaster, PA 17603
Phone: (888) 842-8738
Internet: www.thatpetplace.com

Tuff Products for Pets
(Tuff Oxi)
4035 Wade Street, Suite B
Los Angeles, CA 90066
Phone: (310) 574-3252
E-mail: info@tuffcleaningproducts.com

Vir-Chew-All Enterprizez
Phone: (877) 695-3750
E-mail: presh@vir-chew-all.com
Internet: www.vir-chew-all.com

World's Best Cat Litter
1600 Oregon Street
Muscatine, IA 52761
Phone: (877) 367-9225
Internet: www.worldsbestcatlitter.com

Feline Foundations

American Veterinary Medical Association
1931 N. Meacham Road, Suite 100
Schaumburg, IL 60173-0805
Internet: www.avma.org

Morris Animal Foundation
45 Inverness Drive East
Englewood, CO 80112-5480
Phone: (800) 243-2345
Internet: www.morrisanimalfoundation.org

Winn Feline Foundation for Cat Health
1805 Atlantic Avenue
P.O. Box 1005
Manasquan, NJ 08736-1005
E-mail: winn@winnfelinehealth.org
Internet: www.winnfelinehealth.org

INDEX

Amy D. Shojai is a nationally known authority on pet care and behavior. She is the author of more than a dozen award-winning nonfiction pet books and hundreds of articles and columns. Ms. Shojai addresses a wide range of fun-to-serious issues in her work, covering training, behavior, health care, and medical topics.

Ms. Shojai is a founder and past-president of the Cat Writers' Association, and a member of the Dog Writers' Association of America and Association of Pet Dog Trainers. She frequently speaks to groups on a variety of pet-related issues, lectures at writing conferences, and regularly appears on national radio and television in connection with her work. She and her husband live with assorted critters at Rosemont, their thirteen-acre "spread" in north Texas. Ms. Shojai can be reached through her Web site at www.shojai.com.